A
REALISTIC
PATH
TO
PEACE

2025 EDITION
From Genocide to Global War…
and How We Can Stop It

"Drawing on his lifetime of experience at the front lines of resistance to empire, Dee Knight details the multitude of struggles at home and abroad against the empire, and for building a new, multipolar world in which no single nation dominates, and all nations can live and thrive together. He shows we are now at a tipping point, when the old world of war and exploitation is ending, and a new world is coming into being. Read his book and see the pieces of the new world coming together, piece by struggling piece."

    —*Michael Wong*, National Vice President of Veterans for Peace; Co-founder of Pivot To Peace.

"With the escalating genocide in Palestine, New Cold War on China, and its proxy war against Russia, it's difficult to shake the feeling that the U.S. ruling class has lost any semblance of sanity. Motivated by their mission of hegemony – of creating a 'favorable business environment' around the world – these people are pushing humanity towards World War 3. This volume by veteran campaigner Dee Knight provides a timely and much-needed voice of sanity; a passionate plea for peace, and a call for unity and bold action against imperialism. As Huey P. Newton warned us, 'There can be no real freedom until the imperialist – world enemy number one – has been stripped of his power.' *Essential reading.*"

    —**Carlos Martinez**, Editor, Invent the Future, Co-founder, Friends of Socialist China

"Dee Knight's incisive chronicling of the massacres in Palestine, hybrid war against China, and Ukraine war developments hones closely to one essential truth: the greatest threat to humankind today is the aggressive war-making of the United States, as it desperately seeks to stem the decline of its waning empire. Dee Knight's own experience as a longtime antiwar activist leads us to one inevitable conclusion: We Must Resist!"

—**Gerry Condon**, Vietnam era GI resister and former president of Veterans for Peace, coordinator of VFP's Golden Rule project.

"The corporate media in the U.S. and its NATO allies, and in Australia, South Korea and Japan, mobilized a propaganda campaign to demonize Putin and Russia in Europe, slandering Beijing's policies, and covering up genocide in Palestine. Dee Knight's book combats this propaganda offensive and can serve as a tool in the anti-war struggle. It is an education in how the imperialists move toward war while distorting and disguising their aims."

—**John Catalinotto**, Editor, Workers World

"Dee Knight's book *A Realistic Path to Peace* offers keen insights into the Biden administration's reckless provocations towards Russia and China and morally bankrupt policy in the Middle East, contextualizing it amidst a larger history of U.S. imperialism and war mongering. Knight writes clearly and lucidly and shows the urgency of the need to revitalize the peace movement in the US today."

—**Jeremy Kuzmarov**, Managing editor, *CovertAction Magazine*, author of *War Monger: How Clinton's Malign Foreign Policy Shaped the U.S. Trajectory From Bush II to Biden*

A
REALISTIC
PATH
TO
PEACE

2025 EDITION
From Genocide to Global War...
and How We Can Stop It

by *Dee Knight*

Solidarity Publications
Bronx, New York
info@RealPathToPeace.com

Cover design by Shelley Savoy (shelley@booknook.biz)

Some of the essays in this book were previously published in
LA Progressive or Covert Action Magazine

Paperback ISBN: 979-8-9925306-2-9; Ebook ISBN: 979-8-9925306-3-6;
Kindle ISBN: 979-8-9925306-4-3; Audiobook: 979-8-9925306-5-0
DVD: 979-8-9925306-6-7
Library of Congress Control Number: 2024902057

First Edition June 2023
Second Edition March 2024

Publisher's Cataloging-in-Publication Data
Names: Knight, Dee, author
Title: A Realistic Path to Peace: From Genocide to Global War
and How We Can Stop It / Dee Knight
Description: [Bronx, New York] : Solidarity Publications, [2024]
Includes bibliographic references LCCN and index.
Identifiers: ISBN: 979-8-9925306-2-9 (paperback) | 979-8-9925306-3-6
(Ebook) | 979-8-9925306-4-3 (Kindle) | LCCN: 2024902057
Subjects: LCSH: Ukraine Conflict, 2014- | United States–Foreign relations–
Russia (Federation) | North Atlantic Treaty Organization–Ukraine. | Europe–
Foreign relations–Russia (Federation)–21st century. | United States–Foreign
relations–China–21st century | Europe–Foreign relations–China–21st
century. | United States–Foreign relations–Middle East. | Geopolitics. | World
Politics. | International Relations. | Political Science. | BISAC: POLITICAL
SCIENCE / Peace | POLITICAL SCIENCE / Commentary & Opinion |
POLITICAL SCIENCE / Geopolitics | Imperialism | Political Ideologies /
Democracy |

LC record available at https://lccn.loc.gov/2024902057

DEDICATION

This book is dedicated to the people of Palestine,
and to all of the Global South,
whose centuries-old oppression under colonialism,
is now changing, because they refuse to submit any longer.
Also to the internally colonized people in the Americas –
the Indigenous & Mexican people whose land was stolen,
to the descendants of African slaves dragged here in chains;
and to About Face/Veterans Against the War,
whose lives were significantly damaged,
and often cut tragically short, by the U.S. war machine.

Preface to the Chinese Edition:

Who Is Threatening World Peace?

「调圪娃胃丘畎咎开」

[Editor's Note: A Chinese edition, with the title above, is due in 2026. The following preface provides an update to current historic events that relate directly to this book's core themes and message.]

China is a target of U.S. aggression, whether through hybrid or hot war. It shares this status with a host of friends near and far. Many such allies traveled to Beijing from around the world to celebrate China's 80th anniversary of the defeat of Japanese fascism in World War II and to participate in the Shanghai Cooperation Organization's summit in September 2025. At this display of "unity in multipolarity," Chinese President Xi Jinping stood shoulder-to-shoulder with Russian President Vladimir Putin and North Korean leader Kim Jong Un, among about two dozen others.

These three countries, together with Iran, are constant targets of ongoing war and threats from the United States and its NATO allies. The same is true of the Palestinian people, who have been targets of genocide since October 2023 and apartheid since the founding of Israel in 1948. The perennial U.S. targeting of countries in Latin America and the Caribbean through "gunboat diplomacy" has entered a new phase, with U.S. warships attacking Venezuela illegally in hopes of toppling the socialist government and regaining control of that country's massive oil and gas reserves. The U.S. has also used covert CIA operations to regain control of other governments in South America, including Ecuador, Peru, Bolivia, and Argentina.

Brazil remains in the U.S. crosshairs, especially due to its leading role in BRICS.

At the Shangri-La Dialogue in Singapore in May 2025, U.S. Secretary of Defense Pete Hegseth urged Asian allies to join U.S. efforts "to deter an imminent threat from China." He said the U.S. is "focused on lethality ... and warfighting." Hegseth did not discuss which side is actually posing the imminent threat.

The U.S. defense secretary wants the ASEAN countries to join the Philippines in stepping back from independence toward old-fashioned colonialism as partners in the U.S. military buildup against China. The U.S. seeks more allies like Japan and South Korea, which lost their sovereignty to U.S. military and economic domination in the wake of World War II. But even while U.S. troops and military bases proliferate in these two countries, their people appear resistant. Recent election results suggest the general population, as well as business leaders, reject war policies in favor of peaceful relations with China.

This book delves deeply into the deceptive ways the U.S. leadership engineered a fascist coup d'état in Ukraine, fomenting a proxy war against Russia and dragging its NATO allies into a conflict that could only lead to disaster. These U.S. allies now face constant instability and economic hardship as a result of vassal-like compliance with U.S. warmaking. Their populations want peaceful foreign relations instead of constant war.

In the U.S. itself, President Trump and Secretary Hegseth face difficulty recruiting young people to become "warfighters." The people of the United States are rejecting the "forever wars" of recent decades. Too many young soldiers' lives were lost or ruined by forced combat in wars whose only purpose was the control of oil, gas, and corporate profits. In the case of the U.S.-supported slaughter of Palestinian people, young American soldiers have refused to be involved, with some even committing suicide rather than participate in war crimes.

U.S. service members deployed at bases and on warships surrounding China face extreme danger due to Hegseth's goals to make them combatants in adventures that can only lead to disaster. Just as a majority of people in the U.S. have come to reject ongoing support for "war to the last Ukrainian" and the genocide of Palestinians, an ever-growing share of the U.S. population also rejects war plans against China.

The massive military display at Beijing's V-Day celebration left little doubt that China would never allow itself to be bullied again. More than 35 million Chinese people were killed during Imperial Japan's invasion and occupation from the early 1930s to the end of World War II in August 1945. That is in addition to the USSR's loss of 27 million lives from the Nazi onslaught. Together, these two countries bore the brunt of the global fight against fascism and were the major factors in its defeat.

The U.S.: Sponsor and Protector of Fascists

While China and the USSR achieved major victories against fascism, the U.S. sheltered and rehabilitated Imperial Japan's fascist rulers, helping them form and maintain the country's far-right Liberal Democratic Party, which has ruled virtually nonstop for 80 years. The CIA did the same for the fascists of Ukraine and has sponsored them against Russia. Japan's rulers have always refused to apologize for slaughtering millions during their invasion of China. The same is true for Japan's 35-year colonial hold on Korea from 1910 to 1945. In both countries, Japanese imperialists were notorious for their systems of "comfort women"—sex slaves for occupation forces. This stands in significant contrast to the status of women in China today.

The U.S. has sponsored continual military dictatorships in South Korea, always aimed at threatening China—most notably in the Korean War, which ended in an armistice in 1953 but has continued without a peace treaty. Instead, the U.S. imposed a treaty on its South Korean client, guaranteeing "operational control" of the Korean military in the event of war against either the Democratic People's Republic of Korea (DPRK) or China. This underscores the significance of DPRK leader Kim standing next to President Putin and President Xi at the V-Day event on Sept. 3, 2025.

South Korea's new president, Lee Jae-myung, came to power in June 2025 following months of intense popular struggle to oust the U.S.-backed President Yoon Suk Yeol, who was impeached and jailed after declaring martial law and trying to provoke a war. When President Lee visited Trump in August 2025, he resisted U.S. pressure to join an escalation against China, which remains South Korea's top trading partner.

The leaders from around the world who joined the SCO summit and the Beijing V-Day celebration showed that U.S. efforts to surround China are failing. Most Southeast Asian countries in ASEAN—notably Vietnam, Indonesia, Laos, Malaysia, Myanmar, Thailand, and Cambodia—attended following recent visits by President Xi. The significant exception was the Philippines, where the U.S. maintains a military alliance. However, as in South Korea, the popular movement against U.S. domination is strong, with serious efforts to remove U.S. bases.

Meanwhile, U.S. war theaters have expanded to include Latin America, the Caribbean, and Africa. The devastation caused by "puppet wars" in both Sudan and the Democratic Republic of Congo has caused millions of deaths and massive dislocation. U.S. Tomahawk missiles hit northeastern Nigeria on Christmas Day 2025, near the border with the anti-colonial Alliance of Sahel States.

Threats continue against South Africa. U.S. warships are now deployed against Venezuela on the pretext of preventing drugs from entering the U.S. market. As the U.S. loses its grip elsewhere, it is intensifying efforts to control its "backyard."

The "American Century"

After World War II, the U.S. assumed the role of victor, launching the "American Century" alongside a global war against communism. It has maintained occupation troops in Japan, South Korea, the Philippines, Guam, and other Pacific islands—all of which are deployed today against China. Similarly, NATO continues a proxy war against Russia, with large U.S. bases in nearly every European country.

During the Korean War (1950–1953), the U.S. killed millions of Koreans and flattened every building over one story in a massive bombing campaign. Its threats to extend the war into China were repelled by the mobilization of 500,000 Chinese troops fighting alongside North Koreans. The U.S. war against Vietnam began shortly after the French were defeated in 1954 and lasted until the U.S. was defeated in 1975, at a cost of millions of Vietnamese lives and tens of thousands of U.S. troops. Both wars were also aimed at China, which provided troops and weapons to support its allies.

The war zones of today—in Eastern Europe, West Asia, the Far East, and the Caribbean—are continuations of 80 years of U.S. global domination. The way the U.S. protects its interests has exposed a blunt reality: The official refrain that "America is protecting democracy and human rights" is war propaganda.

Remembering When the U.S. Helped China Against Fascism

During World War II, the U.S. provided strategic support to China's resistance against Imperial Japan. This history is well known in China, but less so in the United States. I personally visited the famous "24-Zig Road" in southwest Guizhou province—also known as the Stilwell Road—which served as a supply line from Burma (now Myanmar) and India to the Chinese resistance. The road was a joint project of U.S. and Chinese forces and a symbol of their united effort. U.S. Gen. Joseph Stilwell had many conflicts with Kuomintang (KMT) leader Chiang Kai-shek, who called for his ouster. Stilwell argued for the unified efforts of the KMT and Red Army forces, which led to his replacement.

Official U.S. support for Chinese resistance was a material factor in defeating global fascism. But the switch to supporting fascist elements after the war, including up to the present day, poses a challenge to the world's progressive forces. The existence of the Shanghai Cooperation Organization constitutes a giant bulwark in that fight. But the struggle continues, as seen in the U.S.-backed assault on Palestine and attacks on Lebanon, Syria, Yemen, and Iran. Just as the world's forces united to stop fascism in the 1940s, history calls on us to unite even more strongly today. Victory against fascism today will spell the end of imperialism and usher in the common prosperity the world needs now.

December 2025

ACKNOWLEDGEMENTS

Ben Norton, editor of the *Geopolitical Economy Report*, together with co-editors Radhika Desai and Michael Hudson were sources and inspiration for much of the analysis that appears here. Scott Ritter, former UN weapons inspector in both Iraq and Russia, and author of *Disarmament in the Time of Perestroika*, provided essential factual support about the ongoing conflict in Ukraine, as did retired U.S. Colonel Douglas MacGregor.

On the genocide in Gaza, I am indebted to *Electronic Intifada, The Palestine Chronicle, and Mondoweiss.*

For analysis of prospects for an effective antiwar movement, I thank Sara Flounders, coordinator of the United National Antiwar Coalition (UNAC), Ajamu Baraka, national director of the Black Alliance for Peace (BAP), Margaret Kimberley, editor of *Black Agenda Report*, and Brian Becker, director of the ANSWER coalition.

Gerry Condon, former national president of Veterans For Peace, with whom I have collaborated since we were part of the *AMEX-Canada* collective in Toronto in the early 1970s, contributed valuable advice, as did Medea Benjamin of CodePink, co-author of *War In Ukraine: Making Sense of a Senseless Conflict*. I'm grateful to both of them and appreciate their patience in spite of some differences of emphasis.

Benjamin Abelow, author of *How The West Brought War to Ukraine*, provided invaluable advice and guidance.

I thank the editors Chris Agee and Jeremy Kuzmarov of *Covert Action Magazine*, as well as Sharon Kyle and Dick Price of *LA Progressive* and *Hollywood Progressive*, for permission to re-publish articles they originally published from 2021 to 2024.

All information and analysis in this book is carefully documented in the text. I take full responsibility for any errors or omissions.

CONTENTS

Foreword: The Threat Continues   xv

Preface: Danger… & Opportunity   xxi

Introduction: The Long Fight Ahead   xxvii

I   Palestine & The End of Apartheid and Colonialism   1

   1   Restore Historic Palestine/End Zionist Apartheid   3

   2   Blinken Blames Hamas for Broken Truce   13

   3   What Does "Strategic Defeat" Look Like?   24

II   Ukraine Conflict: U.S. Proxy War Against Russia   33

   4   Shock and Awe: Then and Now   35

   5   What America Will and Will Not Do in Ukraine   45

   6   Buildup to War: Threats and Counter-threats—
Who's To Blame?   52

   7   "This Battle Will Not Be Won in Days or Months"   58

   8   Showdown at "Credibility Gulch"   66

   9   Anti-Russian Hysteria Limits Peace Prospects   78

III   A Peace Movement Emerges   91

   10   "A Real Path to Peace" – A Movement Is Launched   93

   11   "We Won't Be Silent Anymore!"   103

   12   Pivot To Peace!   110

IV   China Is Not Our Enemy   117

13   Biden's Saber-Rattling Against China Could Lead
     to World War III   119

14   Threats Against China Endanger the World   123

15   Does China's Rise Really Threaten the U.S.?   131

16   "Democracy and Human Rights": China vs. USA   149

17   "Yankees Go Home," Asians Say   159

18   Biden Travels East in Clouds of Mistrust   167

19   "With Us or Against Us" Fails   179

V   What Makes the War Machine So Monstrous?   191

20   Dr. Strangelove Is No Longer Satire   193

21   Why It's So Hard to Stop the U.S. War Machine   202

22   Empire's Debt Trap: How to Resist Gluttonous Greed   216

23   Neoliberalism Has Been Far From "Liberal"   227

24   Sanctions: A Wrecking Ball in a World Economy   238

VI   Looking Backward to See Ahead   248

25   Dissenting Soldiers Challenge the War Machine   249

26   The Socialist Antiwar Tradition   256

VII   From Genocide in Gaza, To Global War?   267

27   From Genocide to Global War?   269

Afterword – 2024 and Beyond   289

About the Author   291

Index   293

Endnotes   303

The Threat Continues

Things are changing fast since Trump came to power. On the home front it's all bad news — roundups and deportations of migrants, firing many government workers, attempts to *reverse everything won in the Civil Rights movement*, and much more. Elsewhere it's mixed.

Trump has shocked the leaders of Western Europe with bold moves to end the U.S./NATO proxy war against Russia — calling for long-delayed elections in Ukraine, signaling that the United States may "no longer need NATO," and declaring the Ukraine disaster was "Biden's war." The famous author of *The Art of the Deal* appears ready to make a deal with Russia's leader, Vladimir Putin.

How fast a deal can happen is uncertain. "President Trump's high-speed effort to end the war in Ukraine is on a collision course with… President Vladimir Putin's goals in the conflict," the *Wall Street Journal* reported February 24, 2025. Trump wants a quick result with substantial "carrots" for the U.S. economy, while Russia wants what it has demanded since before the war began: guaranteed permanent neutrality for Ukraine *outside NATO*, and self-determination for the Donbas and other Russian-speakers inside a Russian umbrella. These were its terms back in December 2021, which the U.S. ignored and then rejected. All this is explained in detail in earlier editions of *A Realistic Path to Peace*, and is just as relevant today for Russia. And Russia is winning on the battlefield.

Meanwhile in the Arab world, Trump has persisted with outrageous, fanciful threats to "own Gaza," and remove the Palestinians, but neighboring Arab countries refuse to go along. Trump has also continued to bolster Israeli threats against Iran. He and his team of neocon re-treads, led by new Secretary of State Marco Rubio, have chosen Saudi Arabia as the key mediator for talks with Russia, and possibly also for *discussions* about the future of Palestine and Israel.

The contrast is stark between the themes of talks with Russia and the Palestine-Israel conflict. A true peace between Palestine and Israel is overshadowed by hopes of a long-sought deal with the Saudis — as if a year and a half of genocidal slaughter hadn't happened. It doesn't seem to register on U.S. leaders that Saudi Crown Prince Mohammed bin Salman (*aka* MBS) has insisted the U.S. must recognize a Palestinian state before anything else can happen. I argue in this book that a real solution is a unitary secular state of Palestine, with equal rights for all, regardless of religious belief or ethnicity.

The Palestinians have established key facts on the ground: their steadfast refusal to move, and the unshakeable strength of their resistance. Unless and until both Israel and the U.S. take them seriously, the Palestinians will continue their long-term struggle to get their land back. Like the Vietnamese half a century ago, they are sure to win, no matter how long it might take. Israel has failed in its aims of forcing the Palestinians out, and of dislodging Hamas and its allies from leadership of the Palestinians.

Regarding Russia, everything is on the table for Trump — ending both the war and sanctions, and re-opening trade in major ways. Trump has expressed hopes of breaking up Russia's close friendship with China, copying the Nixon-Kissinger trick of the 1970s. That trick benefited from an existing Sino-Soviet split at that time, which led to the collapse of the USSR. Both the Russian and Chinese leaders are living a new reality today, as co-leaders of the BRICS coalition, which Trump also wants to break up.

A break-up of NATO is more likely. The leadership of Western Europe is in disarray. The UK has gone from one Prime Minister to another several times in recent years. French President Macron's hold on power is ever more tenuous. In both France and Germany, far-rightists are scheming to scuttle NATO, with likelier prospects of success than ever before.

The economies of Western Europe have been in recession for at least two years. Now Trump is pressuring these "allies" to invest more in "defense," even as he himself scuttles NATO. As Kissinger famously quipped, to be an enemy of the U.S. is dangerous, but to be a friend can be fatal. While new leaders emerge in Europe, only change can be predicted. Will the Europeans end sanctions against Russia? Will they become even more captive to the U.S., both in economic and geopolitical terms? Or will they take the opportunities for a lifeline offered by China?

China's leaders also face numerous challenges. Trump's trade war is already raging, and hot war threatens from nearly every voice in Washington, and also from U.S. military encirclement. To date China has parried every threat, and has made it clear that aggression from the U.S. is unwise. Trump should take the hint, and opt for more deals instead of threats.

That would be good for the world.

Is there any hope for an alternative to more war? Until Trump's arrival in DC, the prospect was for continuing the endless wars of the past quarter century, really the past 75 years. War has, in fact, been a perverse kind of investment for U.S. leaders. The war machine is the most profitable sector of the U.S. economy. It crowds out infrastructure, as well as nearly all people-oriented priorities in the national budget. And wars of aggression can open up markets and sources of raw materials — at least for the winning side. But the U.S. has *not* been the winner since it lost in Vietnam five decades ago, with the rare exceptions of destroying Libya and Yugoslavia.

Trump has made noises about being a "peace president." He has even called for cuts in the military budget. He also signed an order to close USAID, ending billions in U.S. "foreign aid." That has caused panic among hundreds of U.S.-funded media operations and "independent journalists" across the globe. Traditional targets of U.S. regime change campaigns — like Nicaragua, Venezuela, Cuba and China — can hope for a break, though they won't breathe easily as long as Marco Rubio is Secretary of State.

So what's going on? Trump seems to be engaged in retrenchment; for example, recognizing that the U.S./NATO adventure in Ukraine is a lost cause. Perhaps the massive trade deficit and gargantuan public debt are signs of money trouble, especially in view of the rise of China and BRICS. That would explain Trump's penchant for tariffs, which provide a way to pull in much-needed cash, and possibly tip the scales to make U.S. exports more competitive globally.

But there's a problem. Tariffs can backfire. Trading partners may find more attractive alternatives. Even converting the slight boost in cash flow to real gains could prove elusive. The U.S. de-industrialization took place over five decades. Rebuilding can't happen overnight. The economy is shaky.

Trump says he wants to bring back the Monroe Doctrine and Manifest Destiny, reasserting U.S. domination in the Americas, and somehow eliminating would-be competitors. The main competitor is China, which has become the largest trading partner for several Latin American countries. Mexico is poised to launch an EV industry in partnership with China. So is Brazil. Even Canada may find it wise to make some deals with China, if only to hedge bets against U.S. takeover fantasies. Maybe Trump can make deals with China instead of waging war.

Realistic prospects for peace continue to depend on factors outside the control of the U.S. government and its backers on Wall Street and in Silicon Valley. Trump is unlikely to get everything he wants. But ordinary people on the home front need to play a role. We need solidarity, remembering if the sweeps against migrants continue, there will be more to follow, some of it even worse.

Some unions have moved to protect members without papers, realizing that if the government can pick off their most vulnerable members, it won't stop there. Civil rights leaders are thinking much the same. So are families under attack from attempted abortion bans. Gender-variant people are subject to attack on all sides.

Trump is threatening students with visas who express solidarity with Palestine. University administrations are firing professors and suspending students who protest against genocide.

What's next? It's tough to predict. But pulling together all who are threatened may be the most realistic way to stop both the war machine and the fascist juggernaut we're facing. Together we can do it.

Danger... and Opportunity

The world is in a crisis now. As its empire declines toward collapse, the United States leadership is making a series of disastrous errors. The "neocons" in Washington, DC, are determined to maintain U.S. global domination regardless of what it might take. The stakes are high for them. They seem to believe that if they "allow" any other country to challenge their global leadership, their whole system could fall apart. They consider it crucial to control global trade, especially the trade in energy.

So they are prepared to do whatever it takes. Supporting genocide in Israel—by providing weapons, money, and a bizarre "moral justification" for horrific genocidal bombing—is a sign of what it takes. Blowing up the Nord Stream pipeline was another sign of what it can take. That was a desperate, "last-ditch" measure, after efforts to persuade their strongest European ally to cut off Russian energy supplies didn't work. Europeans are now paying much higher prices for natural gas and oil than they did before. The result has been a drastic change in living standards for ordinary people in Europe, and major economic problems across the entire world.

Western European leaders have been rounded up and bludgeoned into a unified NATO alliance against Russia, and in support of Israeli genocide against Palestinians. This alliance—originally composed of "north Atlantic" countries under U.S. leadership at the end of World War II—is now also being extended to Asia. It's a quest to curb China's historic economic success, which threatens Western domination of global trade. Now most countries around the world have stronger trade relations with China than with the U.S. or its European allies. The BRICS coalition, composed of Brazil, Russia, India, China and South Africa—and now also Egypt, Ethiopia, Iran, Saudi Arabia and the United Arab Emirates—has in recent years actually surpassed the Group of 7 rich countries in Gross Domestic Product. Many more countries want to join BRICS. It offers them an alternative to western domination.

The leaders of the G7 countries—the USA, UK, Germany, France, Italy, Japan and Canada—met in Hiroshima, Japan in May 2023, to forge a stronger alliance, and denounce Russian threats of nuclear aggression. U.S. President Biden did not use the occasion to apologize to Japan for the first and only nuclear attacks the world has ever experienced, by the U.S., on Hiroshima and Nagasaki, at the end of World War II. These new super bombs killed hundreds of thousands of people and permanently injured many more. Historians have made convincing arguments that the true purpose of these nuclear attacks was to warn the Soviet Union that it could be next. But the Soviets were able to develop their own nuclear potential. Ever since that time, the people of the world have lived with a "balance of terror," never knowing if one or another of the superpowers would start a global conflagration.

It could be considered ironic, if not obscene, for the United States and its G7 allies to use Hiroshima as the place to denounce Russian nuclear threats. But projection, and big lies, have been a key part of official justifications for war many times. "Weapons of mass destruction" was the rallying cry to invade Iraq at the start of the current century. The real reason for the U.S. invasion was determination to control Iraq's oil resources. At the start of the U.S. war in Vietnam in 1964, there was the "Gulf of Tonkin" incident, in which a North Vietnamese patrol boat was accused of attacking a U.S. Navy ship. It led to the nightmare of war in Vietnam that killed millions of Vietnamese and tens of thousands of young Americans. But the Vietnamese won.

The fact that U.S. Navy ships now surround China, and patrol the Taiwan strait, can be seen as continuation of a pattern. The U.S. fosters and fortifies elements inside a country it wants to dominate, then positions its military dangerously close to its chosen enemy. It then accuses the chosen enemy of aggression. That has been the pattern in the buildup to the current conflict with Russia, starting long before February 2022. In 2004 a "color revolution" in Ukraine toppled a government friendly to Russia. It was "an American creation, a sophisticated and brilliantly conceived exercise in western branding and mass marketing," reported Ian Traynor in *The Guardian* (25 Nov 2004). It included "U.S. consultancies, pollsters, diplomats, the two big American parties and U.S. non-government organizations."[1] The same pattern was used in Serbia, Georgia, and Belarus—all allies of Russia. In December 2013, U.S. Assistant Secretary of State Victoria Nuland told the U.S.-Ukraine Foundation that the U.S. had spent about $5 billion on democracy-building programs in Ukraine since 1991.[2]

The results of the 2004 color revolution were reversed in 2010, which set the stage for the Maidan events of 2013 and early 2014. Meanwhile the U.S. and NATO built up forces in the region. In summer 2021, 30,000 U.S. troops led "Operation Defender Europe 2021," a set of NATO exercises from the Baltic Sea to the Black Sea.[3] In December the U.S. staged simulation bombing raids within 12 miles of Russian airspace. NATO warplanes confronted Russian aircraft 290 times in 2021.

The U.S. strategy of using Ukraine to attack Russia has existed for a long time. Former National Security Adviser Zbigniew Brzezinski summed it up in his 1997 book *The Grand Chessboard:* "Ukraine is a new and important space on the Eurasian chessboard… because its very existence as an independent country [means] Russia ceases to be a Eurasian empire." He proposed a "loosely confederated Russia—composed of a European Russia, a Siberian Republic, and a Far Eastern Republic." He wrote that "what happens with the distribution of power on the Eurasian landmass will be of decisive importance to America's global primacy." He added that "a sovereign Ukraine is a critically important component" of such a policy.

The Eurasian landmass includes both China and Russia, of course. That helps to explain why U.S. leaders tend to link the two countries in their war plans.

In 2013, after the democratically elected leaders of Ukraine decided not to redirect the country's economy away from Russia and toward western Europe, the United States helped foment a *coup d'etat*. It encouraged far-right forces to take over the government and launch an anti-Russian crusade. The Russian language, spoken by about a third of the country's people, was outlawed. The people of the Donbas, where Russian-speakers are the majority, resisted, demanding autonomy and forging independent "people's republics." The people of Crimea broke away from Ukraine, rejoining Russia. A civil war ensued, with fascist-led Ukrainian forces terrorizing the Donbas regions, causing an estimated 14,000 deaths.

In 2021, NATO war games and simulated bombing attacks took place along the Russian border, from the Baltic Sea to the Black Sea. In the seven years prior to Russia's intervention, NATO trainers helped re-shape the Ukrainian military. In December 2021, the Russian government proposed a peace plan based on the Minsk II accords: autonomy for the Donbas regions, separation of Crimea, and strict neutrality for Ukraine. U.S. leaders called the proposal a "non-starter."

A month after the Russian "special military operation" began, the governments of Ukraine and Russia agreed in principle to a peace deal, mediated by Turkey, their Black Sea neighbor. That deal was nixed by the U.S. and UK leaders. The U.S. managed to snatch war from the jaws of peace.

The evidence to prove all this can be found in the chapters of this book. It shows that the conflict in Ukraine didn't have to happen, that China is not an enemy of the U.S., and that the Palestinian people have a right to stop Israeli apartheid. A new peace movement is emerging. It faces enormous obstacles, including a gigantic wave of war hysteria engineered in Washington, magnified exponentially by a captive mainstream media that seems to have abandoned all pretense of critical journalistic independence and objectivity. But as facts emerge and truth surfaces, the movement for peace will intensify. Combined with the horrific results of sanctions and war, these facts and truths can be expected to bring ever greater waves of opposition and resistance into the fray.

Whether efforts to achieve peace can overwhelm the power of the U.S. and NATO war machine is an open question. The alternative is too horrific to imagine. That in itself can be a driving force to build the peace movement we need. And we can be confident that the neocons have made a bad gamble. They are unlikely to win. Their loss could bring about a world free of imperialist war. It's early to know if that can happen, but it's a possibility worth striving for.

The Chinese word for "crisis" is composed of two characters, one meaning "danger," the other meaning "opportunity."

The Long Fight Ahead

Real Peace – Not Pax Americana

"Why the fuss?" That was the apparent reaction of Biden, Blinken and the DC war planners to worldwide horrified reactions at Israel's U.S.-backed genocidal slaughter in Gaza. As pressure built at the UN Security Council in late December 2023 to avoid a U.S. veto of another resolution to stop the bombing in Gaza, Blinken criticized nations calling for a cease-fire.[4] He said he hears almost no calls for Hamas to lay down its arms and surrender, adding "How can it be that there are no demands made of the aggressor and only demands made of the victim?" Instead of surrendering, Hamas has held off an Israeli land invasion of Gaza.

The consequences of "justifying" genocide are difficult to calculate in the midst of the operation itself. How many Palestinians will be killed? How many homes, hospitals and schools will be destroyed? Will there be anything or anyone left in Gaza? Will Israel's goal of "crushing Hamas" be realized? How is this operation different from earlier attacks on Gaza, or the constant attacks on Palestinians in the West Bank now and in recent decades? What is the goal for Israel and its backer, the United States? And the results?

For Blinken and his boss, the Gaza conflict began October 7, when Palestinian forces broke through the apartheid wall caging them in, and staged an "unprovoked" attack in which a reported 1,200 Israelis died. Overlooked is the fact that Israeli forces had made repeated bombing attacks on Gaza almost every other year since 2008. So are Israeli admissions that "friendly fire" caused the majority of Israeli deaths on October 7 and the subsequent fighting, according to the largest daily English-language Israeli news source, Ynet (Ynetnews.com).

Israeli Air Force Colonel Nof Erez admitted on a Haaretz podcast (later reported in *Electronic Intifada*[5]) that October 7 was a "mass Hannibal" event. Hannibal is a code name for Israel's policy of firing to kill hostages and enemy fighters rather than allow the enemy to take hostages. The homes of settlers in the Kibbutz Be'eri were blown up even when occupied by Israelis, if the IDF suspected Palestinians might be inside, the report said.

For Blinken and Biden, Israel was the "victim," despite subjecting Palestinians in both Gaza and the West Bank to decades of constant intense repression and bombing as part of its refusal to allow for an independent Palestinian state.

Switching Victim and Aggressor

Switching victim and aggressor is a favorite U.S. tactic for justifying slaughter in efforts to maintain domination. Back in 1964 it was a "Vietnamese attack" on a U.S. ship in the Gulf of Tonkin that "justified" what U.S. Air Force General Curtis Lemay called "bombing them back to the Stone Age." Years earlier, the U.S. Air Force bombed and destroyed all the cities and most towns in northern Korea rather than allow Korea's revolutionary leadership to take over the country after the Japanese colonialists were defeated at the end of World War 2. This "carpet bombing" was also a warning to China's post-1949 revolutionary leadership. But it backfired as half a million Chinese forces helped the Koreans push back the invaders at the 38th parallel and force an armed truce that continues today.

General Lemay admitted the U.S. killed "about 20 percent of the north Korean population" during that war.[6] And in 2017 then "President Trump Threatened to 'Totally Destroy' North Korea. The U.S. Has Done That Before."[7] It's a reminder of Hiroshima and Nagasaki, where the U.S. used nuclear bombs against Japan *after* Japan was on the brink of surrender. That was a warning to the Soviet Union, which had already defeated Germany and was poised to complete the defeat of Japan. It became the basis of a "balance of terror" between the U.S. and the USSR that lasted until the Soviet collapse in late 1991.

For U.S. war planners, the Cold War's end was not enough. It would have been a disaster for the Military-Industrial Complex if its annual bonanza of military profits were ended for lack of enemies. So U.S. war planners like Zbigniew Brzezinski and Paul Wolfowitz crafted elaborate plans for a New World Order with the U.S. "*uber alles.*" Maintaining control of the oil-rich Middle East—really Western Asia—and aspiring to control "the World Island," especially the Eurasian land mass, would facilitate long-term U.S. hegemony.[8]

Multiple aggressive U.S. and NATO military interventions followed the Soviet collapse: in Iraq, the former Yugoslavia, Afghanistan, Libya and Syria. Millions of people died, and millions more became refugees. The 1999 NATO bombing attacks against the former Yugoslavia destroyed the last vestiges of a socialist country in Europe.

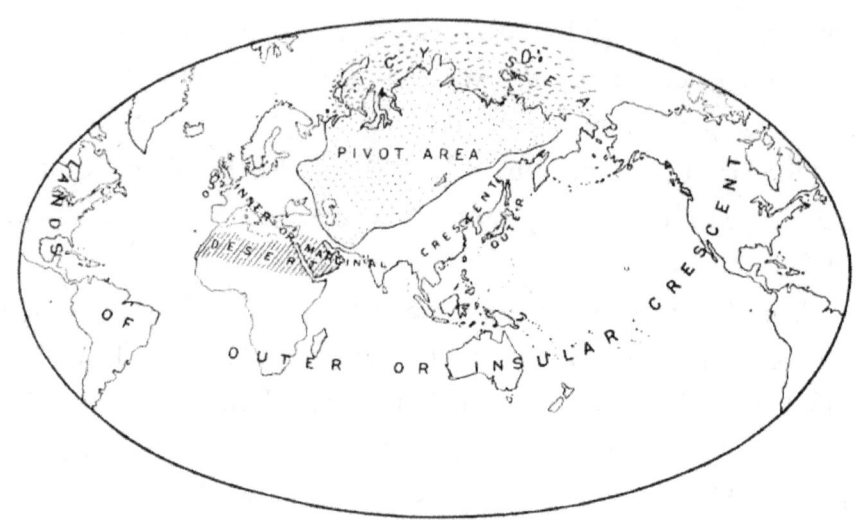

**Mackinder's "World Island," cited by
Brzezinski as key to U.S. global domination.**

Following the events of 9/11/2001, the U.S. declared "endless war against terrorism," falsely claiming it was the "victim" of both Iraq and Afghanistan. U.S. forces achieved little but slaughter and enormous profits. In 2011 the U.S. and NATO launched attacks against Libya, the richest country in Africa at the time. They killed President Muammar Gaddafi, who had provided an economic lifeline to the poorer countries of Africa. Now civil war continues to rage in Libya, spilling over into the countries of the Sahel—Mali, Burkina Faso, Niger, and Sudan. Crisis grips these countries and others across Africa.[9] But U.S. leaders don't really mind collateral damage.

They have bitten off more than they can chew
The endless mess caused by three decades of "endless war" helps to explain the problem facing Biden, Blinken, and their NATO allies,

as well as Netanyahu. They have bitten off more than they can chew. As they face defeat in their proxy war against Russia in Ukraine—a defeat they disguise as a "stalemate"—they are hoping for an easy solution of the Palestine/Israel conflict, one that would maintain the *status quo ante*, as if nothing serious has happened as a result of the current genocidal slaughter. It's a false hope.

Palestine's allies in Yemen and Malaysia closed off the two most crucial "chokepoints" of world commerce following the US veto of the UN Security Council's ceasefire resolution.

"The Yemeni position is clear," a spokesperson of Ansar Allah (*aka* Houthis) told the NY Times.[10] Attacks on ships in the Red Sea will stop "when the Israeli war on the people of Gaza stops." If the U.S. directly attacks Yemen, it could "turn the war in Gaza into an international conflagration," the Houthi representative warned.

Malaysia announced a ban on all Israeli-flagged cargo ships from docking at its port in the Strait of Malacca, in "response to Israel's actions that ignore basic humanitarian principles and violate international law through continuous massacres and atrocities against the Palestinians."[11] So while the oil-rich Arab monarchies have yet to cut off Israel's oil supplies, shipments to Israel of oil and other cargo have slowed to a trickle.

Meanwhile intense diplomatic activity has continued, both at the UN in New York and in Cairo, to at least provide humanitarian aid to Gaza, if not a ceasefire.[12] The U.S. threatened to veto any call for a "suspension of hostilities." And Israel insisted on controlling and inspecting all cargo entering Gaza, which has left hundreds of trucks stalled at the border between Egypt and Gaza. The UN Secretary General's spokesperson said an immediate humanitarian ceasefire would

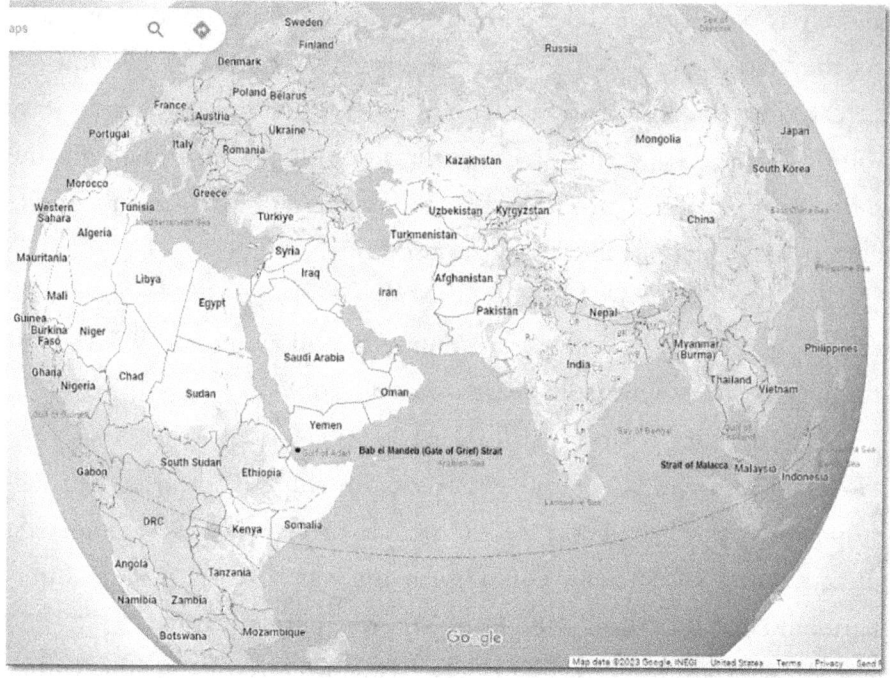

be "the most helpful thing for the delivery of humanitarian aid in a sustained high volume." The U.S. has provided the bombs and other munitions for the Israeli massacre in Gaza.

Building for Peace

Pressure is building for a genuine ceasefire—a permanent one, based on justice for Palestine. The streets are full of protesters almost everywhere. For the first time in decades, many labor unions in the U.S. have called for a ceasefire, and union members and organizers have hit the streets—by the thousands in both New York and Oakland, California, Dec. 16, and thousands more in New York Dec. 22.

Labor for Palestine was the main organizer, with strong support from the United Auto Workers (UAW), American Postal Workers Union, the United Electrical Workers (UE), California and National Nurses Association, United Food and Commercial Workers (UFCW), National Education Association (NEA), Service Employees Union (SEIU), International Longshore and Warehouse Union (ILWU), Unite Here, Association of American Federation of State, County and Municipal Employees (AFSCME), and others. Teachers unions including the Chicago Teachers Union, the San Antonio Alliance of Teachers and Support Professionals, and the Massachusetts Teachers Association were early signers of a ceasefire resolution spearheaded by UE and UFCW.

Labor for Palestine march Dec. 16 in Oakland, CA.
PHOTO: Common Dreams

"Workers have a special ability to stop Israeli genocide," said Michael Letwin of Labor for Palestine. "If workers refuse to load or unload Israeli Zim Line ships, that's worth a thousand resolutions."

Letwin is the former president of United Auto Workers Local 2325, the Association of Legal Aid Attorneys.

The new UAW President Shawn Fain said "we take pride in our history of standing up for justice at home and around the world. I thank our UAW members for speaking out and pushing us to come out in support of a ceasefire." UAW Region 9A director Brandon Mancilla declared Nov. 30, outside the White House where protesters were on hunger strike, "I'm proud today to announce that the UAW international has joined the call for a ceasefire in Israel and Palestine. From opposing fascism in WWII to mobilizing against apartheid South Africa and the Contra war, the UAW has consistently stood for justice across the globe. A labor movement that fights for social and economic justice for all workers must always stand against war and for peace."

Jewish groups like Jewish Voice for Peace, Not In Our Name, and If Not Now have organized numerous disruptive protests, shutting down a highway in Los Angeles, as well as Grand Central Station and three major bridges in New York. Zucotti Park, the scene of the Occupy movement a decade ago, filled on Dec. 28 in a protest organized by Within Our Lifetime, a Palestinian community group that has led numerous protests.

The Shut-It-Down-for-Palestine Coalition has maintained weekly and even daily actions in large and small cities across the country. The coalition includes the Palestinian Youth Movement, National Students for Justice in Palestine, Al-Awda, ANSWER, People's Forum, International People's Assembly, and many other local groups. Demands include an immediate ceasefire, cutting all U.S. aid to Israel, and lifting the siege of Gaza. The coalition is committed to "keep building momentum and increase the pressure with more marches, walk-outs, sit-ins, and other forms of direct action to end collaboration with Israeli genocide and occupation."

The Adalah Justice Project, a Palestinian-led advocacy organization, mobilized more than eighty community-based advocacy groups to "de-link" anti-immigrant repression and money for war in Gaza and Ukraine. They issued a joint statement against a deal Biden offered to send billions to Israel and Ukraine "in exchange" for a draconian anti-immigrant bill. Hundreds of activists occupied the Capitol Rotunda, where they sang and chanted slogans including "not in our name" and held signs reading "stop arming Israel" and "protect immigrants and asylees."

CodePink has also staged numerous disruptions in Congress, and called a national March on Washington for Gaza on January 13, together with a coalition of numerous Muslim and Palestinian groups, and hundreds of local and national antiwar groups. CodePink "recognizes Palestinians as the rightful owners and caretakers of Palestine, their indigenous homeland. We support Palestinians' right to resist the violent Israeli occupation of Palestine. We are committed to supporting Palestinian liberation, using the demands of Palestinians as our guideline for organizing, and we endorse the BDS movement, to Boycott, Disinvest and Sanction Israeli apartheid."

The protests and the news from Gaza have had impact: a December 19 New York Times report said "Voters broadly disapprove of the way President Biden is handling the bloody strife between Israelis and Palestinians, with younger Americans far more critical than older voters of both Israel's conduct and of the administration's response to the war in Gaza."[13]

Global Pressure for Peace

While the U.S. tries to bolster Israel as its proxy in the Middle East, the majority of countries in the world are looking for a different solution. The Arab League and Organization of Islamic States (OIC) met in late 2023 to call for a ceasefire and pursue joint action. This Arab-Islamic summit represents 79 countries, over half the global South. They met together with China, whose five-point peace proposal on Israel-Palestine was launched at the UN security council to coincide with the UN's International Day of Solidarity with the Palestinian people on November 30. China calls for a comprehensive ceasefire; effective protection of civilians; ensuring of humanitarian assistance; diplomatic mediation; and an emergency international conference as soon as possible to forge a political settlement.

China says the root cause of the problem is "the long delay in realizing the dream of an independent state of Palestine and the failure to redress the historical injustice suffered by the Palestinian people."

On December 29, South Africa filed a case against Israel before the International Court of Justice (ICJ), charging "genocidal acts against the Palestinian people in Gaza." Where this can lead is uncertain, but it forces the UN system to grapple with Israel and the U.S.—who are facing total global isolation.

Israel remains determined to crush the Palestinian resistance and expel Palestinians from their land once and for all, and has whole-hearted support in Washington. Their heads are stuck in a racist *status quo* mindset by which they can somehow decide how Palestinians should be governed. But, as Khaled Elgindy wrote in a December 18, 2023 *Foreign Affairs* article, "Israeli and U.S. officials will need to reconcile themselves to the fact that Hamas will, in one form or another, remain a force in Palestinian politics."[14] The author of *Blind Spot: America and the Palestinians, From Balfour to Trump*, Kaligny adds that U.S. and Israeli officials "must abandon the idea that they can reengineer Palestinian politics to suit Israeli (or U.S.) political needs, a conceit that has helped erode the domestic legitimacy of Palestinian leaders since the Oslo process began in 1993."

A New Global Situation

The crisis in Israel/Palestine follows on the heels of U.S. and NATO failure in their proxy war against Russia in Ukraine. The "New World Order" that George Bush Senior announced after the Soviet Union's collapse is now showing cracks. U.S. and NATO planners are slowly awakening from their dream of "weakening Russia" through a proxy war in Ukraine. At his "hastily arranged" visit to Washington December 11, 2023, Ukrainian President Zelensky did not get a Congressional standing ovation as he had a year earlier. And he didn't get a commitment for more billions. Joe Biden pressed hard for the money, declaring the U.S. "should take pride that we've enabled Ukraine's success thanks to the steady supply of weapons and ammunition we've provided them." Biden really did say "success," and then warned of "American troops fighting Russian troops" if Russia "attacks a NATO ally."[15]

Biden's warning caused a reaction which might have led to a White House "walk back" of his reckless remarks. Instead, his Strategic Communications Director John Kirby *repeated* them the next day: "If you think the cost of supporting Ukraine is high now, just imagine how much higher it's going to be—not just in national treasure, but in American blood—if he starts going after one of our NATO Allies."[16]

Meanwhile Hungary blocked proposed new aid to Ukraine from the European Union.

The cost in lives and treasure of its endless wars has not bothered the U.S. leadership ever. In a real sense the question now is what will it look like when they lose—as they are in Ukraine, and as they most likely will in Palestine—as U.S. Defense Secretary General Lloyd Austin has predicted.[17] The Palestinian resistance, and the massive solidarity it has inspired, are sapping confidence in both Washington and Tel Aviv. "Skepticism Grows Over Israel's Ability to Dismantle Hamas," was a NY Times headline December 27. "Critics both within Israel and outside have questioned whether resolving to destroy such a deeply entrenched organization was ever realistic," the article says.[18] At a Dec. 26 Beirut press conference Hamas leader Osama Hamdan said "the decision maker is the Palestinian people alone." They are not literally alone, of course. Support for Palestine has mushroomed everywhere.

"The global mystique of the U.S., after two decades of disastrous wars in the Middle East and the assault on the Capitol on Jan. 6, is as contaminated as its Israeli ally," Chris Hedges says.[19] "The Biden presidency, which ironically may have signed its own political death certificate, is tethered to Israel's genocide. It will try to distance itself rhetorically, but at the same time it will funnel the billions of dollars of weapons demanded by Israel... It is a full partner in Israel's genocide project."

Meanwhile There's China

While crises in Gaza and Ukraine have continued to dominate headlines, China still holds top spot on the US "enemies list." Roger Harris, a member of the U.S. Peace Council's executive committee, visited China with a 2023 Peace Council delegation that met with the Chinese People's Association for Peace and Disarmament.[20] Harris says "the U.S. is preparing for war with China. High-ranking U.S. Airforce General Mike Minihan foresees war as early as 2025."[21] He notes that China is surrounded by a ring of some 400 U.S. military bases.[22] Biden has strengthened:

- the Quad military alliance with India, Australia, and Japan originally initiated in 2007,
- the AUKUS security pact with the UK and Australia founded in 2021,
- the Five Eyes intelligence-sharing with UK, Australia, New Zealand, and Canada dating back to the beginning of the first Cold War, and
- forged a new mini-NATO alliance with Japan and South Korea last August.[23]

Chinese President Xi Jinping has said "How China and the U.S. get along will determine the future of humanity."[24] China wants friendly cooperative relations, based on mutual respect, peaceful coexistence and "win-win cooperation," as opposed to the U.S. "winner take all" approach.[25] Following the official U.S. national security doctrine of "full spectrum dominance,"[26] the RAND Corporation, the Pentagon's think tank, recently completed a study which says it all: "War with China—thinking through the unthinkable."[27] The outcome, they predicted, would be disastrous to both sides. That may be an optimistic assessment for the U.S. war planners.

Ajamu Baraka, chair of Black Agenda for Peace, was also part of the U.S. Peace Council delegation. He shared the definition of peace from the Black radical peace tradition:

> *"Peace is not the absence of conflict, but rather the achievement by popular struggle and self-defense of a world liberated from the interlocking issues of global conflict … through the defeat of global systems of oppression that include colonialism, imperialism, patriarchy, and white supremacy."*

This is the kind of peace we need—not a continued "Pax Americana" imposed as U.S. global hegemony.

Failure upon failure globally and at home is causing a cascade of disasters, not only for the Biden administration, but for the whole U.S. elite, and for the world of its victims. The one positive factor is that the Palestinians have awakened a determination for peace and solidarity across the world and even in the United States. But it will take continued effort to make peace and solidarity a dream that can come true.

January 1, 2024

Snatching War from the Jaws of Peace

The first proposal to end the Ukraine-Russia conflict was agreed in principle by both sides in late March 2022, about a month after Russian forces entered the Donbas region. But Britain's then-prime minister Boris Johnson flew to Kyiv to scuttle that deal. He told Ukraine's President Zelensky the collective West "wasn't ready for the war to end," and "Putin cannot be negotiated with."[28]

Just before the leaders of Russia and Ukraine agreed in principle to that first peace accord, Joe Biden said on March 26, 2022 that "this battle will not be won in days or months, either. We need to steel ourselves for the long fight ahead."

In a June 1, 2022 op-ed statement in the *New York Times,* Biden wrote "I will not pressure the Ukrainian government—in private or public—to make any territorial concessions." He did not say if the U.S. would exert pressure *against* such concessions, which would surely be required for talks to start. Neither the Russian government nor the people of the Donbas, Crimea and nearby areas are likely to accept the terror that was imposed on Russian speakers in Ukraine from 2014 to 2022.

China's top diplomat, State Counselor Wang Yi, told the delegates at the Munich Security Conference in February 2023 "It is imperative to return to the Minsk II agreement... as quickly as possible."[29] That would mean a ceasefire and autonomy for the Donbas, and getting NATO out of Ukraine. Wang said Minsk II "is a binding instrument negotiated by the parties concerned and endorsed by the UN Security Council. Russia and the EU both support Minsk II." He claimed U.S. Secretary of State Blinken had expressed U.S. support. The Chinese diplomat called for "the relevant parties [to] sit down together" to work out a roadmap and timetable for implementation of the agreement.

War Hysteria vs. Mass Revulsion to War

The first year of the Ukraine conflict was gripped by nearly unprecedented war hysteria—remarkable in a country that has experienced nearly continuous war hysteria for generations. The memories of mainstream media publishing major exposures of U.S. war crimes—like the 1969 MyLai massacre in Vietnam and the infamous Pentagon Papers that blew the lid off Washington's hopeless misadventures—are faded blips on a distant radar screen.

But they are reminders of the power of an aroused wave of anti-war protest that swept American society during the U.S. war in Vietnam. It was powerful enough to make all sectors in the country take notice, and ultimately helped the Vietnamese force the U.S. to stop the war. It fostered the "Vietnam syndrome," a mass revulsion to war and war propaganda that put brakes on the war machine, at least for a while.

It can happen again, and it needs to. Over the week marking Dr. Martin Luther King Jr.'s birthday, January 13 to 22, 2022, protest surged across the country to "Stop U.S. Wars." Major national coalitions joined forces to hit the streets of New York and more than 90 other cities. A March 18 national mobilization in Washington, DC, was much larger, with echoes in other cities across the country.

Margaret Kimberley of Black Agenda for Peace, spoke at both the New York rally and a Harlem Speakout to Stop Racism, Poverty and World War III. She denounced NATO as a cabal of white supremacists waging war not only against Russia and China, but the peoples of Africa, the Middle East, Asia and Latin America.

John Parker, former Peace and Freedom candidate for the California State Senate, and national leader of the Socialist Unity Party, gave eye-witness testimony from the Donbas, where he visited in May 2022. He said U.S.-funded Ukrainian fascists committed war crimes that were later blamed on Russia by western media. He pointed to a direct connection between the Ukrainian fascists and the May 14 mass shooting of ten Black people in Buffalo, NY.[30] The killer described himself as a supporter of white supremacy, inspired by Ukraine's neo-Nazi Azov battalion.

Sara Flounders, of the United National Antiwar Coalition (UNAC), said UNAC called protests in more than 90 cities. "Across the country people are beginning to mobilize and speak out against the billions and billions for a new war. Just weeks after [the U.S.] got out of Afghanistan they had a new war prepared, and that war was years in the planning—long before the 2014 fascist coup. It was for one reason only: to bring in a fascist grouping to threaten Russia, to bomb Russia and the Russian population of Ukraine, to expand NATO."

Flounders added: "Now they're doing the same thing against China. Japan has just doubled its military budget. It will soon be the third largest military power, in alliance with the U.S. for war on China. In these wars the Democratic and Republican parties are together: there's one war party. It's only people's movements from below—the grassroots movement—that's going to stop them. So *No to NATO, stop all U.S. wars!*"

The New York march ended with a teach-in at the People's Forum, where Eugene Puryear of *BreakThrough News* said that when the government and liberals blame Russia for the war in Ukraine, "it marginalizes any resistance to U.S. and NATO actions by setting up a framework that puts any anti-escalation or anti-sanctions arguments on the back foot by framing Russia as the aggressor."

Brian Becker, director of the ANSWER Coalition, said at the People's Forum teach-in that "It's quite clear the U.S. is not going to stop the war. It has no intention of negotiating a deal with Russia. But Russia is determined not to lose, because this is an existential war—if it were to lose it would be broken up, like Yugoslavia and the USSR. The U.S. would like to break up Russia and China so they won't have to face great powers."

Becker added: "When Biden *et al* talk about a Green New Deal, their actual policy is the opposite, because they need to produce more oil both in the U.S. and abroad. So if you care about climate change, this is another reason to oppose this war. If you care about the human family you need to oppose this war....

"We're in the beginning of a very big project," Becker continued. "When Rosa Parks didn't give up her seat [in the mid-1950s], she didn't know she was launching the Civil Rights movement." He noted that militant antiwar struggle won in the face of far-right electoral victories in 1968, when Wallace won five states and Nixon 35. It was the intensity of the antiwar and Civil Rights movements that forced the government to concede in spite of far-right electoral victories, Becker said.

Dr. King sparked an escalation of the antiwar movement with his historic April 4, 1967 speech at New York's Riverside Church, when he declared "the greatest purveyor of violence in the world is my own government. I cannot be silent." King also denounced "a triple prong sickness that has been lurking within our body politic from its very beginning. That is the sickness of racism, excessive materialism and militarism." Today the peace movement needs the leadership and prophetic voice King provided, and the elemental force of the Civil Rights movement he led in the 1950s and '60s.

Big Lies

The government learned important lessons from its failure to suppress the historic movements of the sixties—despite massive repression—

and it gradually revived the traditional U.S. war spirit. Ronald Reagan famously declared *"America's back!"* following the glorious 1983 invasion of tiny Grenada to stop a red revolution in "our back yard." Joe Biden again said *"America's back!"* in his first post-election victory lap to Europe in early 2021. In March 1991, after terror bombing Iraq, George H.W. Bush declared *"By God, we've kicked the Vietnam syndrome once and for all!"*

Twelve years later Bush Jr declared *"Mission Accomplished"* after his theatrical landing on the aircraft carrier USS Abraham Lincoln on May 1, 2003. The specter of Iraq's fabled "weapons of mass destruction" had been vanquished in an orgy of mass self-delusion.

The secret of success for the war planners was mass deceit—brazen use of the Big Lie to cover the true nature of the government's misadventure, and harness mass consent. It is now the weapon of choice for Biden and his *neo-cons* in waging the proxy war in Ukraine against Russia, and Israel's genocide in Palestine.

But deceit is not enough. It's combined with a war against "disinformation," designed to suppress anything but the official narrative. Inspired by the torture and imprisonment of whistle blowers like Chelsea Manning and Julian Assange, this war makes it a crime to tell the truth. The whistle blowers have been condemned as "terrorists," with the resulting fear effectively silencing journalists across the western mainstream media. An important by-product is self-censorship among antiwarriors, with a substantial sector denouncing vocal criticism of the official narrative. In October 2022, progressives in Congress quietly retracted a mild letter to Biden suggesting negotiation to stop the war. Instead, progressive leader Pramila Jayapal met with Biden at the White House.

Protesters have been called "Putin puppets" for highlighting the dominant presence of U.S.-backed neo-Nazis in Ukraine. But it has been impossible to suppress memories of the state department's Victoria Nuland blurting "Fuck the EU," in early 2014, while hand-picking the U.S. choice for president of Ukraine, on orders from then-Vice President Biden.

Military Breakdown

U.S. soldiers were a major factor in stopping the U.S. war machine during the Vietnam era. A Marine colonel wrote at the time that the U.S. military had "broken down" in Vietnam,[31] as soldiers refused to fight and combat veterans marched in protest after coming home. Sailors shut down ships that had been ordered to the war zone. Many bomber crews refused to go on raids into Vietnam, after witnessing at least thirty giant B52s crash after they were shot down.

Units of the Army's 101st Airborne Division have been stationed in Poland and Romania,[32] alongside about 70,000 active-duty U.S. troops in the rest of Europe. To date there have been no reports of U.S. troops deserting or refusing duty in Europe, or of European antiwar groups reaching out to them. Such activity was common during the Vietnam era,[33] and during the endless wars in Iraq and Afghanistan.

As of early 2023 about 375,000 U.S. soldiers, sailors and air personnel were stationed in east Asia, surrounding China, or on war ships patrolling the South and East China seas. The largest concentrations are in Okinawa and South Korea. They are bolstered by more than 600,000 regular South Korean Army forces (operationally controlled by the U.S.) and a suddenly resurgent Japanese military force.[34] U.S.

nuclear missile batteries are stationed in both countries, trained to target China and Russia. There is constant civilian protest against these forces in both Japan and Korea. Antiwar groups there often reach out to U.S. military personnel, encouraging them to demand to be sent home. Roughly 100,000 soldiers and family members are stationed in Hawaii, which is frequently used as a transit point between the U.S. mainland and the Asian theater.

In 1969 there was a large and significant *sanctuary struggle* in Honolulu.[35] Soldiers demanded a bill of rights, and sought sanctuary in local churches. The protest impacted the war planners, the soldiers themselves and their civilian supporters. Key organizers were the American Servicemen's Union (ASU), and religious antiwar activists, similar to the GI resistance movement in mainland USA. There were hundreds of GI resistance "coffee houses" near bases across the U.S., in Europe and Asia. Many of these support centers developed their own "underground" presses, publishing leaflets and newspapers encouraging active duty people to resist.

Worldwide Chorus Urgently Calling for Peace in Ukraine

Medea Benjamin and Nicholas Davies reported in late October 2022 on calls for peace[36] from UN Secretary General Guterres,[37] Pope Francis[38] and leaders of 66 countries[39] who were speaking at the UN General Assembly in September 2022, representing the majority of the world's population. They also highlighted former U.S. Ambassador to the Soviet Union Jack Matlock, who wrote an October 17 article in *Responsible Statecraft* titled "Why the U.S. must press for a ceasefire in Ukraine." The Ambassador said the United States "is obligated to help find a way out" of this crisis. The article concluded, "Until the fighting stops, and serious negotiations get underway, the world is headed for an outcome where we all are losers."[40]

Biden Says...

In March 2022 President Biden said "this battle will not be won in days or months... We need to steel ourselves for the long fight ahead." In May he said he was "doing everything within my power" to address "Putin price hikes." Margaret Kimberley, editor of *Black Agenda Report*, wrote that "Joe Biden and his foreign policy team of incompetent ideologues hope to convince Americans to accept food shortages, rising gas prices, and the risk of a hot war. The steady diet of dangerous nonsense is a necessity for them. The game is up if the people begin to question what they are being told.... The average person may not be well versed in the history of U.S. policy towards Russia, but they know when things don't add up.... Rambling, incoherent speeches punctuated by shouts of 'war criminal' and 'genocide' don't cut it when working people can barely afford to put gas in the tank."[41]

In a June 1, 2022 op-ed in the *New York Times*,[42] Biden insisted "We do not want to prolong the war just to inflict pain on Russia." Instead, he said the flood of new weapons, ammunition, and billions of dollars, is meant to help Ukraine "be in the strongest possible position at the negotiating table."

With strong U.S. support, Ukrainian President Zelensky has insisted on a *status quo ante,* meaning Russian troops leaving all the areas they have occupied. Neither the Russian government nor the people of the Donbas, Crimea and nearby areas can be expected to give up the gains achieved in the war.

A Path to Protracted Conflict

In late December 2022, retired Colonel Douglas MacGregor wrote that U.S. "refusal to acknowledge Russia's legitimate security interests in Ukraine and negotiate an end to this war is the path to protracted conflict and human suffering.... Inside the Biden administration, there is growing concern that the Ukrainian war effort will collapse under the weight of a Russian offensive."[43] He cited an *Economist* interview in which Ukraine's armed forces chief General Valery Zaluzhny admitted "Russian mobilization and tactics are working.... Ukrainian forces might be unable to withstand the coming Russian onslaught."[44]

MacGregor said "The Biden administration's unconditional support for the Zelensky regime in Kyiv is reaching a strategic inflection point not unlike the one LBJ reached in 1965. Just as LBJ suddenly determined in 1964 that peace and security in Southeast Asia was a vital U.S. strategic interest, the Biden administration is making a similar argument now for Ukraine. Like South Vietnam in the 1960s, Ukraine is losing its war with Russia."[45]

Faced with this grim scenario, MacGregor predicts "Biden will soon repeat LBJ's performance in 1965," proposing *not* a NATO attack on Russia, but instead a U.S.-led "coalition of the willing" to "establish the ground equivalent of a 'no-fly zone'."

But MacGregor says "NATO's governments are divided in their thinking about the war in Ukraine. Except for Poland and, possibly, Romania, none of NATO's members are in a rush to mobilize their forces for a long, grueling war of attrition with Russia in Ukraine.[46] No one in London, Paris, or Berlin wants to run the risk of a nuclear war with Moscow.[47] Americans do not support going to war with Russia,[48] and those few who do are ideologues, shallow political opportunists, or greedy defense contractors."[49]

'The Edge of Nuclear Catastrophe'

"The world is on the edge of nuclear catastrophe… because of the failure of Western political leaders to be forthright about the causes of the escalating global conflicts," declared Jeffrey Sachs,[50] Columbia University professor and Director of the UN Sustainable Development Solutions Network. "The relentless Western narrative that the West is noble while Russia and China are evil is simple-minded and extraordinarily dangerous. It is an attempt to manipulate public opinion, not to deal with very real and pressing diplomacy.

"There is only one country whose self-declared fantasy is to be the world's dominant power," Sachs continued. "It's past time the U.S. recognized the true sources of security: internal social cohesion and responsible cooperation with the rest of the world, rather than the illusion of hegemony. With such a revised foreign policy, the U.S. and its allies would avoid war with China and Russia, and enable the world to face its myriad environment, energy, food and social crises."

Sachs added that "European leaders should pursue the true source of European security: not U.S. hegemony, but European security arrangements that respect the legitimate security interests of all European nations, certainly including Ukraine, but also including Russia…. Europe should reflect on the fact that the non-enlargement of NATO and the implementation of the Minsk II agreements would have averted this awful war in Ukraine."

The fundamental question is what will it take to get the U.S. government to stop pouring the means of war—money, weapons, mer-

L

cenaries, and its NATO allies—into Ukraine. An all-sided and massive antiwar movement will be required, that does not depend merely on moral suasion or the enlightened words of illustrious sages. Only if there is a gigantic upsurge of opposition determined to stop "business as usual," will it be realistically possible to bring peace. Antiwar forces must directly challenge the "Big Lie" official narrative, and unite with all who want to save the planet and oppose the onset of fascism.

May 1, 2023

I

Palestine
&
The End of Modern Colonialism

1

Restore Historic Palestine, End Zionist Apartheid!

*Millions of people across the planet see that Zionism is the
ideology that perpetuates racism, apartheid and genocide.*

November 26, 2023

As protests surged across the U.S. and the rest of the world against Israel's genocide in Gaza, with polls indicating 68 percent of people in the U.S. support a ceasefire,[1] a call to "End Zionist Apartheid and Restore a Free Palestine" emerged at the United Nations in New York November 20. A contingent of "True Talmud Jews" carried signs saying "Judaism Condemns the State of 'Israel' and its Atrocities," and protesters held placards saying "Land Back: Restore Historic Palestine," and "From the River to the Sea—Single State Now!" This slogan is not "antisemitic," but, as Rep. Rashida Tlaib declared, is "an aspirational call for freedom, human rights, and *peaceful coexistence*."[2]

The group delivered a petition signed by 15 organizations and hundreds of individuals, addressed "to the UN, all relative officials and deliberative bodies," to "revoke the UN partition plan of 1947 which created the State of Israel."[3] The petition said "the British Mandate for Palestine (at the end of WWI) "was never valid," and Israel's "current

**Bronx Antiwar Coalition's Richie Merino summarizes
petition in front of the UN.**
Paul Gilman Photo

escalation of ethnic cleansing and genocide against the Palestinian people of Gaza and the West Bank" should be ended. It should be replaced by "a single state, a unified nation that respects the rights, voices and safety of all, regardless of religion or ethnicity."

The call was an echo of the anti-apartheid movement against the racist colonial state of South Africa, which led to its dissolution in 1994, when African National Congress leader Nelson Mandela became president of the new Republic of South Africa.[4] The parallels between the two struggles are many, including stubborn official U.S. government support and alliance with both racist regimes, which faced decades of struggle by the indigenous people of both countries, with intense and ever-growing worldwide solidarity.

The petition presented to the UN November 20 includes the following demands:

- An immediate Israeli ceasefire
- Open the Rafah crossing to bring in medical aid and fuel supplies for hospitals in Gaza
- Worldwide aid to Gaza refugees
- Free all Palestinian political prisoners held in Israeli jails
- End all aid to Israel—military and otherwise
- Freeze all Israeli assets held in foreign banks
- Cut off all trade to Israeli-held companies
- Demand Israel immediately dismantle and surrender all weapons of mass destruction in its possession: nuclear, biological and chemical.

It also calls for the arrest of Prime Minister Netanyahu, his immediate cabinet, leading members of the IDF and any/all U.S. officials complicit in Israeli's war crimes. It says such individuals "must be remanded to the International Criminal Court (ICC) for prosecution, in the spirit of the 1945-46 Nuremberg trials."

The petition says the UN should facilitate the creation of a new Single Palestinian State, with recognition of the Right of Return to all Palestinians, including refugees from the Nakba who currently reside in other nations.[5] (As enshrined in UN Resolutions 194 and 302) There should be land restitution to all Palestinians (either in land or monetary compensation), and full and equal citizenship to all Palestinians in the new nation. There should be an enforceable timetable for enacting new elections..., and a new constitution for the new nation, including a Bill of Rights with universal guarantees for all citizens, regardless of ethnicity, race or religion.

"All illegal settlements would be removed. In the interest of diversity and peace, current anti-Zionist Israeli citizens [would] not be expelled from the new nation's borders, but rather encouraged to stay and help rebuild, should they so choose." The UN has condemned settlements in the Occupied Palestinian Territories in multiple resolutions, declaring them to be illegal under international law.

"How Could So Many Have Stayed Silent...?"

"As a Jewish kid," said the petition's author, Janet of the Bronx Antiwar Coalition, "I often heard the question asked in my synagogue: how could so many have stayed silent during the Holocaust? What we're seeing now is a Holocaust wreaked by Israel. And what they do now has *nothing* to do with 'Jewish Values.' Zionists *do not*, and never did, speak for us."

She added "The constant refrain we hear now is Ceasefire. That's vital, but *not enough*. We need to address the cause itself. If we don't, I *guarantee* Israel and the U.S. Government (Democrat and GOP) will use a ceasefire to claim everything's fixed... and sweep the continuing Holocaust of Palestinians under the rug. If that happens, the death and suffering will continue."

She called the two-state solution "a fraud, an attempt to institutionalize past injustice, which enables more violence by Israel. Israel has *never* been serious about two states—they admit that in rhetoric you hear from Zionists calling for 'Greater Israel'... And two state denies Palestinians the right to return. Separate but equal doesn't work—we in the U.S. know what an injustice that is. Stolen land deserves restitution. *All* Palestinians—in Gaza, the West Bank, and refugees in other nations—have a *right* to return home to Historic Palestine, and be granted equal citizenship and rights."

Rabbi Dovid Weiss, of True Talmud Jews, said "we feel a religious duty to denounce the state of Israel," adding that for 3,000 years Jews and Arabs lived side-by-side in peace before the Zionists invaded. "Without Zionist state violence, Jews and Arabs can live in peace in a democratic, secular Palestine," he said.

"Israel's One-State Reality" – Foreign Affairs

Foreign Affairs, the flagship publication of the U.S. foreign policy establishment, ran a major article in April 2023 titled "Israel's One-State Reality: It's Time to Give Up on the Two-State Solution."[6] It said Netanyahu's extreme right-wing government "has shattered even the illusion of a two-state solution." It added that the "temporary status of 'occupation' of the Palestinian territories is now a permanent condition in which one state ruled by one group of people rules over another group of people."

The *Foreign Affairs* article says "a one-state arrangement is not a future possibility; it already exists, no matter what anyone thinks. Between the Mediterranean Sea and the Jordan River, one state controls the entry and exit of people and goods, oversees security, and has the capacity to impose its decisions, laws, and policies on millions of people without their consent." It notes that "Netanyahu has written that 'Israel is not a state of all its citizens' but rather 'of the Jewish people—and only it.' The man he appointed as minister of national security, Itamar Ben-Gvir, has declared that Gaza should be 'ours' and that 'the Palestinians can go to . . . Saudi Arabia or other places, like Iraq or Iran'."[7]

Israel's one-state reality, the *Foreign Affairs* article says, reveals a situation of *apartheid.* The term "refers to the system of racial segregation that South Africa's white minority government used to enforce white supremacy from 1948 to the early 1990s. It has since been defined under international law and by the International Criminal Court as a legalized scheme of racial segregation and discrimination and deemed *a crime against humanity*. Major human rights organizations, including Human Rights Watch and Amnesty International, have applied the term to Israel. So have many academics..."

The *Foreign Affairs* article says "the United States bears considerable responsibility for the one-state reality." So far, the article says, "the Biden administration has sought to sustain the status quo while urging Israel to avoid major provocations." That could be considered accurate in April 2023 when this article was published. But now the Netanyahu government is committing genocide in Gaza, and the Biden administration is supporting it with weapons, and vetoing calls at the UN for a ceasefire. This is not what most people in the United States want. The article says "polls show that most American voters would support a democratic Israel over a Jewish one." The authors say "the Israeli-Palestinian issue is increasingly viewed as an issue of social justice rather than strategic interest or biblical prophecy. This has been particularly true in the era of Black Lives Matter."

Legal Action to Block U.S. Aid to Israeli Genocide
In mid-November 2023 the Center for Constitutional Rights brought an emergency motion[8] in U.S. federal court to force President Joe Biden, Secretary of State Antony Blinken and Defense Secretary Lloyd Austin to stop providing weapons, money, and military and diplomatic support to Israel, as it is committing genocide in Gaza. "Our Palestinian clients are asking the court to urgently order Biden, Blinken

and Austin to stop supporting Israel's genocide," said Maria LaHood, CCR's Deputy Legal Director.

The report by Marjorie Cohn, former president of the National Lawyers Guild, appeared November 19 in *Truthout.*[9] The complaint alleges violations of the Genocide Conven-tion,[10] the Genocide Convention Implementation Act[11] and customary international law which forbids genocide. Plaintiffs include Defense for Children International–Palestine;[12] Al-Haq;[13] three Palestinian individuals who reside in Gaza and five Palestinian Americans who have family in Gaza.

Public statements by Israeli leaders constitute evidence of an "intent to destroy, in whole or in part" a "national group," the report says. Senior Israeli officials and politicians have called Palestinians in Gaza "human animals" and "children of darkness," and refuse to distinguish between civilians and combatants. The New York Times reported that "Calls for Gaza to be 'flattened,' 'erased' or 'destroyed' had been mentioned about 18,000 times since Oct. 7[14] in Hebrew posts on X (formerly known as Twitter).

In addition to supplying huge amounts of military hardware to Israel as it commits genocide, the U.S. government is supporting and guiding the Israeli military effort. DOD's Deputy Press Secretary Sabrina Singh admitted that Defense Department and other officials, "all the way up to the president have certainly informed and at least guided some of what the Israelis are doing on the ground in their ground operation," the legal complaint says.

U.S. officials refuse to place any limitations on Israel's use of U.S. military aid. On November 7, Singh admitted that "we don't put conditions on weapons that ... we're sending or that Israel is using." And Biden continues to refuse to call for a ceasefire. On November

9, when asked at a press briefing about the chances of a ceasefire, he replied, "None. No possibility."

Can There Be a Permanent Ceasefire?

A November 23 New York Times report said the Qatari government announced "a pause in fighting," to include an exchange of 150 Palestinian political prisoners for 50 non-military Israeli hostages, as well as the entry of hundreds of trucks of humanitarian aid into the besieged Gaza Strip.[15] Meanwhile the Palestine Information Center reported Nov. 23 that approximately 1,000 boats have gathered in Türkiye November 22 before heading toward Gaza in an attempt to break the Israeli blockade.[16] Organizers said the boats will carry 4,500 people from 40 countries, "including anti-Zionist Jews." The flotilla is part of a massive international campaign to force a permanent ceasefire.

"The steadfast resilience and resistance of the Palestinian people has delivered a four-day pause in the ongoing genocide while securing the imminent release of 150 Palestinian political prisoners," said an early December statement signed by the Palestinian Youth Movement, National Students for Justice in Palestine, The People's Forum, ANSWER Coalition, and the International Peoples' Assembly.[17]

The groups have called on people to remain in the streets around the world, to ensure that a permanent ceasefire is reached: "We must intensify our commitment and efforts until every single one of our demands is fulfilled: a permanent ceasefire, an end to the siege on Gaza, and an end to all U.S., Canadian, and European aid to Israel."

International NGOs are also pushing for a more permanent ceasefire. Joel Weiler, executive director of Médecins du Monde, said "for a medical organization, four days of pause is... band aid, not health care," arguing it would be insufficient time for treatment of serious injuries. Danila Zizi, Handicap International director for Palestine, said "it's a kind of a drop in the ocean if we don't have fuel and we don't have access."

"The only way to meet all these needs," or respect for human rights and access to healthcare, "is a permanent, sustained cessation of humanitarian law violations and a cease fire long enough to restore human rights to millions of people," said Paul O'Brien, Executive Director of Amnesty International USA. "That's why we're joining this call for an immediate and sustained ceasefire."

Mass pressure to stop the genocide is escalating. Activists in Tacoma, Washington, scaled the entrance of a ship in early November to stop weapons shipments to Israel, after people in Oakland gathered to slow down the ship.[18] Indigenous activists used canoes to interfere with the ship, one of dozens of ships carrying U.S. weapons to apartheid Israel. Similar actions have taken place in many other countries. Meanwhile university administrations across the country have waged a campaign of repression against students calling for an end to Israeli genocide, calling it "antisemitic."

Electronic Intifada, a voice of the Palestine solidarity movement, reports a "campaign of intimidation,"[19] especially against university students, who have been called "anti-Semite"[20] and "terrorist supporter"[21] for mobilizing for a ceasefire. "Raising our voices requires a calculation of risk, the report said: Will I be slandered?[22] Will I be prosecuted?[23] Will I be suspended?[24] Will I be fired?[25] Will my job offer be rescinded?[26] Will I be denied tenure?"[27] All of these things have happened. But the solidarity movement continues to grow stronger.

It is in this atmosphere that the petition to abolish apartheid Israel and restore historic Palestine has emerged. It's a movement that will not be stopped. Millions of people across the planet see that Zionism is the ideology that perpetuates racism, apartheid and genocide. The solution is to reverse the U.S.-European settler project in Palestine, and restore a democratic, secular Palestine where Arabs and Jews can live together in peace.

2

Blinken Blames Hamas
for Broken Truce

*During the long South African anti-apartheid struggle
the U.S. government stubbornly maintained support for
apartheid, just as it supports apartheid Israel today.*

December 5, 2023

After meeting with Israeli Prime Minister Netanyahu the night before the truce ended, U.S. Secretary of State Blinken blamed Hamas: the truce "came to an end because of Hamas. Hamas reneged on commitments it made."[1] He also said "Israel has the right to do everything it can to ensure that the slaughter that Hamas carried out on Oct. 7 can never be repeated… Hamas cannot remain in control of Gaza. It cannot retain the capacity to repeat that carnage."[2] Israel has been inflicting brutal terror on Palestinians for 75 years.

The Israeli Prime Minister's office said it was leaving the talks because Hamas "did not fulfill its part of the agreement, which included the release of all children and women on a list that was passed to Hamas and which it approved," the NY Times reported.[3]

Regarding carnage inflicted on Palestinians, Blinken said "before Israel resumes major military operations, it must put in place humanitarian civilian protection plans that minimize further casualties of innocent Palestinians," adding that "it's imperative that Israel act in accordance with international humanitarian law and the laws of war." But he arranged further shipments of tons of bombs immediately afterward.

Israeli Prime Minister Netanyahu defiantly responded "We have sworn, I have sworn, to eliminate Hamas. Nothing will stop us."

Plans for "A Greater Israel"

In September 2023, Netanyahu spoke at the United Nations General Assembly, detailing plans for "a greater Israel." He presented a map of "The New Middle East," showing Israel in 1948 "surrounded by a hostile Arab world. In our first seven years we made peace with Egypt and Jordan, and then in 2020 we made the Abraham Accords—peace with another four Arab states. Now look at what happens when we make peace between Saudi Arabia and Israel: the whole Middle East changes! We tear the walls of enmity."

He took a red marker and drew a line that "connects Asia through the UAE and Saudi Arabia to Israel and Europe." Palestine was gone. During the General Assembly debates in October, both Israel and the United States repeatedly opposed resolutions to stop the Israeli bombing of Gaza and allow aid convoys to enter.

The October 7 Hamas operation broke through the wall of enmity Israel had erected and maintained since 2006.

"Israel Knew Hamas's Attack Plan More Than a Year Ago," reported the New York Times December 2.[4] "The approximately 40-page document, which the Israeli authorities code-named 'Jericho Wall,' outlined, point by point" the *military operation* (not a "terrorist raid") which Hamas carried out. The document "described a methodical assault designed to overwhelm the fortifications around the Gaza Strip, take over Israeli cities and storm key military bases, including a division headquarters. Hamas followed the blueprint with shocking precision," the report said, including "a barrage of rockets at the outset of the attack, drones to knock out the security cameras and automated machine guns along the border, and gunmen to pour into Israel *en masse* in paragliders, on motorcycles and on foot—all of which happened on Oct. 7."[5]

The document circulated widely among Israeli military and intelligence leaders, the Times reported, "but experts determined that an attack of that scale and ambition was beyond Hamas's capabilities, according to documents and officials."[6] They seemed to ignore it.

Targeted Terror Bombing

Israel has conducted repeated terror bombing sorties against Gaza: "Operation Protective Edge" in 2014, another violent escalation in November 2018, and "Operation Guardian of the Walls" in 2021, according to Israeli journalist Yuval Abraham, reporting in *+972 Magazine*.[7] The article, "A Mass Assassination Factory: Inside Israel's Calculated Bombing of Gaza," says the Israeli army has perfected a system of "bombing targets that are not distinctly military in nature. These include private residences as well as public buildings, infrastructure, and high-rise blocks, which sources say the army defines as 'power targets'."[8]

The article says "The bombing of power targets, according to intelligence sources who had first-hand experience with its application in Gaza in the past, is mainly intended to harm Palestinian civil society:

to 'create a shock' that, among other things, will reverberate power-fully and 'lead civilians to put pressure on Hamas'… The Israeli army has files on the vast majority of potential targets in Gaza—including homes—which stipulate the number of civilians who are likely to be killed in an attack on a particular target. This number is calculated and known in advance to the army's intelligence units, who also know shortly before carrying out an attack roughly how many civilians are certain to be killed."

That's *terror bombing*—a program of state terrorism, systemati-cally developed and implemented by the Israeli government with U.S. approval and financing.

Israel wants to crush Hamas, but its actions target all Palestinians. During the seven-day truce, according to the Mondoweiss Palestine Bureau, Israel imprisoned more Palestinians than were released during the hostage swap, and killed at least 20 Palestinians in Gaza, the West Bank, and East Jerusalem.[9] So in reality Israel is waging war against *all Palestinians*, in both Gaza and the West Bank.

While Blinken and Netanyahu condemn Hamas, "Israel's bom-bardment of Gaza and the elation over the prisoners' release have deepened support for Hamas in the Israeli-occupied West Bank," the New York Times reported.[10] The freed prisoners have become "a potent symbol of Hamas's ability to achieve tangible results and its willing-ness to fight for the Palestinian cause. Each night in Ramallah, as new batches of prisoners were released, one refrain echoed across the crowds: 'The people want Hamas! The people want Hamas!'"

New elections are due for the Palestinian Authority, which shares administrative functions with Israel in the West Bank. Hamas could win, replacing Fatah, perhaps in alliance with all the Palestinian groups that have participated in the current *Intifada*, like those in the 1980s and early 2000s. In reality Hamas and its allies are a *national liberation movement,* that has led Palestinians in resistance repeatedly over decades. *Intifadas* are mass popular uprisings against Israeli occupation and repression.

The United Nations Human Rights Council opened Nov. 30 with a call for submissions[11] to its investigation into violations of international law in Israel and the occupied Palestinian territories since October 7. The invitation specified "attacks against and killing and injuring of civilians, including children, attacks on civilian structures and objects, ... collective punishment (including denying access to and availability of essential resources and services), starvation, incitement to violence (ethnic, political, religious), the dissemination of misinformation/disinformation, and other actions constituting a crime under international law."

An Axis of Resistance

Hamas and its allies inside Palestine are far from alone in resisting Israel's attacks, as well as threats from the U.S. to widen the war in support of Israel's ambitions to forge a "greater Israel." According to CodePink's Medea Benjamin and Nicholas Davies, there is an "axis of resistance" that includes the Lebanese-Palestinian front Hezbollah, which repulsed an Israeli invasion in 2006, and recently helped Syria defeat a ten-year U.S. proxy war.[12] In Iraq the Popular Mobilization Forces (PMF) have been fighting against the remnants of the U.S. invasion of the early 2000s. Now rebranded as the Islamic Resistance in Iraq, they have conducted numerous attacks against U.S. bases in both Iraq and Syria. They responded to U.S. airstrikes with two attacks on another U.S. base on Nov. 22 and several more on Nov. 23.

Iranian Foreign Minister Hossein Amir Abdollahian held meetings in Qatar on Nov. 23, first with Hezbollah leader Nasrallah and Lebanese officials, and then with Hamas leader Ismail Haniyeh, the Benjamin-Davies report said. "In the meeting with the leaders of the resistance," the Iranian foreign minister said, "I found out that if Israel's war crimes and genocide continue, a tougher and more complicated scenario of the resistance will be implemented. The leaders of the resistance will not allow the Zionist regime to do whatever it wants in Gaza and then go to other fronts of the resistance."

Another formidable and experienced military force opposing Israel and the United States is the Houthi army in Yemen. The Houthi Deputy Information Secretary Nasreddin Amer told *Newsweek* that if they had a way to enter Palestine, they would not hesitate to join the fight against Israel. "We have fighters numbering hundreds of thousands who are brave, tough, trained, and experienced in fighting," Amer said. "They have a very strong belief, and their dream in life is to fight the Zionists and the Americans."[13]

Cracks in Support for Israel's War

Cracks are appearing in Western support for Israel's war against Palestine. Spanish Prime Minister Pedro Sanchez said November 29, 2023 he had "genuine doubts" regarding whether Israel was complying with international humanitarian law in Gaza, and called for the European Union to recognize a Palestinian state.[14] The Belgian government, according to a November 16 Human Rights Watch report, "questioned the legality of some Israeli airstrikes, condemned its collective punishment of the Palestinian population, and called for targeted sanctions and accountability for those responsible."[15] It also expressed support for an International Criminal Court investigation on the situation in Palestine. The Belgian federal parliament has introduced a bill to ban trade with settlements in occupied territories.[16]

President Recep Erdogan of Türkiye has called the Israeli war on Gaza a massacre amounting to genocide. Turkish civil society groups are spearheading a campaign to send humanitarian aid to Gaza on cargo ships. The Palestine Information Center reported November 23 that approximately 1,000 boats gathered in Türkiye November 22 before heading toward Gaza in an attempt to break the Israeli blockade.[17] Organizers said the boats will carry 4,500 people from 40 countries, "including anti-Zionist Jews."

Chinese Foreign Minister Wang Yi appeared in New York in late November 2023 as part of China's month-long presidency of the Security Council. He announced a proposal to end the Israel-Palestine conflict through intensified diplomatic mediation, and convene a "more authoritative and effective" international peace conference as soon as possible.[18] Chinese President Xi Jinping also hosted an emergency meeting of BRICS countries—including new members Saudi Arabia, Iran, Egypt and Ethiopia, as well as South Africa, Russia and Brazil—with the same message.

A Movement to "Shut It Down for Palestine"

A leader of the Palestinian Youth Movement, Yara Shoufani, told the Real News Network Israel said "the human toll of Israel's latest bombing campaign now officially surpasses the bloodshed and displacement of the initial Nakba of 1947 to 1949, in which Zionist settlers killed more than 15,000 Palestinians, burned down over 500 villages, and drove some 700,000 people from their homes to clear the land for the founding of the state of Israel."[19] The Israeli leadership is mounting "a new Nakba," calling Palestinians "human animals."

The Real News Network report says "a global mass movement in opposition to Israel's genocide in Gaza has mobilized millions of people from Jakarta to Johannesburg, Ottawa to Oslo. Workers in Belgium and Spain have refused to transport weapons bound for Israel. Students have walked out of their schools and universities, activists have shut down arms factories, ports and government offices generating political crisis in many of the nations allied with Israel."

In the U.S. the November 4 national march on Washington DC, was the largest action in favor of Palestine in U.S. history, with estimates of more than half a million. "At the center of this campaign is really a refusal to continue with business as usual while the Palestinian people are facing a genocide that is part of a 75-year long process of colonization," Shoufani said. "And what we've seen in the context of this campaign have been a myriad of direct actions and mass mobilization. We've seen high school and university walkouts; in the Bay Area the shutdown of a highway; in New York protesters shut down the Brooklyn, Manhattan and Queensborough Bridges. We saw the Macy's Thanksgiving parade disruptions, the occupation of BlackRock and the New York Times offices. Across the world, we've seen the shutting down of train stations. We've seen labor organizers refuse to transport weapons to Israel, and block boats with weapons being sent to Israel."

Shoufani said it's "a major watershed moment where the Palestinian Youth Movement has been a part of a movement in North America and Britain to shut down industry and organize mass mobilizations across the world and across North America and Europe." But it goes further, Soufani suggests. "We're building a broad coalition of national liberation struggles, of working class struggles, of left struggles; and Arab and Palestinian and Muslim communities are coming together." Now, she says, "we have work to do to channel this moment into serious political organization. And I think what we're seeing is actually the beginning of that."

Ceasefire has been a central demand of this movement, Shoufani says, "because of its urgency and necessity amidst a violent genocide." But she says "ceasefire cannot be the only demand... We have also been calling for an end to complicity and aid"—over $3.6 billion per year in US aid to Israel, and now an attempt by the US government to approve an additional $14 billion in aid—"showing that the United States government is interested in rewarding Israel for its genocide."

The third demand is to end and lift the siege on Gaza. "For nearly 17 years, the people of Gaza have effectively been held in an open-air prison whereby Israel controls access to air, land and sea, determining what goes in and what goes out; what medicine is allowed in, what building products are allowed in, rationing food that is allowed in." When the truce ended, the flow of urgently needed aid for Gazans stopped. Numerous groups are headed to Egypt to pry open the Rafah crossing to Gaza.

The broader demands are to end the occupation and to release all Palestinian prisoners, Shoufani concluded.

"From the River to the Sea" – Two Views of One Idea

There has been lots of controversy about the popular slogan, "From the River to the Sea, Palestine will be free!" Maha Nassar, a scholar of Palestinian history[20] and part of the Palestinian diaspora, has "observed the decades-old phrase gain new life, and scrutiny, in the massive pro-Palestinian marches in the U.S. and around the world" recently.[21]

Pro-Israel groups, including the U.S.-based Anti-Defamation League, have labeled the phrase "antisemitic."[22] It has even led to a rare censure of House Rep. Rashida Tlaib, the only Palestinian-American member of Congress, for using the phrase.[23] But to Tlaib, and countless others, the phrase isn't antisemitic at all. Rather, it is "an aspirational call for freedom, human rights and peaceful coexistence."

The phrase can be considered a call for a unitary Palestinian state where people of all religions share equally.

Israel's far-right Netanyahu government has a kind of mirror image of the same vision: a *Foreign Affairs* article last April says "Between the Mediterranean Sea and the Jordan River, one state controls the entry and exit of people and goods, oversees security, and has the capacity to impose its decisions, laws, and policies on millions of people without their consent." It notes that "Netanyahu has written that 'Israel is not a state of all its citizens' but rather 'of the Jewish people—and only it.' The man he appointed as minister of national security, Itamar Ben-Gvir, has declared that Gaza should be 'ours' and that 'the Palestinians can go to . . . Saudi Arabia or other places, like Iraq or Iran'." Israel's ruling Likud party uses "from the River to the Sea" to highlight its determination for an exclusively Jewish state in *all* of Palestine.

Israel's one-state reality, the *Foreign Affairs* article says, reveals a situation of *apartheid*. The term "refers to the system of racial segregation that South Africa's white minority government used to enshrine white supremacy from 1948 to the early 1990s. It has since been defined under international law and by the International Criminal Court as a legalized scheme of racial segregation and discrimination and deemed *a crime against humanity*. Major human rights organizations, including Human Rights Watch and Amnesty International, have applied the term to Israel...." Another demand is *Restore Historic Palestine/End Zionist Apartheid!*

So there are competing interpretations of what life can and should be "from the River to the Sea." The anti-apartheid movement against the racist colonial state of South Africa supported the African National Congress in its decades-long fight, which finally won in 1994. During that long struggle the U.S. government stubbornly maintained support for apartheid, just as it supports apartheid Israel today. Few people today would claim that opposing apartheid in South Africa was a form of "anti-white racism." It seems reasonable to conclude that opposing apartheid in Zionist Israel should not be considered antisemitism. It should be considered removing past injustice and forging a better future for everyone.

3

What Does "Strategic Defeat" Look Like?

The genocidal Israeli assault on the people of Gaza and the West Bank could end the Zionist apartheid project and collapse the Israeli state as constituted

December 12, 2023

U.S. Secretary of Defense Lloyd Austin said recently that Israel faced "strategic defeat" if Palestinian civilians were not better protected. What would that look like? And would it be Israel's defeat alone, or would it also belong to the United States, which has provided the bombs, weapons and funds for Israel's determined campaign to "crush" its enemy in Palestine.[1]

"The center of gravity is the civilian population and if you drive them into the arms of the enemy, you replace a tactical victory with a strategic defeat," Austin said in a speech at the Reagan National Defense Forum in Simi Valley, California, on December 2.[2] "It would compound this tragedy if all that awaited Israelis and Palestinians at the end of this awful war was more insecurity, more rage and more despair," Austin said. "Israelis and Palestinians have both paid too bitter a price to just go back to October 6."

A few weeks earlier on November 7th, Jon Alterman, of the Center for Strategic and International Studies (CSIS), a prestigious DC think tank, wrote that Israel could lose:

> *"It is quite possible that the war in Gaza will be the first war in Israel's history that the army has fought and lost. That loss would be catastrophic for Israel and deeply damaging to the United States."* [3]

A senior vice president at CSIS, Alterman holds the Zbigniew Brzezinski Chair in Global Security and Geostrategy. Before joining CSIS in 2002, he was a senior State Department official, serving as special assistant for Near Eastern affairs.

Alterman highlighted "the checkered history that has afflicted the United States since the Vietnam War"—a colossal strategic defeat for the U.S. He also mentioned the post-9/11 wars in Iraq, Afghanistan, and the Syrian-Iraqi border area, which "were serious efforts with serious resources behind them, but years of fighting, billions of dollars, and thousands of U.S. deaths failed to secure victory."

He didn't mention the U.S. proxy war in Ukraine against Russia, which competes with the current crisis for attention, resources and lessons. Alterman asks:

> "What if the lesson that the United States offers is that even weak parties can repel strong ones with the right strategy?"

The lessons from Vietnam are especially relevant. A David and Goliath contest in which David humiliated Goliath, the Vietnam war was the beginning of the end for U.S. invincibility, and a signal to colonized people everywhere. "Our people will always exist," Vietnam's President Ho Chi Minh wrote in his political testament in May 1969.

"With the American invaders defeated, we will rebuild our land to make it ten times more beautiful [...] Our homeland will be reunified."[4] Ho's words resonate among Palestinians, not only in Gaza, but in the West Bank and in refugee camps in Lebanon, Syria, Jordan and Egypt.

Restoring historic Palestine, and rebuilding it as a land of peace where everyone can live together in equality and harmony would be many times more beautiful than the apartheid horror that Israel and the U.S. are currently forcing on the Palestinian people.

The Vietnam war led to the collapse of the U.S. military in Vietnam. The massive rebellions among U.S. youth in response to U.S. genocidal bombing there, the spiraling economic cost of the war, the disarray in the government and society, and growing international isolation all serve as warnings to both Israel and the United States of potential dangers looming in the present crisis. "Knee deep in the big muddy," the iconic description of the U.S. predicament in Vietnam,[5] suddenly seems familiar.

"A Mutiny Brewing"

There is "a mutiny brewing" in the State Department "at all levels," a State Department official told The Huffington Post shortly after Blinken greenlighted Israel's bombing assault on Gaza.[6] Hundreds of Jewish and Muslim congressional staffers signed an open letter urging lawmakers to demand a cease-fire of the bombing of Gaza.[7] A senior

State Department official, Josh Paul, publicly resigned October 18th, saying:

> "I fear we are repeating the same mistakes we have made these past decades, and I decline to be a part of it for longer."[8]

In his resignation letter Paul said "I cannot work in support of a set of major policy decisions, including rushing more arms to one side of the conflict, that I believe to be shortsighted, destructive, unjust, and contradictory to the very values that we publicly espouse."

Paul's resignation came the same day that Joe Biden embraced Israeli Prime Minister Netanyahu in Tel Aviv and "reiterated his steadfast support for Israel,"[9] in spite of condemnations at the United Nations and among human rights organizations and international law scholars, who claim the U.S.-backed Israeli bombing of Gaza is genocide.[10]

The U.S. faced a storm of criticism globally following its sole-vote veto December 8 of a UN Security Council resolution calling for a cease-fire in Gaza.[11] One day earlier the U.S. voted alone (or with a tiny and shrinking circle of allies) in the General Assembly against several resolutions to help the Palestinians with

- Humanitarian assistance to Palestinian refugees
- Support for the operations of the UN agency for refugees that works on the ground in Gaza
- A stop to Israel's illegal settlements on occupied Palestinian territory

France's UN ambassador, voting with the majority against the U.S. in the UN Security Council, called for a "new immediate and lasting humanitarian truce." Other European Union states are going further.

Spain's Prime Minister has called for the European Union to recognize a Palestinian state.[12] And the Belgian government, "questioned the legality of some Israeli airstrikes, condemned its collective punishment of the Palestinian population, and called for targeted sanctions and accountability for those responsible."[13]

Belgium also called for an International Criminal Court investigation on the situation in Palestine.

A Mark of Shame

The U.S. veto of the Security Council ceasefire proposal was "a mark of shame that will follow the United States for many years," declared Mahmoud Abbas, president of the Palestinian Authority,[14] which Washington and others have floated as a potential governing body for postwar Gaza. He called the United States "aggressive and unethical."

An overwhelming majority of U.S. voters—84 percent—are either very concerned (43 percent) or somewhat concerned (41 percent) that the United States will be drawn into a military conflict in the Middle East, according to a Quinnipiac University national poll of registered voters released Nov. 2.[15] A *Reuters*/Ipsos poll released Nov. 13 found that 68 percent think Israel should call a ceasefire in its attack on Gaza.[16]

Meanwhile the leaders of both Russia and China have taken initiatives to help end the crisis. Chinese President Xi Jinping hosted an emergency meeting of BRICS countries—including new members Saudi Arabia, Iran, Egypt and Ethiopia, as well as South Africa, Russia and Brazil—calling for an international peace conference on the crisis as soon as possible. China's Foreign Minister Wang Yi appeared in New York in late November as part of China's month-long presidency of the Security Council. He announced a proposal to end the Israel-Palestine conflict through intensified diplomatic mediation, leading to a "comprehensive, just and lasting" settlement of the Palestinian issue.[17]

Russian President Putin got lavish welcomes in both Saudi Arabia and the United Arab Emirates on a state visit December 6, where he offered to help resolve the crisis.[18] The Saudi and Russian leaders of the world's two biggest oil exporters called for all OPEC-plus members to join an agreement on output cuts "for the good of the global economy." Whether the move was aimed at Israel was not clear.

Massive U.S. financial and military aid to Israel provides a kind of shield for its ally. But any disruption of the global oil market could have unpredictable consequences. "A strategic move, such as embargoing oil exports to Israel and countries that do not support an immediate ceasefire in Gaza, could exert considerable pressure," wrote Yemeni author Karim Shami in *The Cradle,* a Middle Eastern publication.[19]

Inside Israel, in spite of a public show of united rage against Hamas for its daring October 7 attack, there has been much speculation that Prime Minister Netanyahu is fighting for his political life. Many Israelis blame him for ignoring an intelligence report showing "Israel Knew Hamas's Attack Plan More Than a Year Ago," according to a New York Times report December 2.[20] Hundreds of thousands of Israelis have had to leave their homes during the conflict, and many of those with dual nationality have been leaving the country.[21]

The Ground War in Gaza

Palestinian sources describe a situation much different from the official Israeli, U.S. government and mainstream media narrative. Writing in *The Electronic Intifada,* a Palestinian online publication based in the United States, Susan Abulhawa said "Israel tried desperately to control the narrative in a series of fabrications that immediately unraveled... Sensational lies about rape and beheaded babies[22] were quietly retracted despite being uncritically parroted by mainstream western media."[23]

The Electronic Intifada report says Israel's threatened land invasion was repeatedly delayed, "even after the U.S. came to its rescue with two aircraft carriers[24] and America's most sophisticated nuclear submarine[25] to the Mediterranean (along with bombs and other weaponry, plus billions of US tax-funded financial aid)." The report says each Israeli "attempt to roll into Gaza was met with fierce Palestinian resistance... With light armament, men in knock-off Adidas track suits and flip flops are successfully blowing up one Israeli tank after another and taking more and more prisoners, outsmarting the most celebrated Israeli and American military minds."

A spokesperson of the Palestinian Alternative Revolu-tionary Path Movement, Masar Badil, writes that "a small, brave, organized fighting force can defeat a well-equipped, large army. This is a lesson of history, what we have learned and what humanity has learned, from Algeria to Vietnam and today in Palestine."

Despite their grief and outrage at the genocidal assault on the Palestinian civilian population, Masar Badil says "the resistance is unified, completely—Islamic, nationalist and leftist forces, fighting together, on one path, one united front... Palestinians fight together because they know what Israel wants is to erase them. This is a battle of existence for us and for the resistance. And, therefore our people have no choice but resistance, no choice but steadfastness and no choice but unity."

Palestinians in Exile and in the Diaspora Regain Their Role

Palestinians in exile and in the diaspora have also begun to regain their involvement, particularly in Lebanon: "This has already been apparent, and we can expect a rise in the armed struggle in the Golan Heights, potentially in Jordan and elsewhere in the region. This reflects the restoration of the struggle in the Arab region to its compass, to the primary contradiction, with the Zionist regime and with imperialism...." This includes Lebanon, Syria, Iraq, Iran and Yemen, as well as popular forces in other nearby countries.

"We believe that Arab youth across the Arab homeland will join the Palestinian struggle and the Palestinian resistance," Badil says. "We know that our allies are all of those who confront imperialism: the Black Liberation Movements, the Filipino movement, the liberation movements and workers' movements all over the world. We salute all of those who are fighting together against all forms of repression against the illusions promoted by the capitalist media."

It is also possible that friends of the people of Gaza will break through the Israeli blockade at Rafah to force in food, medicine, and fuel. The Palestine Information Center reported November 23 that approximately 1,000 boats gathered in Türkiye November 22 before heading toward Gaza in an attempt to break the Israeli blockade. Organizers said the boats will carry 4,500 people from 40 countries, "including anti-Zionist Jews."[26]

The South African government and people are steadfastly supporting the Palestinian struggle. Their battle against apartheid achieved victory in the early 1990s, after the same decades of struggle the Palestinians have waged since 1947, and even before.

The solidarity movement in the U.S. and EU, as well as globally, have a significant role to play. The massive protests that continue and are intensifying, are having impact. They can be credited, at least partially, for the resignations of staff and interns in the White House, State Department, and Congress. Thousands of protesters flooded Wall Street as the U.S. vetoed the ceasefire resolution on December 8.[27] They called for a shutdown of the New York Stock Exchange.[28] At the same time, thousands were protesting a Biden fundraising event in Los Angeles.[29]

The genocidal Israeli assault on the people of Gaza and the West Bank is being confronted with a very large regional and global response. That response could actually cause not only the defeat of the Zionist apartheid project, but actually lead to the collapse of the Israeli state as currently constituted, and also to further crisis in the United States. It may also lead to fracture of major U.S. alliances in the region, as it has already in Turkey.

The governments of Egypt, Jordan and Saudi Arabia have all rejected the urgings of Blinken (*et al*) to provide an "outlet" for Palestinian refugees. Now a key question is whether the people in these countries can force their official leaders to take it a step further to stop the slaughter and siege of the people of Gaza and the West Bank.

II

Ukraine Conflict:
U.S. Proxy War Against Russia

4

Shock and Awe: Then and Now

March 16, 2022

S hock and awe" was George H.W. Bush's name for his attack on Iraq in 1991. A United Nations report described the effect as "near apocalyptic," sending Iraq back to the "pre-industrial age."[1] But it wasn't enough. After a decade of sanctions against Iraq, which further decimated the country and its people, George Bush junior launched a new invasion in 2003. Together with a parallel war in Afghanistan, the world has seen two decades of wholesale death and destruction at the hands of the U.S. military, at a cost of trillions[2] and countless deaths[3] estimated between one and two million.

When the savagery of the U.S. war was exposed by Wiki-leaks and Chelsea Manning, the official U.S. reaction was to demonize the whistle blowers, as if they were terrorists. Commenting on official U.S. hysterical condemnations of Russia and U.S. coverups of its own aggression elsewhere, Margaret Kimberley wrote that "it is the white supremacist underpinnings of U.S./NATO foreign policy which have created all of Ukraine's suffering. The narrative that only white people deserve peace and security is all the more shameful because the Global South suffers from war and privation as a direct result of U.S./NATO actions. It is NATO that destroyed the nation of Libya, NATO which attempted to do the same in Syria, NATO that occupied Afghanistan, NATO which wages war across African countries with U.S., French and British troops deployed across the continent."[4]

Kimberley added that "Ukraine has been pushed to the forefront of American thought in order to defend the imperialist foreign policy which led to the current conflict with Russia. If the blue eyed nation is suffering it is because of U.S. and NATO arrogance and aggression. Ukraine's current situation is a direct result of the 2014 coup engineered by the U.S. and its EU partners. An elected president was dispatched and a civil war began that has killed some 14,000 people. Ukraine is a U.S. colony with a puppet government now under military attack."

Cartoon: Patreon/Tim Murphy

John Mearsheimer, a leading proponent of the "realist school" of international relations, echoes Kimberley on the cause of the current crisis. In 2014, after the coup that brought far-right Ukrainians to power, Mearsheimer wrote that "the United States and its European allies share most of the responsibility for this crisis." He told the *New Yorker* "all the trouble in this case really started in April 2008, at the NATO Summit in Bucharest, where afterward NATO issued a statement that said Ukraine and Georgia would become part of NATO. The Russians made it unequivocally clear at the time that they viewed this as an existential threat, and they drew a line in the sand."[5]

Despite intense war hysteria and propaganda, the BBC admitted on February 28, 2022 that many of the viral claims about "Russian atrocities" were false.[6]

In the Donbas, the UN High Commissioner for Human Rights found that more than 14,000 people had been killed between 2014 and early 2022, with another 50,000 non-fatal casualties.[7] About two million Ukrainian refugees escaped to Poland and other European countries in early 2022. Another million eastern Ukrainians were evacuated to Russia, which is seldom reported in western mainstream media.

Official U.S. government claims—echoed by the main-stream media—of global condemnation of Russia are not validated by reality. Much of the Global South, led by China, India, Pakistan, Middle Eastern and African countries, and a substantial number of Latin American ones, have "abstained" from the avalanche of condemnations of Russia by the U.S. and its European allies.

The U.S. is waging a new "shock and awe" campaign, shipping countless tons of war material, mobilizing neo-fascist "volunteers" to join an "insurgency" against Russia, and urging NATO ally Poland to lend Soviet era bombers to Ukraine. President Zelensky of Ukraine is demanding a "no fly zone," with strong support from many U.S. members of Congress. That would mean U.S. fighter jets shooting down Russian aircraft—"it means starting World War III," according to Senator Marco Rubio.

Sanctions Threaten Global Economy

Sweeping sanctions imposed on Russia by the U.S. and western Europe threaten the global economy. The Biden administration has imposed an embargo on Russian oil, frozen Moscow's central bank assets and attempted to cut off most Russian banks from the SWIFT bank transfer system, not including the banks European countries use to pay for Russian gas they urgently need. All civilian air traffic between Europe and Russia has ended, and shipments of virtually all commerce to and from Russia have been frozen. U.S. and European companies have pulled out of Russia, with uncertain consequences.

Who gets hurt by this shock and awe campaign? It may be too early to tell. Starvation looms in north Africa, which depends on wheat from Russia and Ukraine. The COVID19 pandemic paralyzed the economies of many countries. As they struggle now to recover, this new hit could be a major blow. Gasoline prices and general inflation are rising everywhere.

European countries may not continue going along with the sanctions. Economist Michael Hudson argues the U.S. war on Russia is actually a U.S. war on Europe, to keep the EU subordinated to U.S. capital. Now European industry is shutting down as energy prices soar due to sanctions. Hudson says U.S. sanctions aim to "prevent America's NATO and other Western allies from opening up more trade and investment with Russia and China," to keep them "firmly within America's own economic orbit."[8]

To offset the loss of Russian oil on the global market, the U.S. has rushed to reopen negotiations with Iran and Venezuela. This is a sign of over-extension: one set of U.S. sanctions complicates or even cancels others.

Russia Offers Ceasefire and Peace Talks

On March 7, 2022 *Reuters* reported that Russia offered to immediately cease hostilities—to end its military actions "in a moment"[9]— if Ukraine and the West would do four things:

- Cease military action as part of a wider ceasefire;
- Change Ukraine's constitution to enshrine neutrality, and pledge to stay out of NATO;
- Acknowledge Crimea as Russian territory;
- Recognize the separatist republics of Donetsk and Luhansk as independent states.

A *New York Times* report on March 10, 2022 said "talks fail to stop the fighting."[10] Russian Foreign Minister Lavrov said Russia remained open to talks, suggesting a meeting between the presidents. Lavrov highlighted Ukrainian President Zelensky's recent comments that he was prepared to make concessions over Ukraine's aspirations to join NATO to stop the war.

"We are ready to discuss security guarantees for the Ukrainian state along with security guarantees for European countries and, of course, for the security of Russia," Mr. Lavrov said. "And the fact that now, judging by the public statements of President Zelensky, an understanding of just such an approach is beginning to take shape, inspires a certain optimism." *The Times* reported that the White House press secretary said "the United States also speaks to Mr. Putin's interlocutors before and after all these conversations."

Medea Benjamin and Nicholas Davies reported[11] that after President Zelensky's election in 2019, Ukraine's extreme right threatened him with removal from office, or even death, if he negotiated with separatist leaders from Donbas and followed through on the Minsk Protocol, which would grant autonomy to the Donbas region.[12] Zelensky had run for election as a "peace candidate," but under threat from the right, he refused to even talk to Donbas leaders, whom he dismissed as terrorists.[13]

John Mearsheimer said he thinks "the Russians would be willing to live with a neutral Ukraine, and that it won't be necessary for Moscow to have any meaningful control over the government in Kyiv... They just want a regime that is neutral and not pro-American."[14]

A Role for China?

U.S. Secretary of State Blinken has called Chinese Foreign Minister Wang Yi numerous times during this crisis, pressing China to use its leverage on Russia. Each time the Chinese have emphasized "rock-solid" friendship with Russia. Wang told *Global Times* March 10, 2022, "we would like to see an early ceasefire and cessation of fighting, which is also the common aspiration of the international community."

The *Global Times* report said "the major consensus reached by Chinese, French and German leaders during a virtual summit" was "the sovereignty and territorial integrity of all countries must be respected, the purposes and principles of the UN Charter must be fully observed, the legitimate security concerns of all countries must be taken seriously, and all efforts that are conducive to the peaceful settlement of the crisis must be supported."

Concerning the rounds of negotiations between Russia and Ukraine, Wang said that although there remain obvious differences between the two sides, the differences will be reduced each time the two speak, the hope for peace will increase, and the goal of a ceasefire and cessation of fighting will be further advanced. "China... is ready to step up communication with France and push the UN Security Council to reach a relevant consensus," Wang said.

Zelensky phoned Chinese President Xi in late April 2023. Xi told the Ukrainian president that China would send a special representative to visit Ukraine and other countries "to conduct in-depth communication with all parties on a political settlement to the crisis."[15]

A United Antiwar Movement?

The Ukraine crisis has taken its toll, at least for the moment, on the still modest forces of the U.S. and international antiwar movements, according to Jeffrey Mackler, a founder and leader of the United National Antiwar Coalition (UNAC).[16] He said two poles are emerging with counterposed strategic conceptions. "In the U.S., a growing minority, perhaps a majority, feels compelled to denounce with equal fervor both sides, Russia on the one, and U.S./NATO on the other." In sharp contrast, he said, "organizations representing the major antiwar coalitions demand: 'No to U.S./NATO War in Ukraine! No wars with Russia! No sanctions! No to NATO and NATO expansion' – a central cause of the present crisis – and, 'Fund human needs, education, housing, the environment and healthcare, not war!'"

That group includes UNAC, Black Alliance for Peace, ANSWER (Act Now to Stop War and Eliminate Racism), CodePink, International Action Center, Popular Resistance, U.S. Peace Council, Black Alliance for Peace, Women's International League for Peace and Freedom, Veterans For Peace, World Without War, and Global Network Against Weapons and Nuclear Power in Space.

These groups agree that "the U.S. imperialist government, with 1,100 military bases around the world in 110 countries is by far the world's greatest purveyor of force and violence. This all-encompassing violence includes an Orwellian-like U.S. and worldwide surveillance system, cyber wars aimed at disrupting or disabling vital communication and power generating systems, drone wars, sanction wars against 40 nations, embargo-blockade wars, CIA Special Operation wars, death squad assassination wars and open military interventions aimed at 'regime change' and conquest.

"It also includes wars of multi-lateral UN-sponsored 'humanitarian' interventions in the name of 'democracy' as is the case of the present U.S./UN occupation of Haiti."

The Biden administration, in a required report to the U.S. Congress a few months ago, listed 158 countries where U.S. military operations are underway. And the U.S. AFRICOM (African Command) conducts military operations in 53 African countries, where there have been five *coups d'etat* just in the past year.

In contrast China maintains a single military base outside its borders—in Djibouti, at the Horn of Africa—while Russia maintains six military bases, mostly in the former Soviet Republics and one in Syria.

The U.S. spends more on its military, at least $1 trillion annually, including the CIA budget, than most of the rest of the world combined. Russia's military budget is $60 billion. China's is about $232 billion. China and Russia are near-totally surrounded by U.S. military bases.

Who Are the Imperialists?

Mackler says defining China and Russia as imperialist countries along with the U.S., and concluding that they must be equally condemned, is wrong. "U.S. imperialism planned and orchestrated a fascist-led coup aimed at obliterating the minority Russian-speaking people, 30 percent of the population, and the same U.S. government seeks to orchestrate Ukraine's affiliation to NATO, replete with nuclear weapons on Russia's doorstep."

Ukraine's oppressed Russian-speaking population has asked for Russian aid in this crucial matter, Mackler says. "We support this right of all poor and oppressed nations to be free from imperialist war and conquest. This includes their right to seek aid from other nations… to help defend their sovereignty, if not their very existence."

Oil wars are the U.S. stock-in-trade, Mackler says, from the outright theft of Iraq's oil via the U.S. war against Iraq, to the sanctions, coup attempts and hot wars against Venezuela, Syria, Iraq, Libya and Iran, all aimed at keeping their competitive oil off the world market, or transferring it outright to U.S. corporations.

Michael Hudson adds that "the aim of U.S. sanctions is to keep the world oil trade firmly under U.S. control, because oil is energy and energy is the key to productivity and real GDP."

"U.S. imperialism lit the fuse that ignited and sustains the present war in Ukraine," Mackler concludes. "The U.S. antiwar movement's simple demand 'U.S./NATO Out Now!' remains central to its future success." He calls for a united front, democratic and mass action antiwar movement capable of defeating the U.S. warfare state's endless atrocities. "U.S. working people, allied with the nation's oppressed and exploited have a key role to play in the coming struggles."

5

"What America Will and Will Not Do in Ukraine"

June 8, 2022

To deal with the recently changed situation in Ukraine—where Scott Ritter says "Russia is achieving its military objective of liberating the entire territories of both Lugansk and Donetsk"[1]—Biden issued a carefully crafted message as an op-ed in the June 1, 2022 *New York Times*.[2]

The message appears to reflect conciliation, focusing on potential negotiations. "We do not want to prolong the war just to inflict pain on Russia," he insists. And "we do not seek a war between NATO and Russia." But Biden says the flood of new weapons, ammunition, and billions of dollars, is meant to help Ukraine "be in the strongest possible position at the negotiating table."

This reflects a new reality both on the ground and in the economic war against Russia. As the *Guardian*'s economics editor Larry Elliott wrote on June 2, 2022, things are not "going according to plan. On the contrary, things are going very badly indeed." His conclusion is that "sooner or later, a deal will be struck."

Guardian columnist Simon Jenkins adds that the sanctions policy "has blatantly failed… sanctions are clearly hurting countries in western and central Europe who are imposing them." A major recession threatens in both Europe and the U.S., as prices for fuel and food skyrocket. "The victims are overwhelmingly the poor," Jenkins says.

African Union leader Macky Sall, President of Senegal, met with Russian President Putin in Russia on June 3, 2022.[3] After talks on food shortages allegedly caused by the war, the leader said "I found Vladimir Putin committed and aware that the crisis and sanctions create serious problems for weak economies, such as African economies." He said he was leaving Russia "very reassured and very happy with our exchanges."

President Putin said Russia is "always on Africa's side," and is now keen to ramp up cooperation. He said Russia is ready to look for ways to ship grain stuck at Ukrainian ports, which western media falsely claims that Russia is blocking, but demanded the West lift sanctions. Russian Foreign Minister Sergey Lavrov planned to visit Turkey June 8 for talks on creating a "security corridor" to unblock grain exports from Ukraine.

A June 2, 2022 *New York Times* report said "Western nations like the United States, as well as Ukraine, oppose lifting sanctions imposed on Russia."[4] A UN report says around 25 million tons of grain from last year's Ukraine harvest are stranded in silos, and another 50 million tons are expected to be harvested in coming months. David Beasley, executive director of the World Food Programme, said: "Right now, Ukraine's grain silos are full. At the same time, 44 million people around the world are marching towards starvation."[5] The *Times* report said Turkey has proposed using its ships to transport grain from Odessa which, in addition to getting Ukraine to demine the port, would require an agreement from Russia.

In a June 3, 2022 interview, President Putin said Ukraine "must clear the mines and raise the ships they sunk on purpose in the Black Sea to make it difficult to enter the ports to the south of Ukraine... we will not use the demining process to initiate an attack from the sea."[6] He added there are numerous ways grains from Ukraine could be exported by rail or by sea, with full Russian cooperation.[7]

On June 6, 2022, the *New York Times* lead front-page headline was "Putin Peddles Stolen Grain To Needy World, U.S. says."[8] The "stolen" grain comes mainly from the Donbas and regions of Kherson and Zaporizhzhia, which are occupied by Russian forces, the *Times* article says. There is no mention of Russia itself as a possible source. According to UC Davis professor Aaron Smith's Ag Data News, Russia produces 11% of the world's wheat and Ukraine produces 3%. Russia accounts for 19% of the global wheat export market and Ukraine 9%.[9] Africans and Russians have a shared interest in moving the wheat.

African countries are unlikely to hesitate before buying Russian-supplied grain, no matter where it comes from, said Hassan Khannenje, director of Kenya's HORN International Institute for Strategic Studies, according to the Times report. Any Western pressure over Russian supplied grain is likely to backfire, he said. A Kenyan Foreign Affairs ministry spokes-person asked "Why would they need to warn us in the first place? This sounds like a propaganda ploy." Which is clearly what it is, given that the population in Donbas and in Kherson and Zaporizhzhia largely welcomes integration with Russia and does not consider its grain to have been stolen.

Negotiations?

All this underscores the urgency for negotiations to end the current war. But whether Washington and its NATO allies on the one hand, and Russia on the other, will decide to talk is an open question. Biden wrote in *The New York Times* op-ed: "I will not pressure the Ukrainian government—in private or public—to make any territorial concessions."

He did not say if the U.S. would exert pressure *against* such concessions, which would surely be required for talks to start. Most recently, Ukrainian President Zelensky has insisted on a *status quo ante,* meaning Russian troops leaving all the areas they have occupied. Neither the Russian government nor the people of the Donbas, Crimea and nearby areas can be expected to give up the gains achieved in the war.

Biden said "Ukraine's talks with Russia are not stalled because Ukraine has turned its back on diplomacy." He said, instead, that it is Russia's fault. He may actually believe that.

On June 4, 2022, the same week Biden's op-ed appeared, the *Times* ran a lead editorial by Christopher Caldwell saying "the administration is closing off avenues of negotiation and working to intensify the war." It also said the U.S. "is trying to maintain the fiction that arming one's allies is not the same thing as participating in combat," adding that the massive U.S. and NATO support is "a powerful incentive not to end the war anytime soon."

Scott Ritter wrote May 30 that Russia's early major battlefield successes in the Donbas "will leave Russia with a number of unfulfilled political objectives"[10]—including denazification, demilitarization, permanent Ukrainian neutrality, and western acceptance of a new European security framework. Whether these objectives can be achieved in negotiation or only continued war is an open question.

Ritter emphasizes that Russia linked its special military operation to Article 51 of the UN Charter, claiming "preemptive, collective self-defense."

This claim is supported by Ellen Taylor, daughter of Nuremberg prosecutor Telford Taylor, who wrote recently that "Russia, convinced that an attack was imminent, despairing of negotiations, persuaded by information contained in a hacked email, and aware of the danger of waiting any longer, launched its 'special operation'."[11]

Taylor cites reports from the Organization for Security and Cooperation in Europe (OSCE) that from February 15 to 24, 2022, Ukrainian army shellings in the Donbas increased daily from 41 to more than 2,000 on successive days. Taylor says "NATO's intention was to precipitate an attack. From a legal perspective it was imperative not to be identified as the aggressor. Russia was aware of this too." She adds that Russian leadership had "the responsibility to protect" its people.

Taylor concludes that "the crime of conspiracy to commit a war of aggression… has to be laid at the feet of NATO and the U.S." She adds that "the often-repeated claim that Russia's aggression was unprovoked, is preposterous."

"Stay the Course"

Biden's essay ends with some pontification, saying the U.S. will "stay the course with the Ukrainian people because we understand that freedom is not free. That's what we have always done whenever the enemies of freedom seek to bully and oppress innocent people."

In some parts of the world—like Africa, Asia, the Middle East and Latin America—it has been the United States that has sought to bully and oppress innocent people. It is happening now, in Yemen and

Somalia, and continues in Syria, Iraq and Afghanistan. Many Latin American governments claim it is also happening in their region.[12] Some in Western Europe feel their governments have been bullied by the U.S. to go along with the self-destructive economic war of attrition there. In the second half of the 20th century U.S. interventions in Asia, Africa, the Middle East and Latin America caused millions of deaths, and condemned millions more to extreme poverty and misery, according to *The Jakarta Method,* by Vincent Bevins.

The U.S., especially the CIA, has teamed up with local oligarchies to suppress democratic initiatives across Latin America: an attempted coup against Venezuela's Hugo Chávez in 2002, and against his successor Maduro in 2020; successful coups in Haiti in 2004 and Honduras in 2009; "lawfare" (fake legal scandals) leading to impeachments in Paraguay in 2012 and Brazil in 2016; a "self-coup" in Ecuador by President Lenin Moreno in 2017; and a *temporarily* successful coup against Bolivia's President Evo Morales in 2019. It is a pattern dating from the 1960s.[13]

This lived experience by the peoples who live outside the NATO alliance makes it increasingly difficult for Biden and his neocon advisers to make credible claims about protecting innocent people from the enemies of freedom. The question is: Who will protect us from Biden and the neocons?

In a May 2022 *Black Agenda Report* article, contributing editor Danny Haiphong says "Joe Biden is in trouble. The crisis of legitimacy afflicting his administration continues to worsen." A new AP-NORC poll in May 2022 pegged Biden's approval rating at 39%.[14] Rising inflation and shortages in basic needs, such as baby formula, have played a major role in Biden's declining popularity, as has an undue focus on prolonging the Russia-Ukraine conflict. The Biden administration is set to send billions in military aid to Ukraine despite the fact that the war does not make the list of major issues of concern for voters,[15] let alone the general population.

It may be pressure from below—from ordinary people in the U.S., Europe, and the countries of the Global South—that will finally bring enough pressure to achieve a durable peace, one which recognizes the sovereignty of Donbas and the post-2014 status of Crimea, and demilitarization and denazification of a new Ukraine.

6

Buildup to War: Threats and Counter-threats—Who's To Blame?

January 14, 2022 *(before February 24, 2022)*

Threats and counter-threats flying between Washington and Moscow over Ukraine have caused a flurry of fear and confusion that escalates and expands daily. Is the world on the brink of war? What's it about and who's to blame?

At this writing, the standoff in Ukraine between the U.S. and Russia had lasted for most of a year. Each side insisted the other is threatening a war reminiscent of the Cuban missile crisis of the early 1960s.

After three negotiating sessions in January, Russia's Deputy Foreign Minister Sergei Ryabkov declared it "absolutely mandatory" that Ukraine "never, never, ever" become a NATO member. In response U.S. Deputy Secretary of State Wendy Sherman said "we will not allow anyone to slam closed NATO's open door policy."

When U.S. Defense Secretary Lloyd Austin met with Ukraine's President Zelensky in Kyiv in October 2021, he promised U.S. support for Ukraine's future NATO membership, and blamed Russia for "perpetuating the war in Eastern Ukraine."

Russian President Putin declared December 23, 2021, that "Further movement of NATO eastward is unacceptable. They are on the threshold of our house."

On March 24, 2021, the Ukrainian president decreed Ukraine would take Crimea back from Russia, with "military measures" to achieve "de-occupation."[1] The U.S. and NATO voiced "unwavering" support. In April 2021 NATO backed a Ukrainian offensive in its civil war against Russian-allied separatists in the eastern provinces, Donetsk and Luhansk. That's when Russia moved thousands of troops to its borders with Ukraine, signaling it would defend its allies.

A January 11, 2022 report in Covert Action Magazine shows the Russian troop buildup is defensive. "The U.S. and Ukraine are secretly preparing for all-out war while advancing propaganda to make it appear that Russia is the aggressor," reported Russell Bentley, January 11, 2022 from the "Donbas People's Republic" (DPR).[2] DPR is a former eastern Ukraine province which declared its independence in 2014 after a U.S.-supported far-rightist coup government attacked Russian speakers in eastern Ukraine. Bentley claims U.S. war hawks and neo-Nazi Ukrainian officials are plotting a "false-flag" chemical warfare attack to blame on Russia as a pretext for declaring war. He says "Turkey has provided Bayraktir attack drones which have been used in combat against the DPR forces."[3] He adds that Ukrainian government "fracking" operations near Donetsk have caused tap water in the DPR to be unsuitable for cooking or drinking.

In summer 2021, 30,000 U.S. troops led "Operation Defender Europe 2021," a set of NATO exercises from the Baltic Sea to the Black Sea, according to the U.S. Peace Council.[4] In December the U.S. staged simulation bombing raids within 12 miles of Russian airspace. NATO warplanes confronted Russian aircraft 290 times in 2021. On December 7, Undersecretary of State Victoria Nuland told the Senate Foreign Relations Committee the U.S. has given $2.4 billion to Ukraine since 2014 "in security assistance" – $450 million in 2021 alone.[5]

As of January 2022 there were 10,000 NATO "instructors" in Ukraine, including 4,000 from the United States, Bentley reported. He added that in early December, 2021, the Greek port of Alexandroupolis received the largest shipment of U.S. military equipment in its history, including helicopters, UAVs, tanks, IFVs and artillery for a spring 2022 NATO exercise "Atlantic Resolve."

Nuland helped orchestrate the 2014 coup in Kyiv, the Ukrainian capital, that toppled a government friendly to Russia. The new far-rightist government ended language rights for Russian speakers who form the majority in the Ukraine's eastern provinces. Donetsk and Lugansk voted to separate, as did Crimea. Russia then annexed Crimea, to protect Russian speakers there and secure its Black Sea naval base. Russia provided humanitarian aid and trade to Donetsk and Lugansk, and stationed troops on their eastern border for protection.

A *New York Times* January 6, 2022 report said "Russia intervened militarily in Ukraine in 2014 after *pro-democracy protests* erupted there."[6] [emphasis added] The coup was actually carried out by fascist gangs, according to a May 2, 2018 report in The Nation by Stephen Cohen.[7] The gangs, including self-declared neo-Nazis, were egged on by Nuland, Biden, and other prominent U.S. politicians. The neo-Nazis were integrated into Ukraine's official military, which since 2014 has been trained, armed and reorganized by the U.S., Britain, Canada and other NATO countries. Stephen Cohen wrote that "the pogrom-like burning to death of ethnic Russians and others in Odessa later in 2014 reawakened memories of Nazi extermination squads in Ukraine during World War II." These horrors have all been whitewashed from the American mainstream narrative, despite being well-documented.[8]

Cohen added that "stormtroop-like assaults on gays, Jews, elderly ethnic Russians, and other 'impure' citizens are widespread throughout Kyiv-ruled Ukraine, along with torchlight marches reminiscent of those that eventually inflamed Germany in the late 1920s and 1930s... The police and official legal authorities do virtually nothing to prevent these neofascist acts or to prosecute them. On the contrary, Kyiv has officially encouraged them by systematically rehabilitating and even memorializing Ukrainian collaborators with Nazi German extermination pogroms and their leaders during World War II, renaming streets in their honor, building monuments to them, rewriting history to glorify them, and more."[9]

The people of the self-declared people's republics of Donetsk and Lugansk in eastern Ukraine face a complete economic blockade by Ukraine and its Western allies. Historically known as the Donbas region, eastern Ukraine is a mining and industrial center. Donbas miners played a crucial and heroic role in the defeat of the German invasion of the Soviet Union in World War 2. Many Russians revere the Donbas as "the heart of Russia."[10]

The Most Dangerous Problem in the World

A November 15, 2021 article by Anatol Lieven in The Nation says Ukraine is "the most dangerous [immediate] problem in the world, and also in principle the most easily solved."[11] The solution "has already been proposed and accepted—in principle: the Minsk II agreement, adopted by France, Germany, Russia and Ukraine in 2015, and endorsed unanimously by the UN Security Council."

Key elements of the Minsk II deal are full autonomy for Ukraine's eastern regions in the context of decentralization of power in Ukraine, demilitarization, and restoration of Ukrainian sovereignty. Despite agreement by all parties, Lieven says "because of the refusal of Ukrainian governments to implement the solution and refusal of the United States to put pressure on them to do so," the settlement is a kind of "zombie policy."

In mid-December 2021 Russia took a diplomatic initiative and presented a list of security proposals to the United States. According to the Wall Street Journal they include ending NATO's expansion further eastward to include Ukraine, a promise for each side to refrain from hostile activities, and an end to NATO military activities in all of Eastern Europe, Transcaucasia and Central Asia.[12]

"There is no other option," Russian Deputy Foreign Minister Sergei Ryabkov told reporters, "since a characteristic feature of the current stage of relations between Russia and the collective West is a complete lack of trust."

A *New York Times* December 16, 2021 report said President Biden is threatening "severe consequences" should Russia send troops into Ukraine.[13] The *Financial Times* on December 9 said Russia's Nord Stream 2 gas pipeline to Germany was "top of the list" when US officials brainstormed potential sanctions against Russia.[14] Germany and the rest of western Europe are already facing an energy crunch, with skyrocketing prices for natural gas.

Europeans need energy security and are wary of war. They want the Nord Stream 2 natural gas pipeline as soon as possible, while the Biden Administration calls it a "bad deal" and claims that it makes Europe vulnerable to Russian "treachery."[15] Texas Senator Ted Cruz has pressed hard against the pipeline, which offsets opportunities for U.S. energy companies to supply gas to the European market. U.S. foreign adventures have often constricted Europe's energy sources.

A 2021 survey by the European Council on Foreign Affairs found that most Europeans want to remain neutral in any U.S. war against Russia or China. But new NATO member states align with the U.S. against Russia. They have installed terminals to receive U.S. liquid natural gas deliveries, to reduce dependence on Russian gas.

Despite all the diplomatic efforts, powerful institutional and economic forces in the U.S. – the military industrial complex and big energy companies among others – are eager for a new cold war with Russia, which would provide them with boundless opportunities for profitable deals. "The U.S. military-industrial complex needs enemies like human lungs need oxygen," the saying goes. "When there are no enemies, they must be invented."

The demonization of Vladimir Putin and Russia by the U.S. media is part of this policy of inventing enemies. There is a long list of foreign leaders and nations whose attempts to pursue an independent foreign policy, defying the dictates of Washington, have brought down on them the wrath of the Empire.

7

"This Battle Will Not Be Won in Days or Months"

Biden on the Long Fight Ahead

The U.S. goal in Ukraine is regime change in Russia, no matter how long, or how many Ukrainian and Russian lives it may take or how many people become refugees

[BOB KNIGHT / APR 4, 2022]

April 4, 2022

Joe Biden "sparked a global uproar" on March 26, 2022, declaring Russian President Vladimir Putin "cannot remain in power."[1] He also said "this battle will not be won in days or months, either. We need to steel ourselves for the long fight ahead."

This was public confirmation that the U.S. goal in Ukraine is "regime change" in Russia, no matter how long, or how many Ukrainian and Russian lives it may take—or how many people become refugees, or how the world economy will be damaged.

"The words of a president matter," Biden said. "They can move markets. They can send our brave men and women to war. They can bring peace." In this case Biden's words helped move markets for the military-industrial complex and big U.S. energy companies. They were not intended to bring peace.

Biden's remarks came after a triple summit in Brussels of NATO, the European Union and the G7 big capitalist countries. There he "coaxed a display of unity" among U.S. allies, but "limited practical outcomes... underlined the limited options," according to *Agence France Presse-AFP*.[2] European powers stopped short of sanctions against Russian gas supplies, the report said, "fearing the consequences for their own energy security."

"Why I asked for this NATO meeting," Biden said, "is to be sure that, after a month, we will sustain what we're doing, not just next month, the following month, but for the remainder of this entire year," according to the AFP report. Speaking afterwards in Warsaw, Poland, Biden expressed the aggressive tone he hoped for in Brussels—to fire up his most militant NATO ally, and chat with members of the U.S. 82nd Airborne Division stationed there.

PR War "Off Message"

Biden's statement "went further than even U.S. presidents during the Cold War," according to a Washington Post report: It "immediately reverberated around the world as world leaders, diplomats, and foreign policy experts sought to determine what Biden said, what it meant—and, if he didn't mean it, why he said it." White House aides "were adamant the remark was not a sign of a policy change." But "they did concede it was... off message," the report said.[3]

Message control is a key weapon for U.S. war planners and their Ukrainian clients. CIA Director William Burns testified March 3 that "we have had a great deal of effect in... demonstrating to the entire world that this is premeditated and unprovoked aggression..."[4] The effort involves a super-professional message management operation, described by Dan Cohen, that "has produced a steady stream of sophisticated propaganda aimed at stirring up public and official support."[5] The international effort is led by PR Network of the UK.[6]

The PR campaign helped the Ukrainian Foreign Ministry produce a set of "key messages." It ruled out use of the terms "civil war in Donbas," "internal conflict," "conflict in Ukraine" and "Ukrainian crisis" to describe the Ukrainian government's war against the secessionist republics of the Donbas region. The UN Human Rights Office estimates that 14,200 people, including 3,404 civilians, have been killed in combat in eastern Ukraine between early 2014 and February 2022.[7]

Recent U.S. Regime Change Wars

U.S. message managers try to avoid comparison to recent U.S. regime change wars in Iraq, Afghanistan, Libya and Yugoslavia. It was 23 years ago that NATO countries, without UN Security Council authorization, ordered attacks on Yugoslavia—NATO's first target in Europe after the collapse of the USSR.[8] The air strikes lasted 78 days, from March 24 to June 10, 1999. About 1,000 NATO aircraft hit Serbia and Montenegro with thousands of cruise missiles and 80,000 tons of bombs, killing thousands and destroying countless buildings, hundreds of miles of roads, railroads and airfields, bridges, schools and hospitals. It also bombed the Chinese embassy in Belgrade, killing three Chinese citizens. The Chinese government protested vigorously without escalating the crisis, getting a U.S. apology and several million dollars of reparations.

"This war did not come out of nowhere," commented Serbian filmmaker Emir Kusturica. "This is a continuation of something sown long before. You can see the continuity of Russophobia in the West." He added that NATO's military intervention was followed by a color revolution that led to the overthrow of Yugoslav President Slobodan Milosevic. The same coup strategy was then used in Ukraine in 2004 and 2014. NATO's objective was the disintegration of the Yugoslav state. This is happening now against Russia, Kusturica said.

Biden's message includes intense demonization of the Russian President, calling him a war criminal and a "butcher," among other things—not likely to facilitate peace talks. That has not been the top priority for Washington, which has used Poland as a prime staging area for countless tons of military hardware, as well as mercenaries recruited from around the world.

New Round of Peace Talks

Russian and Ukrainian delegations planned a new round of face-to-face negotiations between March 28 and 30, 2022, reported China's Xinhua news agency.[9] Since February 28, the two sides held three rounds of face-to-face peace talks and a series of online discussions, failing to reach a major agreement.

The new round of talks took place after the Russian military announced on March 26 that "the main tasks of the first stage of Russia's special military operation in Ukraine had been completed." That stage focused on securing eastern Ukraine's Donbas region, demilitarizing and de-Nazifying Ukraine as Russia's priorities—not taking

Kyiv or other cities outside eastern Ukraine. The U.S. interpreted the Russian message as a "scaling back" of its original war objectives. It could also be interpreted as a new opportunity for peace.

Some observers have said China could play an effective mediator role in peace talks, since it has substantial trade with all parties—Russia and Ukraine, the EU countries and the U.S. China has "Belt and Road" projects in numerous European countries, including Ukraine, giving it an interest in an early resolution to the conflict. But U.S. pressure on China to "switch sides" against Russia complicates the issue.

The Chinese newspaper *Global Times* editorialized March 27, 2022 that "NATO, under the leadership of Washington, is the real initiator and driving force behind the conflict between Russia and Ukraine... What the U.S. really needs is tense and conflicting Russia-Europe relations," the editorial said. "It is NATO's eastward expansion that has triggered Ukraine's desire to join NATO and greatly triggered Russia's concerns over territorial security, which directly led to the current Russia-Ukraine conflict..."

Global Times raises the question: "do major European countries like Germany and France – also NATO members – really hold a stance over the Russian-Ukrainian conflict that is in line with Washington's interests? Unlike the past security crises in Europe, the EU will become the biggest victim of the Russia-Ukraine conflict. It will have to bear the brunt of the conflict. Therefore, as the Ukraine crisis develops, the differences between the US and Europe will become inevitable once the public opinion in major EU countries changes."

NATO leaders at the Brussels summit called on all states, including China, to abstain from supporting Russia's "war effort," *Global Times* reported, "and to refrain from any action that helps Russia circumvent sanctions. They also said China is engaged in spreading lies and misinformation to support Russia." Chinese Foreign Ministry spokesperson Wang Wenbin said "We oppose groundless accusations and suspicion against China, and will not accept any pressure or coercion."

A "Permanent State of Precarity"

Economist Michael Hudson agrees with the Chinese analysis, adding that U.S. policy is to control the world, and "to sort of repeat in Ukraine and Europe what it was doing in Syria and Libya."[10] John Mearsheimer, the noted exponent of the realist school of international relations, says "the West bears primary responsibility" for the disaster in eastern Europe, which "will cause a wrecked global economy."[11] In the Global South, with much of the world's population, many countries rely on grain imports from Ukraine and Russia, and worry about major shortages caused by supply chain disruptions.

South Africa's ANC Youth League spokesperson, Sizophila Mkhize, told *Breakthrough News* on March 25 that "Our countries were invaded, led by the western countries, led by NATO itself; and we did not hear anyone say 'pray for Libya,' for instance… They could have avoided this war, like the president of South Africa said. But they're arrogant, they're self-serving and they're selfish. And they don't care about many of the lives that are going to be lost." She added that "we have also realized the racism with which the people of Africa who were trapped in Ukraine were treated."[12] South African President Cyril Ramaphosa has offered to help mediate the crisis.

Ajamu Baraka of *Black Agenda Report* says "The war being waged against global humanity by the U.S./EU/NATO Axis of Domination is a hybrid war that utilizes all the tools it has at its disposal—sanctions, mass incarceration, coups, drugs, disinformation, culture, subversion, murder, and direct military engagement to further white power." He adds that on the heels of the 2008 financial crash and the crisis of the Covid pandemic, today millions "are experiencing a permanent state of precarity with evictions, the continued loss of medical coverage, unaffordable housing and food costs, and a capitalist-initiated inflation." He says U.S. rulers hope that "with the daily bombardment of war images, U.S. workers and the poor will embrace rising costs of gas and even more increases in the cost of food."

The Brown University Costs of War Project estimates that the wars waged by the United States in this century have cost millions of lives, at least $8 trillion and counting,[13] with another $8 trillion that will be spent over the next ten years on the military budget if costs remain constant from the $778 billion just allocated.[14] The Costs of War Project also notes that "38 million people have been displaced by the post-9/11 wars in Afghanistan, Pakistan, Iraq, Syria, Libya, Yemen, Somalia, and the Philippines."[15] Are the architects of NATO expansion ready to accept responsibility for more huge numbers of Ukrainian refugees?

CodePink's Open Letter

The anti-war group CodePink says:

"The U.S., which played a major role in exacerbating the conflict that led up to Russia's invasion of Ukraine, must now play a major role in the negotiations between Ukraine and Russia to achieve a ceasefire." It adds that the United States must be ready to make compromises and support negotiations between Ukraine and Russia by committing to the following:

- Rejection of a no-fly zone over Ukraine;
- No NATO expansion;
- Recognition of Ukraine as a neutral country;
- Sanctions on Russia to be lifted;
- Support for an international security agreement to protect the interests of all people on the European continent to remain free from war and occupation;
- Support for Ukrainian demilitarization to the degree that missiles would be banned;
- Supply humanitarian aid to Ukraine and support Ukrainian refugees.

8

Showdown at 'Credibility Gulch'

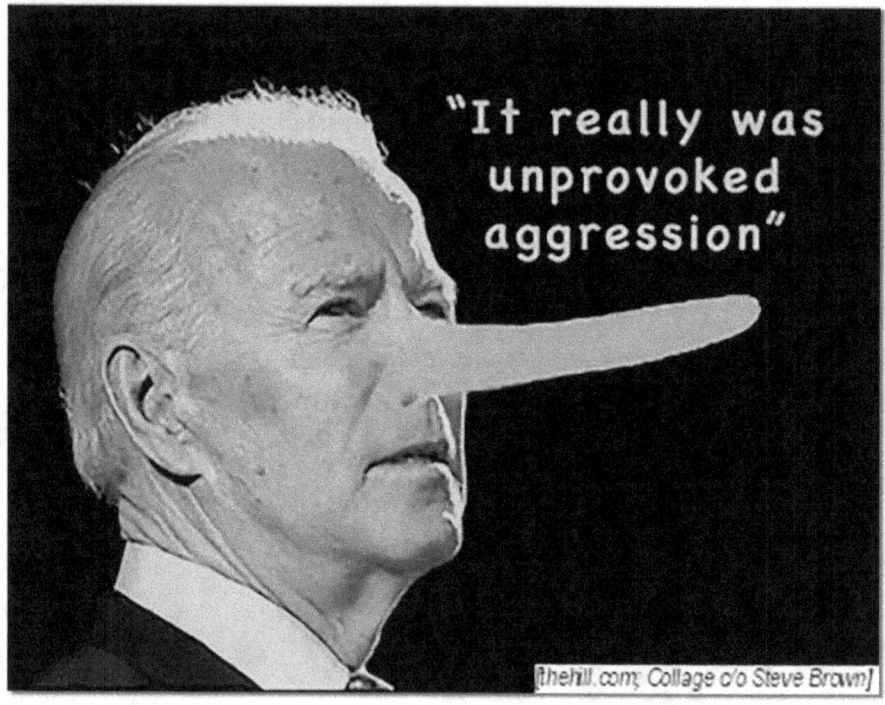

May 6, 2022

Back in the 1960s and 1970s during the war in Vietnam, everybody knew about the "credibility gap," which morphed into "Credibility Gulch" as the official story stretched ever-farther from reality.

We are seeing it again in the current war between the United

States/NATO and Russia, being fought out mainly in Ukraine. It is becoming "the Mother of All Energy Wars," according to Charlotte Dennett,[1] who highlights U.S. determination to cut Western Europe off from Russian gas and oil. She also links it to the recent endless wars to control the world's energy supply in Iraq, Afghanistan, Syria, Libya and Iran, and to dominate the Eurasian landmass with its enormous deposits of fossil fuels and other rich resources.

So when Joe Biden says he is doing "everything within my power" to address "Putin price hikes,"[2] he is stretching truth to the breaking point. He is really saying we need to endure higher prices for gas—and food, rent, clothes, and everything else—because of the reckless draconian sanctions war on Russia. It is an economic war of attrition against Russia, but it is hitting the whole world. So far Western Europe is suffering more than Russia, and the poorest people in the world, especially in Africa and the Middle East, are likely to be hurt the most. This hurt will turn into a massive showdown with Biden's "reality."

About the war itself, there is just one acceptable narrative in the mainstream media: that it is an unprovoked and illegal aggression by Russia. Any alternative views are "far-fetched claims from Russia" to "discredit international concerns about... war crimes," in the words from the April 12 *New York Times*.[3] In the online version of that article Ben Norton, editor of *Multipolarista.com*, is shown with a red line across his face, tweeting on Chinese media. It says Norton "claimed that a coup sponsored by the United States government took place in Ukraine in 2014 and that U.S. officials had installed the leaders of the current Ukrainian government."

How Far-fetched is This Claim?

According to Scott Ritter, the former Marine intelligence officer who served as a UN inspector of "weapons of mass destruction" in Iraq, it is *exactly* what happened. He takes it further back: During World War II, he says, "many Ukrainians joined the Waffen SS and fought for the Germans. They murdered, committed atrocities against Poles, Russians and Jews. In Babi Yar more than 30,000 Jews were gunned down."

In an interview with Joe Lombardo of the United National Antiwar Coalition (UNAC)[4] and Margaret Flowers of *PopularResistance.org*, Ritter tells of the Ukrainian fascist movement led by Stepan Bandera, who today has become an official hero to the far-right Ukrainian government. After 1944, Ritter notes, "Bandera began a resistance against the Soviets, which killed over 300,000 Russians."[5]

Ritter says that the CIA continued to fund, support and nurture the Bandera movement as part of its anti-Soviet activity right up to 1990. This is well-documented: "CIA intervention in Ukraine has been taking place for decades," write Richard Breitman and Norman Goda in *Hitler's Shadow: Nazi War Criminals, U.S. Intelligence, and the Cold War*,[6] published by the U.S. National Archives.[7]

In "Seven Decades of Nazi Collaboration: America's Dirty Little Ukraine Secret," in *The Nation*, March 28, 2014, Paul Rosenberg and *Foreign Policy In Focus* write that "the key organization in the coup that took place [in Kyiv in January 2014] was the Organization of Ukrainian Nationalists [OUN], or a specific branch of it known as the Banderas [OUN-B]. They're the group behind the Svoboda party, which got a number of key positions in the new... regime."[8]

The report says the U.S. has had a long-standing tie to the OUN. In 2004 they became part of the so-called Orange Revolution, heavily funded by the U.S., which brought Viktor Yushchenko, a close Svoboda ally, to the presidency from 2005 to 2010. "The United States was very aggressive in trying to keep the nationalists in power, but they lost the election. The U.S. was spending money through the National Endowment for Democracy," the *Nation* article says.

Ritter summarizes, saying of the Ukrainian far right, "The CIA grew it, owned it, controlled it." He says the U.S. organized a *coup d'etat* in early 2014 on the heels of the rightist protests demanding European Union membership for Ukraine.

He highlights that U.S. Assistant Secretary of State Victoria Nuland was caught in a phone call that was recorded, handpicking the U.S. choice to lead Ukraine. "We brought in the Banderistas," Ritter says. "They came in armed, and overnight they turned a peaceful demonstration into a violent revolution that killed scores of people—horrible acts of violence. That's what an insurrection looks like; it was orchestrated by the U.S. Biden got on the phone and told [the elected president] he 'had to go.' Now you've empowered these neo-Nazis, immediately passing laws at the expense of Russian language and culture. Slaughter in Odessa, attack on Crimea, move on Donbas. Thus began the Ukrainian civil war in Donbas."

Former NATO Military Analyst Backs Up Ritter

Jacques Baud, a former officer in the Swiss armed forces who was the Head of Policy and Doctrine for the United Nations Department of Peacekeeping Operations, backs up Scott Ritter's analysis and takes it further. He says, "Western countries have... clearly created and supported Ukrainian far-right militias. In October 2021, the *Jerusalem Post* sounded the alarm by denouncing the Centuria project.[9] These militias have been operating in the Donbas since 2014, with Western support," Baud says.[10] "These militias, stemming from the far-right groups that led the Euromaidan revolution in 2014, are made up of fanatical and brutal individuals. The best known of these is the Azov regiment, whose emblem is reminiscent of that of the 2nd SS *Das Reich* Panzer Division... So the West supports and continues to arm militias that have been guilty of numerous crimes against civilian populations since 2014: rape, torture and massacres."[11]

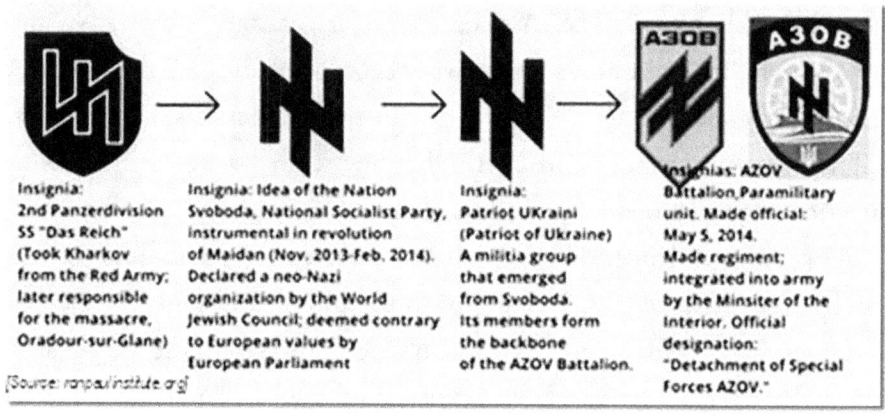

Insignia:
2nd Panzerdivision
SS "Das Reich"
(Took Kharkov
from the Red Army;
later responsible
for the massacre,
Oradour-sur-Glane)
[Source: ronpaulinstitute.org]

Insignia: Idea of the Nation
Svoboda, National Socialist Party,
instrumental in revolution
of Maidan (Nov. 2013-Feb. 2014).
Declared a neo-Nazi
organization by the World
Jewish Council; deemed contrary
to European values by
European Parliament

Insignia:
Patriot Ukraini
(Patriot of Ukraine)
A militia group
that emerged
from Svoboda.
Its members form
the backbone
of the AZOV Battalion.

Insignias: AZOV
Battalion, Paramilitary
unit. Made official:
May 5, 2014.
Made regiment;
integrated into army
by the Minster of the
Interior. Official
designation:
"Detachment of Special
Forces AZOV."

These forces occupied the port city of Mariupol on the Azov Sea. It is strategically located at the southwestern edge of the Donbas, on the highway to Crimea and Odessa. Mariupol has a significant Russian majority, and the 15,000 troops of the Azov regiment deployed there (but who do *not* live there) are seen as brutal occupiers, Ritter said.

The Russians have done everything possible to create humanitarian corridors, in accord with international law, Ritter said. "But the Ukrainian government and Azov have tried to close them. Azov used civilians as human shields, which meant the Russians had to assault residential buildings. The Ukrainians have said it's 'indiscriminate shelling—like the case of the maternity hospital, which is off limits by international law 'unless used for unpermitted purposes,' for instance, as a civilian target. Azov was using it for military purposes." Jacques Baud cites the testimony of civilians from Mariupol who said that the maternity hospital was taken over by the militias of the Azov regiment, who chased out the civilian occupants, threatening them with their weapons.

The other case is a large historic theater in Mariupol. Ritter said the narrative is that 1000-plus civilians were there; the Russians said "we know they're there and ordered our military to not attack it. No airplanes flew over the theater." Ritter said Azov blew off the roof to create a scandal of atrocity. "When you examine forensically the destruction doesn't look like the result of a bomb but of explosives in the roof—a false flag operation," he said.

"Most of the civilians are dying because Ukrainians are digging into civilian neighborhoods, forcing the Russians to blow up buildings, put down artillery barrages, and so on, killing civilians," Ritter said. "But the numbers would be even lower if the Ukrainians obeyed the law of war... There's one side that says we're trying to preserve civilian lives and civilian infrastructure. We have the other side that says 'if you collaborate with the Russians you will be killed'."

Whose War Crimes?

The cases of Bucha and Kramatorsk are especially notable. In both cases the Ukrainian government accused Russians of unspeakable atrocities, which were immediately echoed by Western governments, politicians and media, calling for Putin to be tried in The Hague for war crimes.

What really happened?

In late February Russian and Ukrainian troops fought on the outskirts of Bucha, northwest of Kyiv. Russian troops took control of the city, then on March 30 the Russians withdrew. While they were there for several weeks, Ritter says the Russians "had good relations with the local people. It was peaceful. The Russians said 'we traded our dry rations for their dairy products.' The citizens of Bucha would give them eggs, milk and cheese, and the Russians would give them dry rations—flour, salt, sugar, meat, and so on. This was going on, then the Russians left. Anybody who engaged in that type of interaction with the Russians was now viewed as a collaborator," Ritter said.

On March 31 Bucha's mayor declared the city "liberated" from Russians, calling it a major victory for Ukrainian defenders, with no Russian troops left in Bucha. The announcement made no mention of murdered civilians in the locality. On April 1—two days after the Russians left—the Ukrainian national police announced they were going into Bucha "to carry out a cleansing operation to liquidate the collaborators." Ritter said there is a videotape of a senior political figure announcing on social media to the citizens of Bucha, "'stay in your homes. The national police are carrying out a cleansing operation. Do not panic. Stay in your homes.' She repeats it over and over again. Why? Because the police are in the streets, gunning people down, kicking in doors of people who were collaborating, and killing them."

On April 2 the Ukrainian foreign minister claimed Russian troops shot and killed civilians before they left on March 30. Within minutes Western politicians were condemning Russian "war crimes" *before* looking at evidence and before there could be an investigation. The Russian government immediately demanded a UN Security Council meeting and called for a forensic investigation. The UK, as interim president of the Security Council, blocked the request.

Western media photos of the Bucha massacre show most of the deceased bodies wearing white armbands. Civilians used these to signal they were not hostile to Russia. The corpses were lying next to bags of humanitarian aid provided by Russian forces. In some photos fresh blood is visible, Ritter said. The corpses had *not* been there for days.

On April 8 in Kramatorsk, a small Donbas city, a missile in use by Ukrainian forces hit a train station while civilian populations were evacuating. Reports said 50 people died and another 100 were wounded. Kyiv immediately blamed the attack on Russia, but pictures of the missiles quickly made their way onto social media and were identified as Tochka-U missiles, which are currently used only by Ukrainian forces. Following this attack, the Investigative Committee of Russia announced they would open a criminal case to investigate the premeditated dissemination of false news about the Russian armed forces at the site.

Who's To blame?

Jacques Baud says "the American and European political leaders deliberately pushed the Ukraine into a conflict that they knew was lost in advance—for the sole purpose of dealing a political blow to Russia... The objective was the closure of the Nord Stream 2 gas pipeline, announced on February 8, 2022 by Joe Biden, during the visit of Olaf Scholz; and which was followed by a barrage of sanctions."

Now the question is when and how will it end. The U.S. and its NATO allies are rushing weapons and other equipment, including anti-aircraft and anti-ship missiles, and drones to Ukraine. Military officials, politicians and the press mainly talk of sending more weapons—not of finding a lasting, diplomatic solution to the crisis.

Biden has said "this battle will not be won in days or months, either. We need to steel ourselves for the long fight ahead." That was after declaring Russian President Putin "cannot remain in power."

This was public confirmation that the U.S. goal in Ukraine is "regime change" in Russia, no matter how long, or how many Ukrainian and Russian lives it may take—or how many people become refugees, or how the world economy will be damaged.

There is also a danger that the war will expand. All too many U.S. and NATO politicians are ready to send troops into Ukraine, risking nuclear war. Meanwhile, the U.S. also seems poised to extend the war to include China. These options are recipes for even greater disaster. Russia will continue to defend Russian speakers in eastern and southern Ukraine who have been victimized by neo-Nazi assaults. It will stop when Ukraine has been demilitarized and "de-Nazified."

It is possible the people of Western Europe will press for an end to the sanctions, which threaten to strangle their economies. The Chinese view is that "the EU will become the biggest victim of the Russia-Ukraine conflict. It will have to bear the brunt of the conflict. Therefore, as the Ukraine crisis develops, the differences between the U.S. and Europe will become inevitable once the public opinion in major EU countries changes."

China may have a role as mediator, based on its very significant trade relations with all parties to the conflict. That could help.

What Will Change Public Opinion?

Cutting through the propaganda that keeps people believing the official narrative has only begun. The testimony of authoritative and credible observers like Scott Ritter and Jacques Baud has not yet surfaced in mainstream media anywhere in the West. It has to be suppressed, as part of the Big Lie strategy the U.S. government and media have used in war after war from 1898 to now. From "Remember the Maine" (Cuba 1898) to the "Gulf of Tonkin Incident" (Vietnam 1964) to "Weapons of Mass Destruction" (Iraq 2002), the Big Lies have been enough to "justify" truly unprovoked aggression by the U.S.

The official phrase "unprovoked invasion of Ukraine" appears constantly. Noam Chomsky found that a Google search for this phrase returned "about 2,430,000 results" in less than half a second.[12] Searching for "unprovoked invasion of Iraq" yielded about 11,700 results in even less time. In fact, as Max Parry wrote in *Covert Action Magazine*, "If there was ever to be an end to the ongoing ethnic cleansing and war crimes in the Donbass region, a Russian intervention became almost inevitable."[13]

Bipartisan Big Lie

"We lied, we cheated, we stole... It's part of the glory of the American experiment," declared former U.S. Secretary of State Michael Pompeo back in 2019, bragging to a college audience in Texas. That unusual admission reflects the long-term, ongoing bipartisan official U.S. approach to both war and peace.

The case of Julian Assange is part of the pattern. Assange is now facing extradition from England to the U.S., after years of torture, charged with "espionage" because he publicized information about

U.S. crimes in Iraq. Assange faces up to 175 years in prison (a virtual death penalty) for practicing honest journalism. His case is barely mentioned in the mainstream media. If the U.S. cared about honest journalism, Assange would get a prize.

The U.S. strategy of using Ukraine to attack Russia has existed for a long time. Former National Security Adviser Zbigniew Brzezinski summed it up in his 1997 book *The Grand Chessboard*: "Ukraine is a new and important space on the Eurasian chessboard... because its very existence as an independent country [means] Russia ceases to be a Eurasian empire."

Victoria Nuland, currently U.S. Under Secretary of State and former foreign policy adviser to Dick Cheney, has been the key U.S. point person for using Ukraine to attack Russia. She coordinated spending billions to foster and finance the 2014 fascist coup in Kyiv, and famously handpicked a new Ukrainian president. From passing out cookies to the fascists to saying "Fuck the EU," Nuland has been the loose cannon that makes it hard to keep the official narrative believable.

How all this will end remains difficult to predict. Margaret Kimberley, editor of *Black Agenda Report,* says "Joe Biden and his foreign policy team of incompetent ideologues hope to convince Americans to accept food shortages, rising gas prices, and the risk of a hot war. The steady diet of dangerous nonsense is a necessity for them. The game is up if the people begin to question what they are being told."[14] She adds that a January 2022 opinion poll shows Biden with a 33% approval rating.[15] "The average person may not be well versed in the history of U.S. policy towards Russia, but they know when things don't add up," Kimberley says. "Rambling, incoherent speeches punctuated by shouts of 'war criminal' and 'genocide' don't cut it when working people can barely afford to put gas in the tank. We are left with a mass gaslighting effort that has created the desired effect of generating fear and or hatred towards Russia, but that hasn't increased satisfaction about the country's direction."

Public opinion, both in the U.S. and Europe, will eventually turn against the official Big Lie. The question remains: can public opinion—and pressure—change soon enough to prevent global disaster?

9

Anti-Russian Hysteria Limits Peace Prospects

July 26, 2022

As the U.S. and its NATO allies met in Spain and Germany during the last week of June 2022 in the midst of four full months of war in Ukraine, they were confronted with frustration and hard choices. Russian and Donbas militia forces controlled most of the Donbas region and a large part of the Black Sea coast. Deadly

Ukrainian shelling continued to kill people in the Donetsk area, but there was little doubt of the outcome for that region, regardless of how long it might take.[1]

Meanwhile, Ukraine's President, Volodymyr Zelensky, is reluctant to negotiate peace, hoping that a flood of U.S. and NATO weapons and money might help reverse some of the heavy losses his regime has endured. Zelensky claimed Ukraine was suffering between 200 and 500 combat losses each day. Western media repeated that claim but, like Zelensky, without offering any evidence. Perhaps it is true, but perhaps it is part of the effort to press for more reinforcements from NATO. Desertions and refusals to fight are also high, and Russian artillery is destroying new NATO weapons even before they can be deployed.[2]

The West's capacity to supply Ukraine's weapon needs is in doubt, as reported by British analyst Alexander Mercouris.[3] Only a fraction of the $53 billion in U.S. aid approved in May 2022 in Washington actually leaves the U.S.[4] Most of it goes instead to U.S. military contractors, while a shocking portion goes to fund Ukraine's government operations, which would grind to a halt without it. It is now clear that only massive U.S./NATO support keeps the war going.

European Unease

NATO "unity" has been overstated: Turkey has ceased dragging its feet on NATO membership applications from Sweden and Finland (new members into the alliance require unanimous approval by existing members) but Hungary, Spain and Portugal have opposed sanctions against Russia or raised doubts, due to a boomerang effect on their fragile economies.[5]

British Prime Minister Boris Johnson, the loudest U.S. ally, was forced to resign soon due to a series of political scandals. In France, President Macron lost his party's parliamentary majority in the June 2022 legislative election. Jens Plötner, foreign policy adviser to German Chancellor Olaf Scholz, declared on June 20, 2022 that Germans need to have a serious discussion about the "exciting and relevant" issue of a long-term relationship with Russia—a signal that Germany may wish for a more conciliatory approach with Moscow. In the U.S., President Biden and his Democratic Party face an electoral debacle in the fall of 2022, as polls show their electoral support continuing to drop.

German and French leaders continue to play a double game, just as they did with the 2015 Minsk 2 accord—feigning interest in "peace" while condemning Russia and imposing harsh sanctions. In fact, *all* Western European leaders are torn between slavish subservience to the U.S. and the economic hardships caused by the sanctions boomerang.

Meanwhile in Madrid, Biden said NATO would be "ready for threats in all directions."[6] He announced a permanent headquarters for the U.S. 5th Army Corps in Poland plus two more F-35 fighter jet squadrons to the United Kingdom. Further "air defense and other capabilities" will go to Italy and Germany, and there will be additional rotational deployments of NATO forces in Romania and the Baltic region. The new UK army chief announced plans for what amounts to *more war against Russia.*

Yes to Peace! No to NATO!

Across Europe and North America, broad peace forces mobilized, saying "Yes to Peace! No to NATO!" The "Peace Summit 2022 Madrid" issued a declaration on June 25 saying "the Russian Federation and the People's Republic of China are singled out as military adversaries and, for the first time, the Global South appears within the scope of the Alliance's intervention capabilities… The new NATO has certified that from north to south and east to west, it is prepared to intervene outside the imperative mandates of the UN Charter, as it did in Yugoslavia, Afghanistan, Iraq and Libya."[7]

In the United States, the Peace in Ukraine website says "This devastating war is killing thousands, displacing millions, and causing hunger, inflation, unrest, and increased militarism globally. It is not far-fetched to foresee a protracted war that goes on for years."[8] (To be clear, it is the *sanctions* boomerang of the West that is causing economic pain and dislocation in the West along with humanitarian tragedy in Ukraine. The war and the economic and political disruptions it is causing could end very quickly were the U.S. and NATO to urge Zelensky to sue for peace.)

The Peace in Ukraine statement denounces "the decades-long U.S. wars in Afghanistan and Iraq, the seven years of fighting in the Donbas, and the interest the U.S. has in bleeding the Russian economy dry."

Anti-war protests took place in many places in the world (notably in Madrid where NATO held a summit meeting on June 29 and 30), in many U.S. cities, and spanning the globe via a 24-hour "Peace Wave" streaming on Zoom. The main slogans at most of them are "End the War in Ukraine; No War with Russia; Ceasefire Now; Negotiate, Don't Escalate."

"Confusion of the American People"

The Peace in Ukraine call highlights the "confusion of the American people. They have tremendous sympathy for Ukrainians, but don't understand that the way to save Ukrainian lives is to stop the war."

Too many peace advocates in the world focus first on denouncing what is termed Russia's "criminal invasion" of Ukraine. That approach neglects to inquire into the *sources* of the conflict and ends up simply echoing the neocons in Washington and the mainstream media. In May, it led *all* members of the "Squad" (liberal members of Congress) to vote with the rest of congressional Democrats for the Biden administration's humongous military aid package to Ukraine.[9] This meant endorsing the official narrative condemning Russia's intervention in Ukraine, which aimed to crush the neo-Nazi presence in Ukraine's political life and oppose NATO expansion up to Russia's western border with Ukraine.

The "aid" vote in May was, in reality, a vote for more endless war, for regime change in Russia, and even for risking a global conflict with unthinkable risks. And of course, it was a vote to shelve the Build Back Better package of social and economic reforms introduced by the Biden administration in October 2021.

In Canada, an anti-Russia approach is absent from a statement by the Peace and Justice Network. It urges "Stop the Weapons; Stop the War; Stop NATO." It goes on to explain, "We will be standing in solidarity with the European activists who are organizing a major demonstration against NATO outside the [NATO] summit [in Spain] and with dock workers who are blocking weapons shipments to Ukraine."[10] Even better would be to more directly explain how the war is NATO's fault, not Russia's.

Russia's "Isolation" Overstated

Outside the United States, the "blame Russia" big lie has little credibility. On June 20, only four of 55 invited African leaders joined a Zoom call with Ukraine's President Zelensky that was organized by France and Germany. Multipolarista's Ben Norton reports "Western governments have tried to rally the nations of Africa to join their war on Russia. But the vast majority of the continent has ignored their pressure campaign."[11] *(Multipolarista* is now *GeoPoliticalEconomy.com)*

France's major newspaper *Le Monde* described Zelensky's message on Zoom as "an address that the African Union (AU) has delayed [receiving] for as long as possible and has been keen to keep discreet, almost secret."[12] This was a clear sign of Africa's overwhelming neutrality in the proxy war between the West and Russia.[13]

A March 28 report in the UK daily *The Guardian* said many African countries "remember Moscow's support for liberation from colonial rule, and a strong anti-imperialist feeling remains." The report said a significant number of African leaders are "calling for peace but blaming NATO's eastward expansion for the war, complaining of Western 'double standards' and resisting all calls to criticize Russia."

The *Multipolarista* report adds that "Global South nations representing the majority of the world's population have either blamed U.S./NATO for the Ukraine war or are neutral"—including China, India, Pakistan, Brazil, Ethiopia, Bangladesh, Congo, Iran, South Africa, Mexico, Tanzania and Vietnam.[14]

Western sanctions have not worked out as planned. "Like all battle plans, the original trans-Atlantic blueprint for imposing severe and crippling sanctions on Russia collided with reality after the war actually began," Andrew Weiss, of the Carnegie Endowment for International Peace, told *The New York Times.*[15]

In mid-June 2022, the St. Petersburg International Economic

Forum (SPIEF) attracted representatives from 141 countries and more than 1,500 companies from across Russia and Eurasia. A report by the Forum on its proceedings said commercial agreements worth trillions of rubles were signed, as well as international and inter-regional cooperation agreements in the areas of banking, high tech, education and science.[16]

"Step by step, we will normalize the economic situation," Russian President Vladimir Putin told the gathering. "We have stabilized the financial markets, the banking system and the trade network. Now we are busy saturating the economy with liquidity and working capital to maintain the stable operation of enterprises and companies, employment and jobs."

Putin also said, "The rising prices, accelerating inflation, shortages of food and fuel, petrol, and problems in the energy sector are the result of system-wide errors the current U.S. administration and European bureaucracy have made in their economic policies... It is not difficult to foresee coming developments. A shortage of fertilizer means a lower harvest and a higher risk of an under-supplied global food market. Prices will go even higher, which could lead to hunger in the poorest countries. And it will be fully on the conscience of the U.S. administration and the European bureaucracy."

He added that "this problem did not arise... in the past three or four months. And certainly, it is not Russia's fault as some try to declare, shifting the responsibility for the current state of affairs in the world economy to our country."

The Russian president added that "Russia is also able to scale up its food and fertilizer exports... Grain exports in the next season can be increased to 50 million tons." He said that, "as a priority, we will supply the countries that need food most of all, where the number of starving people could increase—first of all, African countries and the Middle East."

Right after the SPIEF Forum, there was a BRICS summit in Beijing of the leaders of China, Russia, India, South Africa and Brazil. Along with a full range of economic issues, the summit "discussed the situation in Ukraine and [said] we support talks between Russia and Ukraine. We have also discussed our concerns over the humanitarian situation in and around Ukraine and expressed our support to efforts of the UN Secretary-General, UN Agencies and International Committee of the Red Cross to provide humanitarian assistance in accordance with the basic principles of humanity, neutrality and impartiality," as established in the UN.[17]

Russian Aggression or NATO Aggression?

The avalanche of Western propaganda charging "Russian aggression" does not change the fact that Russia responded to years of provocations, after millions of Russians living inside the existing borders of Ukraine became targeted for choosing political autonomy from Ukraine's fascist-infiltrated national government. Some 14,000 soldiers and civilians have been killed between 2014 and early 2022 by the internal war launched by Kyiv in the spring of 2014 to crush resistance to the *coup d'etat* of that year and crush demands for autonomy.

Ellen Taylor, daughter of Nuremberg prosecutor Telford Taylor, wrote recently that "Russia, convinced that an attack was imminent, despairing of negotiations, persuaded by information contained in a hacked email and aware of the danger of waiting any longer, launched its 'special operation'." Taylor highlighted that, from February 15 to

24, 2022, Ukrainian army shelling in the Donbas region increased daily from 41 to more than 2,000 on successive days. "NATO's intention was to precipitate an attack," Taylor wrote.[18]

"From a legal perspective it was imperative not to be identified as the aggressor. Russia was aware of this too." She added that Russian leadership had "the responsibility to protect" its people, in terms of the 2005 UN World Summit.[19]

Taylor concluded that "the crime of conspiracy to commit a war of aggression... has to be laid at the feet of NATO and the U.S." She added that "the often-repeated claim that Russia's aggression was unprovoked, is preposterous."

U.S. Goal: Dismember Russia

Much of Ukraine was part of the Russian Tsarist empire for centuries. Donbas is considered by many to be "the heart of Russia," as a propaganda poster by the new, Soviet republics issuing from the 1917 Revolution put it in 1921. And the people of Donbas played a decisive role in the defeat of Nazi Germany.[20]

Following the demise of the USSR in 1990-91, future U.S. Vice President Dick Cheney wanted to slice up Russia into several smaller countries.[21] Former U.S. National Security Adviser Zbigniew Brzezinski proposed a "loosely confederated Russia—composed of a European Russia, a Siberian Republic, and a Far Eastern Republic."[22] He wrote, "what happens with the distribution of power on the Eurasian landmass will be of decisive importance to America's global primacy." He added that "a sovereign Ukraine is a critically important component" of such a policy.

Recent events have revealed that a key goal of U.S. foreign policy is to dismember Russia. On June 24, the U.S. government's "Helsinki Commission" held a congressional hearing plotting ways to break up Russia. This was discussed in the name of a supposed "decolonization" of parts of the Russian Federation. Participants at the hearing urged more support to separatist movements inside Russia.[23]

The prospect of fracturing and weakening the Russian Federation is a key reason why the U.S. is demonizing Russia, especially the country's president, Vladimir Putin. The U.S. followed a similar playbook against Saddam Hussein of Iraq, Slobodan Milošević of Yugoslavia[24] and Muammar Gadhafi of Libya. The "Big Lie" strategy uses the power of mass media to establish a narrative that becomes irrefutable through constant repetition.

Russia's defense of the Donbas and other Russian-speaking parts of Ukraine portends a reversal of this U.S. strategy. This is a large reason why Russia has concentrated its military efforts in these parts of Ukraine. It has completed much of the objective of its intervention to "liberate" Donbas from Ukraine's army and its paramilitary, extreme-right battalions.

Of note is that Ukraine's electoral map from 2007 simultaneously reflects the country's ethnic composition almost exactly. (See the following two maps.) Ukraine's current leadership and its U.S./NATO backers would like to avoid a settlement that reflects the demographic and historical reality of the country. But this is precisely one key issue that should guide negotiations for a peace agreement. A peace agreement reflecting Russia's legitimate concerns (voiced for many months and years) would establish a viable basis of cooperation by Russia with Ukraine and with Europe.

Ukraine's 2007 Electoral Map, showing vote breakdown by party

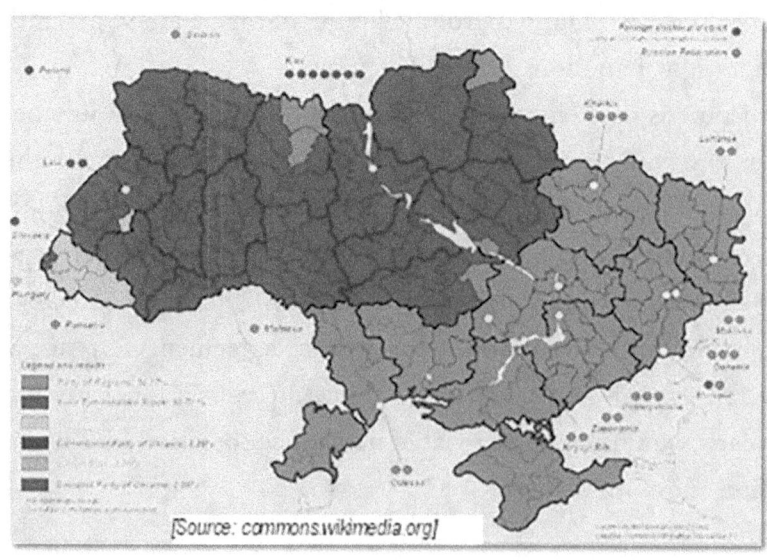

Getting to this type of truly viable peace requires complete withdrawal of NATO forces from Ukraine and an end to sanctions against Russia. It would require recognition of political self-determination for the Russian-speaking regions of Ukraine. (Ideally, a peace settlement in Ukraine would see the dismantling of NATO.)

NATO History is Covered With the Blood of Millions of Civilians

One of the groups participating in the Madrid Peace Summit is the Internationalist Anti-Imperialist Front. In a statement it says "the history of NATO and the U.S. is covered with the blood of millions of civilians, victims of the bombing of cities, towns and villages, of the pain of populations condemned to hunger, misery and forced migration due to the dozens of wars promoted by the sinister political-military alliance or by some of its partners using all its infrastructure. Added to this are the coups d'état and military dictatorships promoted by imperialism, the criminal blockades and the open or covert aggression against nations and peoples who fight for their sovereignty. And its consequences in failed states, after their military intervention, which facilitate the plundering of resources and monopolization of markets for Western imperialism."[25]

The statement continues, "NATO's relentless eastward expansion, the increasing militarization of the European Union under pressure from NATO, and the recent request by Sweden and Finland to join the Alliance add more instability and risk to the world.

"Faced with the serious danger that the warmongering spiral of NATO and the U.S. fuels new wars and provokes the division of the world into two blocs that will lead to a third nuclear world war, the

89

Internationalist Anti-Imperialist Front demands:

- Immediate withdrawal from NATO and closure of U.S. bases.
- Drastic reduction in military spending.
- The cessation of all military activity outside our territory.
- No to the shipment and trade of weapons to countries in conflict and war.
- Signing of the 2017 'Treaty for the Prohibition of Nuclear Weapons.'
- Measures against the growth of fascism that fuels wars."

U.S. "Must Remain Dominant Force in World" –Pompeo

Michael Pompeo, U.S. Secretary of State under Trump, said June 24 the US-EU-NATO alliance is seeking to "prevent the formation of a pan-Eurasian colossus" that could challenge Washington's empire. The United States must remain "the dominant force in the world," and "for an awfully long time to come," Pompeo insisted.[26]

The new cold war between the US-EU-NATO bloc on one side and the Eurasian bloc led by China and Russia on the other is a battle over "economic hegemony," and is rooted in control over fossil fuels and other resources, Pompeo declared.

The former CIA and State Department chief's speech, "War, Ukraine, and a Global Alliance for Freedom," was delivered at the Hudson Institute, a neoconservative Washington think tank.[27] The Hudson Institute is financed by the Pentagon and large corporations such as ExxonMobil and billionaire oligarchs like the Kochs and Walton family.[28]

III

A Peace Movement Emerges

10

"A Real Path to Peace" – A Movement is Launched

"For as long as NATO and U.S. imperialism exist, we'll be mobilizing and organizing against it. People power is the only thing that can stop the war machine!"

—Manolo de Los Santos

November 22, 2022

Y ou don't have to be Ukrainian or Russian to demand the U.S. stop instigating, escalating, and funding the war in Ukraine," declared People's Forum co-director Claudia Cruz at "The Real Path to Peace in Ukraine" event Saturday November 19 in New York.[1] Her comment was an answer to President Biden's clever trick of saying peace "is up to the Ukrainians." That gives him a pretext to continue the flood of military aid and "trainers" that keep the war hot and endless.

"We demand the U.S. government stop its brutality across the world," Ms. Cruz said. She scoffed at the official U.S. government claim that its proxy war in Ukraine was "unprovoked"—adding "we can see the difference between the narrative and the fact! We need to "shut down the war machine—NATO, Africom, every instrument of war across the globe."

"We have a collective responsibility to remember the four waves of NATO expansion," she said, explaining that when NATO's original "defensive" role against the USSR ended, it morphed from a dozen European and North American countries into an aggressive alliance of 30 countries, designed to surround Russia, and extend imperial power to the Middle East, central Asia, Africa and the Far East. "We need to remember *all* the imperialist interventions," Claudia said, "financing dictatorships and attacking people's movements in Central America in the 1980s, the invasion of Panama in 1990, terror bombing of Yugoslavia in 1999, invasions of Iraq, Afghanistan, Libya, and Syria; sanctions, coups and regime change operations in Cuba, Bolivia, Zimbabwe and Venezuela." [She later said the same and more about the U.S.-backed Israeli genocidal assault on Gaza.]

The event was called to launch a major intensification of antiwar activity across the U.S., starting on Saturday, January 14, as part of Martin Luther King Jr's birthday weekend. Sponsored by the People's Forum and the ANSWER coalition, the call was echoed by a large array of groups including Black Alliance for Peace, U.S. Peace Council, United National Antiwar Coalition, Black is Back Coalition, Popular Resistance, International Action Center, World Beyond War, BAYAN USA, Green Party, Sanctions Kill Campaign, Students for a Democratic Society, Global Network Against Weapons and Nuclear Power,[2] and dozens of others, including groups in Canada, Europe and Africa.

Manolo de Los Santos of People's Forum chaired the event, which was packed with people at the forum site, with hundreds more online. Manolo said "for as long as NATO and U.S. imperialism exist, we'll be mobilizing and organizing against it. People power is the only thing capable of stopping the war machine!" Brian Becker, director of the

ANSWER coalition, said "we have to organize *tens of millions*—if you're a worker, a young person, all who are suffering because all the money is going to the war makers and not the people—we need to unite to fight against the war makers. We're building a worldwide movement." Other speakers were Medea Benjamin of CodePink, Noam Chomsky, Jill Stein of the Green Party, Eugene Puryear of *BreakThrough News*, and VJ Prashad of the Tricontinental Institute.

Confusion in Washington

Medea Benjamin highlighted confusion in Washington, where "the most cautious people in DC are the military, with top General Milley calling for negotiations while "Biden and Blinken push the illusion that Ukraine can get back all of Donbas and Crimea." Meanwhile, she said, "not one Democrat opposed massive amounts of money for Ukraine," and thirty supposedly "progressive Democrats" had to retract a friendly letter to Biden gently suggesting it might be time for peace negotiations. She said the most extreme right-wingers are "feeling pressure from their base" against the "blank check" for Ukraine. [Democrats and Republicans have united against both Russia and Palestine. They are now losing on both fronts.]

Benjamin clarified that the antiwar movement should not align with the far right. Rather, it should reach out to people concerned about climate change, and the faith-based movement, including the Pope, calling for a Christmas truce.

Noam Chomsky said the war can end "in one of two ways—surrender or a negotiated settlement." The U.S. wants to continue the war to weaken Russia, then impose conditions on a "defeated" Russia worse than those imposed on Germany at the end the first world war, he said. The consequences of this "vast gamble" is the war must go on as long as it benefits the U.S. as the world's dominant power. He contrasted U.S. "shock and awe" war methods with Russia's more cautious approach, which has involved far less suffering and bloodshed than U.S. wars in Vietnam, Iraq, and Afghanistan. He said the U.S. "gamble that Russia will accept defeat" is based on illusion. He added that the euphoria in the executive offices of fossil fuel companies is unrestrained, but could lead to the end of organized human life on the planet, as the possibility of nuclear war is now casually discussed.

"Every possible path to diplomatic settlement should be pursued," Chomsky said, "but the U.S. and UK have sabotaged the Minsk II process and the deal between Ukraine and Russia in Istanbul in spring 2022. "As the war continues, options become very narrow," he concluded.

The End of the Colonial, White Supremacist Project, but "Full Spectrum Dominance"

Jill Stein, twice presidential candidate of the Green Party, said "we cut our teeth on fighting 'manufactured consent' in Vietnam and Iraq, and we're facing a social-economic system run by elites in the end stage of their colonial, white supremacist project." She pointed to recent polls showing that most ordinary people focus on basic issues like health and housing, inflation and economic desperation, and not "defense and security"—the favorite of DC politicians. The people's second concern is betrayal by government officials. War in Ukraine and against Russia rank between one and two percent, she said. But the U.S. federal budget allots more than a trillion dollars for the military, which "leaves a pittance for human needs and the climate crisis, while fifty million people are facing acute starvation. This is a crisis of war, a crisis of climate, and a crisis of justice, she said.

"The U.S. elites insist on 'full spectrum dominance'," Stein observed. "The U.S. is determined to not allow competitors to emerge—neither among enemies or allies"—referring to how the Biden gang bludgeoned its NATO allies to sanction Russia, causing economic disaster for themselves. The U.S. has disrupted or cancelled all nuclear treaties, endangering everyone. "The solution is to get rid of the nukes," she said. Meanwhile water levels are rising everywhere while fossil fuels are the engines of war. She said the explosion of the Nord Stream pipelines caused the "biggest ever" release of poisonous methane gas. "Now there are ten new LNG terminals in the U.S., and another ten in the EU—*we're gonna stop it!*"

The U.S. Wanted This War…

Brian Becker said "the U.S. pumped in billions for military aid to Ukraine after rejecting Russian peace proposals in December 2021. They wanted this war because of their imperialist objectives. First, the EU was becoming independent of U.S. imperialism by dealing with Russia and China—ending post-WW2 dependence on the U.S." The U.S. strategy was to use Ukraine to weaken Russia. Then the U.S. plan was for Russia to invade Ukraine. "If you're Russia, what should you do? We can't ignore that the U.S. imperialists wanted it." He added that "our enemies are not in Ukraine or Russia, they're on Wall Street, in the Pentagon and Langley [CIA headquarters]."

Becker said "the path to peace is to negotiate—not escalate." But he warned that "if you stand for peace against the war makers, you're an existential threat to them." He recalled that when Socialist leader

Eugene Debs called on people to oppose World War I in 1917, he was "tried, convicted and sent to prison." When Martin Luther King declared "the U.S. government is the greatest purveyor of violence in the world, and we need to stand with the Vietnamese people," he was assassinated a year later on April 4, 1968. Then a year and a half later in December 1969, Chicago Panther Fred Hampton was killed by police, he said. Still, Becker said a massive national and worldwide movement can stop the war makers.

Even though the EU countries became partners with the U.S. against the Global South following World War II, the anti-colonial struggles and revolutions across the world weakened the western alliance, Becker said. As the U.S. became bogged down in wars in Vietnam, Iraq, Afghanistan, Syria and Africa, the Europeans reached out to Russia and China for business. The U.S., under the neocon advisers to both Trump and Biden, have worked to force Europe back into tight dependency, even if it hurts the Europeans.

Realistic Basis for Peace

Ukraine's current leadership and its U.S./NATO backers want to avoid a settlement reflecting the demographic and historical reality of the country. But this is one key issue that should guide any effort at peace. A peace agreement reflecting Russia's legitimate concerns (voiced for many months and years) would establish a viable basis of cooperation by Russia with Ukraine and with Europe.

Getting to this type of truly viable peace would require complete withdrawal of NATO forces from Ukraine and an end to sanctions against Russia. It would require recognition of political self-determination for the Russian-speaking regions of Ukraine, that recently voted to join Russia. Ideally, it would also involve dismantling NATO, which was originally formed as a defense alliance against the USSR, but has morphed into an aggressive global force.

Why the Russian Intervention Happened

Russia's need to defend itself against NATO's increasing threats from the Baltic to the Caspian seas was just one of its problems. Protecting Russians and Russian-speakers in the Donbas was another. As Ellen Taylor, daughter of Nuremberg prosecutor Telford Taylor wrote recently, the Russian leadership "had the responsibility to protect its people."[3]

The Donbas is "the heart of Russia," as acknowledged by the Atlantic Council's reporter Irena Chalupa.[4] "We Won't Abandon Them," was the headline cited by Chalupa from a leading Russian business magazine, *Ekspert,* in June 2014. The people of Donbas played a decisive role in the defeat of Nazi Germany. Russians remember the USSR suffered about 27 million deaths and inestimable economic losses to the Nazis in World War 2. Their determination to prevent anything like that happening again should be understandable.

"Russia, convinced that an attack was imminent, despairing of negotiations, persuaded by information contained in a hacked email and aware of the danger of waiting any longer, launched its 'special operation,'" Taylor wrote. From February 15 to 24, 2022, Ukrainian army shelling in the Donbas region increased daily from 41 to more than 2,000 on successive days. "NATO's intention was to precipitate an attack," she stated.[5]

The avalanche of Western propaganda charging "Russian aggression" does not change the fact that Russia responded to years of provocations. Millions of Russians living inside the existing borders of Ukraine were targeted for choosing political autonomy from Ukraine's fascist-infiltrated national government. Some 14,000 soldiers and civilians were killed between 2014 and early 2022 in the internal war launched by Kyiv in the spring of 2014 to crush resistance to the violent *coup* of that year and smother demands for autonomy.

Conspiracy by NATO and the U.S. in a War of Aggression

Medea Benjamin and Nicholas Davies called Russia's intervention an "illegal, brutal assault," "criminal," and "the worst strategic decision that any Russian government has made" since the Russo-Japanese war of 1904-5. In their new book, *War in Ukraine: Making Sense of a Senseless Conflict,* they say "Russia was the aggressor." But Ellen Taylor states bluntly that "the crime of conspiracy to commit a war of aggression… has to be laid at the feet of NATO and the U.S." She added that "the often-repeated claim that Russia's aggression was unprovoked, is preposterous."

The United States investment in bringing anti-Russian fascists to power was not merely "over $5 billion to assist Ukraine," as Assistant U.S. Secretary of State Victoria Nuland bragged. Another part of the "investment" was to "fuck the EU," as Nuland said. By sabotaging French and German efforts to sustain the Minsk II accords granting autonomy to the Donbas region, and cutting western Europe off from Russian energy supplies, the U.S. forced a conflict between NATO and Russia. The September 26 explosion of the Nord Stream pipelines can be seen as a guarantee, at least for now, that Europe cannot depend on Russian gas. Meanwhile the U.S. and NATO flooded Ukraine with military hardware and "trainers," effectively converting Ukraine's military into a NATO force.

All this makes it clear the U.S. wants the conflict in Ukraine to last, and to "weaken Russia," as Defense Secretary Lloyd Austin said. That's a version of former Vice President Dick Cheney's dream: he "wanted to see the dismantlement… of Russia, so it could never again be a threat,"[6] as former Defense Secretary Robert Gates wrote in his 2014 memoir. (Cited by Ben Norton in *Multipolarista,* now known as *GeoPolitical Economy Report.*[7]) Cheney and former U.S. National Security Adviser Zbigniew Brzezinski wanted a "loosely confederated Russia – composed of a European Russia, a Siberian Republic, and a Far Eastern Republic." Brzezinski wrote that "what happens with the distribution of power on the Eurasian landmass will be of decisive importance to America's global primacy." He added that "a sovereign Ukraine is a critically important component" of such a policy. [8]

Russia's intervention in the Donbas and other Russian-speaking parts of Ukraine countervails the U.S./NATO strategy. It has completed much of its objective to "liberate" Donbas from Ukraine's army and its paramilitary, extreme-right battalions. But this also makes clear that talk of Russian withdrawal from the territories it now holds is not a basis for peace. Western claims that "Ukraine is winning," and Ukrainian President Zelensky's fantasies of "regaining Ukraine's lost territory" are hopeless.

In May 2022 the *NY Times* editorialized that "A decisive military victory for Ukraine over Russia, in which Ukraine regains all the territory Russia has seized since 2014, is not a realistic goal… Unrealistic expectations could draw [the U.S. and NATO] ever deeper into a costly, drawn-out war."[9]

How to Stop the War

The question of how to avoid a drawn-out war that could become nuclear is now a topic of debate. There are calls for negotiations from a variety of sides. Talks will of course take place. Biden takes the position that negotiations are up to the Ukrainians, whose war effort is totally dependent on the U.S. and NATO. Meanwhile Zelensky has insisted that Russia surrender and withdraw its forces. This doesn't sound like a basis for negotiations, and makes calls for talks meaningless. Instead, the peace movement should call for an end to U.S./NATO funding, training and arming of Ukraine. As Manolo de Los Santos declared at the People's Forum event, "people power is the only thing capable of stopping the war machine!"

11

"We Won't Be Silent Anymore!"

[SOURCE: LA PROGRESSIVE]

A massive and militant Poor People's Moral March and rally brought thousands from across the country to Washington, DC on June 18, 2022. The crowd was "a diverse mix of Black and White, Latino and Asian, young families with babies, retirees, union members and college students," a Washington Post report said. The Post report was itself news—authored by four reporters, together with striking color photos of activists with signs and placards.[1]

Black Lives Matter activists were joined by young and old peace movement marchers, trade unionists and many others in a mix of anger and joy, demanding a 'Third Reconstruction' to reverse decades of attacks on the poor, immigrants, indigenous people, the environment and people in countries across the globe. The joy was an expression of the amazing victory that such a coalition had come together to change the country's direction.

The first Reconstruction followed the U.S. Civil War; it saw former slaves take power and control of their lives across the South. They won the 13th, 14th and 15th amendments outlawing slavery and guaranteeing basic civil rights, before being crushed by Klan violence and betrayal by President Andrew Johnson, who came to power after Abraham Lincoln was assassinated. The second Reconstruction was the Civil Rights movement led by the Reverend Dr. Martin Luther King, Jr., in which millions of African Americans and their allies rose up marching and braving racist violence to win the promise of the first Reconstruction.

"We are not an insurrection, but we're a *resurrection,*" declared the Reverend Bishop William Barber, co-chair of the Poor People's Campaign (PPC). The campaign harks back, in revival mode, to the 1968 Poor People's March on Washington, led by Ralph Abernathy of the Southern Christian Leadership Conference in the wake of the King assassination on April 4 of that year. The reference to *insurrection* recalled the proto-fascist assault on the capitol on January 6, 2021, which has dominated headlines and TV news in recent weeks and months.

Speakers From Nearly Every State

The day-long rally heard a parade of speakers from nearly every state, telling personal stories of their experiences with poverty, oppression and injustice. The dozens of speakers addressed homelessness, environmental injustice, challenges faced by Indigenous people, gun violence, women's right to choose abortion, and the shameful treatment of veterans, among others. Prominent "interpreters" also spoke. Dr. Bernice King, daughter of the civil rights leader, emphasized that today's poor people's campaign is part of her father's legacy. She declared "we *can* create the Beloved Community, a society of justice and love. Dr. Cornell West, of Columbia's Union Theological Seminary (formerly of Harvard and Princeton), highlighted the common message of oppression, resurrection *and revolution* in all the speakers' talks. Phyllis Bennis of the Institute for Policy Studies declared that all the problems of the day could be solved by ending the endless U.S. wars everywhere, and cutting the Pentagon budget. (Maybe allot $53 billion to people's needs instead of war elsewhere.)

A special June 18 *Democracy Now* report highlighted that the Moral March comes "as the United States experiences its worst inflation in decades with skyrocketing food, gas and energy prices," suggesting the movement will grow as the economic crisis worsens. *Democracy Now* host Amy Goodman interviewed Poor People's Campaign co-chairs Rev. Barber and Rev. Liz Theoharis, about the background and goals of the campaign. "We are... a resurrection of thousands, of every race and creed and color and kind and geography," Barber said, "who are coming nonviolently to Washington, DC, from all across this great land, to say that the 140 million poor and low-wealth people in this country, 43% of this nation, 52% of the children, 60% of Black people, 30% of white people, 68% of Latinos... 87 million people who are uninsured or underinsured, 32 million people that get up every morning and work jobs that do not pay a living wage, less than $15 an hour – we won't be silent or unseen anymore."[2]

Barber said "poor people are coming to say not only do we need a moral reset – and low-wage workers are saying it – we represent 32% of the electorate now, poor people do, and 45% of the electorate in battleground states. And it's time for that power to be organized, mobilized and felt in every election throughout this country."

"What you saw January 6 was the insurrection. What you see on Saturday is a resurrection of people coming together," Barber said.

Reverend Liz Theoharis mentioned a study by the PPC and Columbia University professor Jeffrey Sachs that showed between two and five times the number of poor people from poor communities died from the pandemic than richer communities and richer people. "How is it," she asked, that "this rich nation… still has the kind of poor health outcomes, still has 87 million people who before the pandemic were uninsured or underinsured, and even tens of thousands who have lost their healthcare coverage in the worst public health crisis in generations?"

At the start of the march, a group of doctors and medical professionals from North Carolina, White Coats for Social and Health Justice, staged a "die-in" highlighting that "poverty is a public health problem," as Dr. Howard Eisenson of Durham, NC, said. "The problem with physicians," he said, "is too often we stick to our exam rooms and operating theaters and don't get out and support organizations fighting for affordable housing, quality education, environmental Justice and other platforms."

Weapons: Roots of Inequality

The antiwar group CodePink carried hand-made signs and placards saying "Cut the Pentagon," and "Demilitarize Everything." CodePink's

San Francisco chapter coordinator Cynthia Papermaster said "Weapons are really one of the roots of all this inequality."

The PPC's Reconstruction Agenda demands the government "prioritize peace by reducing military spending, redirecting those resources" to people's priorities. Over the past 20 years the U.S. government has spent more than $21 trillion on war, militarizing the border, surveillance and a war economy that kills, incarcerates and criminalizes the poor at home and around the world, the Agenda says.

Walter Hales of the Black Political Empowerment Project in Pittsburgh said he believes advocating for those in poverty is the most prevalent issue of the day. "It's an intersectional issue that energizes racism and causes families to fall apart," he said. "But it affects education and hurts those who can't participate in a democracy."

Months and Years of Organizing

The June 18 Moral March was the culmination of months of protest marches in 45 states. There were major rallies earlier this year in Los Angeles, Memphis, Louisiana, Philadelphia, West Virginia, North Carolina, Wisconsin, Ohio, and on Wall Street in New York City. Major unions in all industries across the country endorsed the Poor People's Campaign, as have the organizing drives of low-wage workers in fast food and retail.

At a June 6 press conference Rev. Barber said "Our nation is experiencing a historic wave of labor uprisings led by the workers who are demanding that the value of their work be represented in their pay, their working conditions, and in our nation's laws."

The unions share the campaign's agenda demanding a minimum wage of at least $15 an hour, a universal single-payer national health care system for everyone, and an end to homelessness, evictions and foreclosures. The agenda also calls for expanded food security programs, universal access to clean water, utilities and high-speed broadband; cancellation of student debt, an end to school segregation, and increased funding for early childhood programs. The agenda demands that immigrants' rights be respected and protected, that the southern border be demilitarized, with a timely citizenship process for all who seek citizen status, and an end to deportations. The agenda also calls for "fair taxation on the ultra-rich, corporations and Wall Street," noting that fair taxation combined with cutting the military budget would make the entire people's agenda very affordable.

Rev. Liz Theoharis quoted Dr. King, that "war, in all its forms, is a war on the poor, and it's cruel manipulation of the poor." She added, "we don't have a draft in this country, but we have a poverty draft. And 22 veterans commit suicide every day in this country because of the moral costs of war. And if we look at our military budget, 53 cents of every discretionary dollar goes to the military. We can't even spend 15 cents on healthcare and living-wage jobs and investments in our children and in anti-poverty programs combined. This disproportionately impacts poor people. That's poor people in the United States, and poor people across the world. As Dr. King said, you have poor people come together from this rich nation to go and kill poor people across the world. And we're seeing this across the world in this moment as well."

At the June 18 rally, Barber announced plans to return to DC in September after continued organizing during the summer months. Will the plans include more than elections?

"Our job is to run all the way to the finish line," Rev. Barber said. Where is that "finish line"? Maybe if all the forces aligned in the Third Reconstruction Agenda join together at the same time across the country, the resurrection the campaign calls for can really happen. But it might take more than a rally in DC. We may want to learn from other high points in the people's movement—like Occupy Wall Street, and the Longshore Union's shutdown of the West Coast. Or the "red for ed" teacher wildcats of a few years back. Or the student strikes across the country back in 1970. Or the plant occupations and strikes in the 1930s that gave birth to the CIO. All of that together could get us to the finish line and then some.

12

Pivot To Peace!

Asian Americans & Peace Allies
Mobilize vs. Anti-China Aggression

Dee Knight
Oct. 22, 2022

[SOURCE: LA PROGRESSIVE]

Washington's most recent anti-China hostility and aggression got a strong counterpunch from Pivot to Peace co-founder retired San Francisco Judge Julie Tang and CodePink on October 18, 2022. The Taiwan Policy Act, which made it out of the Senate Foreign Relations Subcommittee in September 2022, would recognize Taiwan diplomatically as a de facto nation, not a part of One China, as established by existing treaty law. It would also add $16.5 billion to an already enormous—and illegal—amount of U.S. military aid to Taiwan. Pivot To Peace and CodePink are fighting to stop it.

"The U.S. is engulfing itself in a war in the Pacific, which neither

China nor Taiwan want," Tang declared. She cited an October 2022 by the Chicago Council on Global Affairs that "sixty percent of U.S. residents agree the U.S. needs to learn to live with China." With the Taiwan Policy Act, Tang said, "the U.S. is appointing itself to implement a range of Taiwan's policies—military and civilian aspects—meaning Taiwan is now being colonized *again.*

Taiwan has been part of China for hundreds of years, since the Qing Dynasty of the 17th century.[1] Imperial Japan grabbed it as booty in 1895, after defeating China in the Sino-Japanese War. China regained control at the end of World War 2; then the ROC government under the defeated Kuomintang party (KMT) withdrew to Taiwan[2] where its leader Chiang Kai-shek ruled until the 1980s.[3] Chiang always claimed Taiwan as part of China.

"A war in the Pacific would have horrendous consequences and would not be easy for the U.S. to win," Tang said. "There is so much corruption—in a wheeler-dealer fashion—in this act. The sponsors were pushing for the interests of Boeing, for Taiwan to buy 16 Boeing airplanes; Taiwan couldn't say no."

Wang Wulan, leader of the Taiwan Labor Party, said the Taiwan Policy Act is "typical hegemonism and imperialism—filling their own pockets... In the name of 'helping Taiwan' the U.S. wants to make Taiwan a 'major non-NATO ally'—to make it an arsenal at the front of the war theater... The U.S. government is trying to cause regional tension. China's government has been constantly incited to take action."

Two other panel members spoke. Professor Wei Yu of New York's Hunter College/City University of NY, said "we're trying to stop a war that has already started in east Asia." Hideki Yoshikawa, a leader of Okinawan efforts to stop construction of U.S. military bases there, said the U.S. is stoking tension between China and Japan, which is trying to intensify militarization of Okinawa. Those bases help form a U.S. "noose" hanging over China.

CodePink said "long before Russia invaded Ukraine, the U.S. funneled weapons to Ukraine to escalate tension with Russia. Now Congress is about to repeat the same scenario with Taiwan. [This] act risks further inflaming U.S.-China relations by funneling [billions[4]] in weapons and military training to Taiwan to prepare for war with China."

In August, retired Judge Julie Tang led a San Francisco rally to protest Nancy Pelosi's trip to Taiwan, calling it "reckless and unreasonable" with "no apparent usefulness or benefit to Americans or the world." Pelosi met with Taiwan leader Tsai Ing-wen, hoping to transfer much of Taiwan's enormous semiconductor industry to the U.S. Pelosi and her husband own a large stake in the U.S. semiconductor industry. In 2017, Tang helped co-found the Comfort Women Justice Coalition that built the Comfort Women Memorial in remembrance of the girls and women sexually enslaved by the imperial Japanese Army.

Retired Judge Tang's leadership in the fight against anti-Asian hate was recently recognized at the Smithsonian National Museum in Washington. Theodore Gonzalves, curator of Asian Pacific American History at Smithsonian, adopted a banner saying "Fight the Virus, NOT the People," as part of a six-month showing at the museum.

Retired Judge Julie Tang was the lead organizer who initiated and led the march. In addition to the Asian community, participants included members of Veterans For Peace, Code Pink, ANSWER (Act Now to Stop War and End Racism), and the CWJC (Chinese Women's Justice Coalition).

Part of a Global and National Movement

Peace rallies are emerging everywhere. "'Yankees, Go Home': U.S.-China Rift Rattles South Korea" was the banner headline of the *NY Times* international section October 19.[5] It reported a protest of thousands of South Koreans who fear war between the U.S. and China will impact them. The article quoted a resident of a tiny hamlet 135 miles south of Seoul: "Now, if there is war, our village will become the first target because of that machine up there." She pointed at the THAAD missile system perched on a hill above the village.

"THAAD has brought nothing but harm to South Korea, causing economic damage and heightening tensions," said Kang Hyunwook, another protester quoted in the article. "If South Korea sides with one party in the rivalry between the U.S. and China, we could suffer the fate of Ukraine." THAAD stands for Terminal High Altitude Area Defense System. The U.S. calls it an "anti-missile" system, and says it's deployed against North Korea. The Chinese government considers it an offensive weapon against China and calls for its removal.

In Europe, large strikes are surging across the continent. "Tens of Thousands March in Paris to Protest Rising Living Costs," reported the *New York Times* October 16, 2022. The demonstration occurred on the heels of strikes at oil refineries, adding to a tense political atmosphere, the report said. Jean-Luc Mélanchon, leader of the opposition "France Unbowed" party (La France Insoumise[6]), vowed to bring a vote of no confidence against the Macron government over the crisis. In Britain, Prime Minister Liz Truss announced her resignation October 20 after just six weeks in office, following the ouster of Boris Johnson, NATO's principal "cheerleader" in goading Ukraine to reject peace talks with Russia. The UK foreign minister was forced to resign in mid-October in the wake of widespread strikes against the government's failed economic policies responding to surging inflation. Strong anti-NATO strikes have also hit Italy; thousands of Germans and Czechs have mobilized against the austerity forced on them by western sanctions against Russian gas, oil and wheat.

Pivot To Peace was formed in response to the so-called "Pivot to Asia" announced in 2011, which has developed into a pivot toward war and confrontation. Pivot To Peace insists that the government and mass media turn away from the anti-China Cold War.[7] Its goal is to educate and mobilize public opinion about the benefits of a policy that facilitates cooperation and mutual respect between the United States and China. Pivot to Peace is a coalition including military veterans, public sector workers, professors, healthcare professionals, public officials, legal professionals and others who are concerned about the future of relations between the U.S. and China.

In its mission statement Pivot To Peace says "We reject the escalation towards global conflict and instead urge peace and cooperation with China. We believe in the fair and open communication of information about China, its economic, social, and political affairs, free of the biases and distortions which dominate much of mainstream media in the United States. We support the frank exchange of views based on facts and evidence, rather than fear mongering and the revival of old racist stereotypes and Cold War political bugbears. We want to build support for peace and prosperity and a shared future of mutually beneficial development for both the American and Chinese people. We believe that friendship and engagement between our countries is the better path towards that future.

In the United States, protests took place in dozens of cities during the week of October 15 to 22.[8] The actions targeted U.S. aggression against China, Cuba, Iraq, Russia, Somalia and Syria, from Venezuela to Palestine to North Korea – "any U.S. action against any country attempting to stay independent of the U.S."

A Minneapolis Anti-War Committee (AWC) speaker, Autumn Lake, denounced the decades-long effort led by the United States to isolate and undermine the People's Republic of China.[9] She said "the U.S. has long spread anti-Chinese propaganda, accusing the People's Republic of human rights violations, of suppressing right-wing 'pro-democracy' protests, and even outright genocide." She said accusations of genocide of ethnic minority Uyghur Muslims in China, spread by the U.S. government and corporate media propaganda machine, are part of a long-term project of manufacturing consent for a "humanitarian intervention" in China.

Mike Madden of Minneapolis Veterans for Peace and the Assange Defense Committee spoke of the history of NATO intervention in Ukraine and the rest of Eastern Europe. He said it's critical for anti-imperialists to fight back against U.S. efforts to escalate the war in Ukraine and lead the world into another World War. "Perhaps the most common adjective used to describe the Russian invasion of Ukraine has been 'unprovoked'," Madden said. "In fact, it was deliberately provoked."

The Bronx Anti-War Coalition organized a demonstration in the heart of the South Bronx in New York City.[10] The rally on Fordham Plaza centered local community leaders speaking from La Peña del Bronx, TBS New Direction and United We Stand, United We Stronger, who proclaimed, "Where's the $60 billion+ for the Bronx?"

A wide range of groups were involved in these protests. In Minnesota, it was Antiwar Advocates of Minnesota, the Anti-War Committee, Bikers Riding Against Police Brutality, the Climate Justice Committee, Freedom Road Socialist Organization, Minnesota Immigrant Rights Action Committee, Minnesota War Tax Resistance, Minnesota Workers United, Movement for a People's Democracy, the Party for Socialism and Liberation, Socialist Action, Socialist Party USA, St. Paul Eastside Neighbors for Peace, Twin Cities Assange Defense, Twin Cities Coalition for Justice 4 Jamar Clark, Twin Cities CPUSA, Twin Cities Nonviolent, Veterans For Peace, Welfare Rights Committee, and Women Against Military Madness.

In the Bronx, speakers were from Black Alliance for Peace, Amazon Labor Union, A Call to Action on Puerto Rico/Puerto Rico Not For Sale, *Cuba Sí* Coalition, Bronx Green Party, Haiti Liberté, People's Power Assembly, Struggle/La Lucha, United National Antiwar Coalition, Workers World Party, and Workers Assembly Against Racism.

Up to now the war makers in Washington have been virtually unanimous in calling for more war. Their sponsors in the military-industrial complex and the energy companies—together with their *stenographers* in the mainstream media—have made it all too easy to stick together for war. But the fissures in their NATO coalition in Europe, and the surging antiwar sentiment across Europe, Asia and the U.S., suggest the unanimity will not last.

IV

China Is Not Our Enemy

13

Biden's Saber-Rattling Against China Could Lead to World War III

It fits a long pattern of war-mongering and provocations that are a feature of the American Century

June 8, 2022

When U.S. President Joe Biden speaks about war and peace, we have to listen carefully whether we like it or not. Regarding Taiwan, when asked in Tokyo on May 23, 2022 if he was "willing to get involved militarily to defend Taiwan," Biden said without hesitation, "yes, that's the commitment we made."[1] White House staff rushed to say "our policy has not changed," but others found it part of escalating Cold War chatter.[2]

The U.S. does not have a security alliance with Taiwan. Rather, it officially recognizes it as part of China. The U.S. State Department website says "The United States has a long-standing one China policy.... We oppose any unilateral changes to the status quo from either side; we do not support Taiwan independence; and we expect cross-Strait differences to be resolved by peaceful means."[3]

But the "no change" claim contrasts with Biden's meeting with Quad Alliance members, two of whom are equipped with nuclear weapons, U.S. warships passing through the Taiwan Straits and nonstop anti-China rhetoric from Washington. "War Games: The Battle for Taiwan,"[4] a 27–minute segment ran in early 2022 on NBC's *Meet the Press*—quite likely a co-production with the State and Defense departments, according to columnist Patrick Lawrence.[5]

China reacted strongly to the Biden statements. "On issues that bear on China's sovereignty, territorial integrity, and other core interests," Wang Wenbin, a foreign ministry spokes-person, said "no one shall expect China to make any compromise or trade-offs."[6]

"Defending Taiwan Would Be a Mistake," was the headline of a May 27 *New York Times* op-ed by China expert Oriana Skylar Mastro of Stanford University. "Simply put," she wrote, "the United States is outgunned. At the very least a confrontation with China would be an enormous drain on the U.S. military without any assured outcome that America could repel all of China's forces." She highlighted a 2018 assessment warning that the U.S. could face a "decisive military defeat" in a war over Taiwan, citing China's increasingly advanced capabilities and myriad U.S. logistical difficulties.[7] "Several top former U.S. defense officials have reached similar conclusions," she wrote.[8]

CGTN, China's Global TV Network, gave another answer. "The Warmonger's Legacy" appeared on YouTube on May 27.[9] Starting with the Gulf of Tonkin episode of August 1964 off the coast of North Vietnam, then cycling through the endless U.S. wars in the second half of the 20th century, it lets a parade of U.S. presidents make the case. Jimmy Carter comes off best, stating "we know which is the most warlike country on earth—my country, the United States."

It shows that LBJ's defense secretary, Robert McNamara, admitted to dishonesty about the Gulf of Tonkin—where the U.S. had provoked the North Vietnamese into attacking the U.S.S. Maddox—saying "our judgment that we'd been attacked…was wrong." George W. Bush's defense secretary, Colin Powell, is heard testifying at the UN about "weapons of mass destruction" in Iraq, and Bush himself declaring that "Saddam Hussein…must leave Iraq within 48 hours."

Barack Obama shows up to say "the Gadhafi regime is coming to an end." Trump appears announcing a bombing of Syria, claiming "chemical weapons." Papa Bush says "air attacks are under way in Iraq" to take out "Saddam Hussein's nuclear bomb potential." Bill Clinton declares military victory in Yugoslavia, while two super-imposed screens state that, "In 78 days of bombing, NATO dropped approximately 20 kilograms of explosives for every person in the targeted areas," and "By supporting Kosovan separatism, NATO showed scant concern for national sovereignty and territorial integrity."

Harry Truman appears to say "We're fighting in Korea for our own nation's security and survival." (This one is of special interest to the Chinese, who recently celebrated their role in the Korean War with the blockbuster hit, "The Battle of Lake Changjin."[10])

Richard Nixon shows up declaring that the 1970 invasion of Cambodia was "for the purpose of ending the war in Vietnam." The movie doesn't show the killings of anti-war students at Kent State and Jackson State universities, but it does show several protests, with the familiar slogans "Money for Jobs Not War," and "No Blood for Oil."

Saving the best for last, Joe Biden is presented at a recent NATO conference proclaiming "quite frankly that America is back." Russian President Vladimir Putin appears, stating "The People's Republics of

Donbas asked for help from Russia." And European Commission President Ursula von der Leyen heroically declares "our airspace will be closed to every Russian plane." Russian Foreign Minister Sergey Lavrov appears calmly affirming that the Ukrainian government's war policy "is determined in Washington and London."

The basic message of this CGTN feature is that China should not be expected to "play nice" in the face of U.S. efforts to extend its war with Russia to include all of Eurasia.

14

Threats Against China Endanger the World

October 19, 2021

In the buildup to the World Climate Change summit, slated for Halloween and the first week of November 2021 in Glasgow, a NY Times report said "China must pivot away from coal immediately" to avoid climate disaster. The article says "attention is riveted on China and whether it will do more to cut emissions." It quoted a British member of Parliament saying "China is responsible for almost a quarter of all global emissions right now."[1]

The Times article acknowledges that China leads the world in hydroelectric, solar and wind power. But it insists that "China is the biggest current emitter now by a wide margin," while also admitting the United States has released more human-generated carbon dioxide over the past century than any other country. On a per capita basis, China's emissions are less than half the U.S. total. And China is converting to renewables much faster than the U.S.

An October 15, 2021 report said the plan to replace coal- and gas-fired power plants with renewable energy will be dropped from

President Biden's "Build Back Better" bill, thanks to Joe Manchin of West Virginia, and his energy lobby backers.[2] "This will create a huge problem for the White House in Glasgow," David Victor of UC San Diego's Deep Decarbonization Initiative told the Times. Biden had hoped to point to the clean electricity program as evidence the U.S., which is historically the world's largest emitter of planet-warming pollution, is serious about changing course, the report said.

Meanwhile hundreds of people were arrested October 11 and 12 in Washington[3] while protesting a record number of new oil and gas leases on U.S. public lands.[4] According to Oil Change International, 21 major fossil fuel infrastructure projects under review in Washington "would be the emissions equivalent of adding 316 new coal fired power plants – more than are currently operating in the United States."[5] That would equal 17% of total 2019 U.S. greenhouse gas emissions.

The gargantuan role of the U.S. military in global emissions is not included in these reports. But a June 2019 report on "The Costs of War" by Brown University's Watson Institute of International and Public Affairs shows the military is by far the largest part of U.S. federal government energy consumption – nearly 90 percent of the total.[6]

A study by Lancaster University's Environment Centre found "the U.S. military is a bigger polluter than as many as 140 countries."[7] The "Costs of War" report says "with an armed force of more than two million people, 11 nuclear aircraft carriers, and [thousands of] the most advanced military aircraft," the Department of Defense "is the world's single largest institutional consumer of petroleum." About 30 percent of this goes to maintaining 800 U.S. military bases around the world, many of them bristling with nuclear warheads. The other

70 percent is "operational"—bombers, fighter jets, air tankers, aircraft carriers, airlift operations, and so on.

The picture suggests a simple a solution: *ground the bombers and save the planet.* Pulling back the nuclear aircraft carriers cruising in the South China and East China seas would improve the planet's safety in myriad ways. But the most significant one is reducing the danger of a war that could wipe out the planet even faster than climate disaster. (The two dangers reinforce each other, of course.)

Reducing the Pentagon budget even modestly could also help clean up the planet. The Congressional Budget Office released "Illustrative Options for National Defense Under a Smaller Defense Budget." The October 1, 2021 report found three modest, super-cautious ways to cut $1 trillion, or 14 percent off the Pentagon budget between 2022 and 2031. That amount could finance a substantial portion of Biden's "Build Back Better" and Infrastructure bills. (Bernie Sanders and Barbara Lee proposed even more modest cuts to the Pentagon budget in September. The proposal was crushed by a near unanimous majority against it.)

Is Taiwan Next?

Immediately following U.S. withdrawal from Afghanistan, tensions began boiling over in the Taiwan straits. An October 9 NY Times report said "Taiwan is now at the heart of the deepening discord between China and the United States," with massive buildups on both sides.[8] The Biden administration approved a $750 million arms sale to Taiwan in August 2021—just the latest batch of billions worth of armaments of all kinds, including fighter jets, tanks, missiles and training.[9] China has responded with its own force buildup. "To us, it's only a matter of time, not a matter of if," said Rear Admiral Michael Studeman, director of intelligence with the U.S. Indo-Pacific Command, according to the Times report.

"Congress must untie Biden's hands on Taiwan," wrote Rep. Elaine Luria in an op-ed published in the Washington Post October 11, 2021.[10] She called for an act that would allow President Biden to bypass Congress to declare war on China. The Pentagon's Stars and Stripes daily newspaper ran a story headlined "Retired Marine colonel says U.S. should weigh nuclear war with China over Taiwan."[11]

On October 3, a U.S. carrier group was joined by war ships from the UK and Japan for joint operations. The U.S. Navy said the deployment is "designed to uphold the international rules-based order: multilateralism and shared values, freedom of navigation, democracy and human rights in the Indo-Pacific region." (Multilateralism is not a favorite U.S. "shared value.")

On October 8, China's Foreign Ministry "vowed to take all necessary measures" to safeguard China's sovereignty and integrity, and "urged the U.S. to fully recognize the high sensitivity of the Taiwan question." It also called for an explanation after a U.S. nuclear submarine accident in the South China Sea. It demanded details, including the intention of the sub's navigation. The Chinese Foreign Ministry spokesperson called the lack of information irresponsible, and expressed concerns about a nuclear leak.[12]

This followed China's protest of the USAUK nuclear submarine deal: "The nuclear submarine cooperation between the U.S., the UK and Australia has seriously undermined regional peace and stability, intensified the arms race and undermined international non-proliferation efforts," the statement said. It also accused the U.S. and UK of holding double standards with their stances on nuclear weapons.[13]

"Hong Kong Today, Taiwan Tomorrow"...

In August 2021 a NY Times Magazine special feature by Sarah Topol appeared, titled "Is Taiwan Next?" It said "Hong Kong today, Taiwan tomorrow" is a rallying cry in Taiwan. "First Tibet, then Xinjiang, then Hong Kong. The edges of empire had been dutifully absorbed. Taiwan was the only one remaining." The choice of words is important. "Edges of empire" suggests these places are not really part of China. Hong Kong, of course, was stripped away from China and colonized by Britain as spoils of the Opium War of 1839, which was the start of China's century of humiliation. Hong Kong's reincorporation under the "One Country Two Systems" deal in 1996 signaled the end of that colonial humiliation. So official calls by British and U.S. leaders for "self-determination for Hong Kong" ring ironically hollow.

The U.S. CIA conducted a "Tibetan program" in the 1950s and '60s that was part of a concerted U.S. push to partition and shrink China[14]—similar to U.S. efforts today in Xinjiang.[15] But Tibet has been part of China for centuries, in spite of 19th century British imperial efforts to link it with "British India." The CIA's Tibet program was shut down in 1972 after then-President Nixon became the first U.S. president to visit China.

The U.S. signed the "one China" agreement in January 1979, saying "The United States acknowledges that all Chinese on either side of the Taiwan Strait maintain there is but one China and that Taiwan is a part of China. The United States Government does not challenge that position. It reaffirms its interest in a peaceful settlement of the Taiwan question by the Chinese themselves."

When Chiang Kai Shek led the defeated Kuomintang forces to Taiwan in 1949, he established his "Republic of China" government there, insisting with U.S. support that it was the government of all of China. According to the legendary I.F. Stone's "Hidden History of the Korean War" (published by Monthly Review Press in 1952, now out of print), President Truman stated in January 1950 that the U.S. would not "give military aid or advice" to Chiang, and would not "pursue a course which would lead to involvement in the civil conflicts in China." This non-intervention policy was reversed by the outbreak of war in Korea, Stone wrote. Intense machinations between January and June 1950 by the maverick General Douglas MacArthur, U.S. supreme commander in Japan, with collaboration from Wall Street attorney John Foster Dulles, led to an alliance of Chiang's and U.S. forces. Stone cites MacArthur's August 6, 1950 declaration that "The United States ought to take a vigorous position against Communism everywhere in Asia, and Korea ought not to be an isolated case." Eleven days later, on August 17, 1950, MacArthur ordered a bombing raid on Rashin, a North Korean seaport bordering both China and the USSR, a short distance from the Soviet far-east port of Vladivostok.

General MacArthur fought a political battle in 1950 with President Truman over war with China. MacArthur argued that by "holding Formosa" (the colonial name for Taiwan), the U.S. could "dominate with air power every Asiatic port from Vladivostok to Singapore," Stone wrote. President Truman ultimately fired the insubordinate MacArthur, but it was too late. The maverick general's anti-communist war campaign galvanized enough right-wingers to plunge the U.S. into its first major battle to "contain Communism in Asia." The Chinese Red Army pushed the U.S. forces back to the 38th parallel, dividing Korea in two. Meanwhile Dulles became Eisenhower's Secretary of State after the Republicans defeated Truman in 1952, and conducted a decades-long campaign to realize MacArthur's vision.

It's an irony of history that Eisenhower's vice president, Richard Nixon, was the U.S. leader to reverse the U.S. war against China in 1972. But it is no accident that the long-term imperial U.S. goals of ending communism in Asia and restoring U.S. domination there would resurge. The question remains, as vice admiral Robert Thomas, former commander of the U.S. Seventh Fleet said: "How far are you willing to go to defend Taiwan? I don't know if the United States is willing to see U.S. young people coming back in body bags for the defense of Taiwan."

The war danger is all too real. An October 8 editorial in China's Global Times says: "We must resolutely define the deployment of U.S. troops in Taiwan as an 'invasion.' The mainland has the right to carry out military strikes against them at any time. We will not make any promises over their safety… We must make Washington understand that it is playing a dangerous game that is destined to draw fire onto itself and it is risking the lives of young U.S. soldiers."[16] Pentagon Papers author Daniel Ellsberg revealed in May 2021 that U.S. officials considered using nuclear weapons against China during a Taiwan crisis in 1958. "As the possibility of another nuclear crisis over Taiwan is being bandied about this very year, it seems very timely to me to encourage the public, Congress and the executive branch to pay attention."[17]

"What would happen to the world," asks retired Judge Julie Tang of San Francisco-based Pivot To Peace, "if the United States and China were to go to war? The price of war would be calamitous. We need to aim for peace, not war."[18] The anti-war group CodePink and Pivot for Peace are waging an all-out campaign saying "China is Not Our Enemy."[19]

15

Does China's Rise Really Endanger the U.S.?...Or Just Its Sociopathic Power Elite?

[SOURCE: globalvillagespace.com]

August 14, 2021

Government-sponsored 'fake news' is brainwashing the American public into accepting a new U.S./NATO-sponsored Cold War with China.

A massive blitz of Western propaganda is behind the escalating U.S. cold war against China.

President Biden and most of the U.S. Congress say China has become a serious threat that must be countered in every way and in every corner of the globe. The U.S.-led cold war against China has escalated quickly and dramatically. President Biden is trying to harness the G7 and NATO to isolate China, and Congress is fast-tracking bills to counter China's Belt and Road Initiative and punish China for alleged human rights violations.

This escalation is not new. Barack Obama launched the U.S. "pivot to Asia." Now the seas around China bristle with U.S. aircraft carriers and nuclear submarines; missiles and super-bombers are aimed at China from Japan, Korea, Thailand, the Philippines, Indonesia and Australia, with hundreds of thousands of troops.

The U.S. recently forged the "Quad Alliance" with Japan, India and Australia, to further challenge China. But it is not enough. Biden wants *all* U.S. allies to join sides against China.

There is a problem with this strategy. A *NY Times* report of June 16 said "Not all countries in NATO or the Group of 7 share Mr. Biden's zeal to isolate China."[1] Germany, France, Italy, Greece, and several other European countries have major economic ties with China. French President Emmanuel Macron told *Politico* "NATO is an organization that concerns the North Atlantic. China has little to do with the North Atlantic."[2] It was a casual comment, even as France also joined EU gestures to isolate China.

The people of Europe do not want war. A survey by the European Council on Foreign Affairs in January 2021 found that most Europeans want to remain neutral.[3] Only 22% would want to take the

U.S. side in a war on China, and just 23% in a war on Russia. The Alliance of Democracies Foundation (ADF), in Europe, conducted a poll of 50,000 people in 53 countries between February and April 2021, and found that more people around the world (44%) see the United States as a threat to democracy in their countries than China (38%) or Russia (28%).[4]

That makes it hard for the U.S. to justify war in the name of democracy. In a larger poll of 124,000 people ADF conducted in 2020, countries where large majorities saw the United States as a danger to democracy included China, Germany, Austria, Denmark, Ireland, France, Greece, Belgium, Sweden and Canada.[5]

ADF also studied the disparity between those who believe in democracy and those who think they live in one. This chart shows 73% of Chinese think their country is democratic, while just 49% in the U.S. believe their country is democratic.

Another report, from Harvard University's Ash Center for Democratic Governance and Innovation, finds that more than 90% of the Chinese people like their government, and "rate it as more capable and effective than ever before."[6]

"Interestingly, more marginalized groups in poorer, inland regions are actually comparatively more likely to report increases in satisfaction." It says Chinese people's attitudes "appear to respond to real changes in their material well-being." Elevating 800 million people out of extreme poverty probably helped.

This contrasts with people's attitudes in the United States, which are polarized politically, racially and economically. Public trust in government is in crisis. This could be a reason for politicians to whip up a cold-war fever—and an urgent reason to take the danger seriously.

There are very real human rights concerns at home, where police killings, homelessness and mass incarceration are at pandemic proportions.

In the U.S. Congress, there has been bipartisan support for the Innovation and Competition Act, which demonizes China's economic successes across the globe. Charges fly that China favors its companies, both private and state-owned, in China and elsewhere, through subsidies and special financing, while subjecting Western trade partners to forced technology transfer, theft of intellectual property, and more.

The proposed response is for the U.S. government to do much the same. In Europe Biden announced a "build back better" Western version of global infrastructure development, but when and whether it will happen are unclear.

Bernie Sanders wrote in *Foreign Affairs* in June 2021 that "a fast-growing consensus is emerging in Washington that views the U.S.-Chinese relationship as a zero-sum economic and military struggle …"[7]

Sanders also stated that "the rush to confront China has a very recent precedent: the global 'war on terror.' In the wake of the 9/11 attacks, the [U.S.] political establishment quickly concluded that antiterrorism had to become the overriding focus of U.S. foreign policy. Almost two decades and $6 trillion later, it's become clear that national unity was exploited to launch a series of endless wars that proved enormously costly in human, economic, and strategic terms and that gave rise to xenophobia and bigotry in U.S. politics—the brunt of it borne by American Muslim and Arab communities. It is no surprise that today, in a climate of relentless fearmongering about China, the country is experiencing an increase in anti-Asian hate crimes."

Media Bias and Human Rights Part 1: Hong Kong

The media's demonization of China has been apparent in biased coverage of the 2019 Hong Kong protests where the norm has been to present the protesters as heroic champions of human rights and democracy and police and pro-Chinese government authorities as adherents of an authoritarian social order.

Missing from this assessment, among other things, is the influence of the United States.

Hong Kong native Julie Tang, now a retired judge of the San Francisco Superior Court, said recently that the 2019 riots began as a political protest against the extradition of a confessed murderer, but were supported by "a shadow power"—the National Endowment for Democracy (NED), a CIA offshoot—in an attempt to destabilize China through destruction and violence.[8]

In 2018, the NED gave $155,000 to the anti-Beijing solidarity center in Hong Kong which helped instigate the protests and $200,000 to the National Democratic Institute and Hong Kong Human Rights Monitor.[9]

Rioters killed a 70-year-old man by hitting him with a brick, and doused another with gasoline and burned him. They broke into the parliament building—much like the January 6, 2021, fascist riot in Washington, DC.

Tang observes that Hong Kong ranks in the top three on the Fraser Human Freedom Index, while the United States is in 17th place.[10] She quotes Hong Kong journalist Nury Vittachi that "Hong Kong's civil unrest was the most reported news story of 2019—yet every salient detail presented was incorrect ... The city's freedoms had not been removed... Police killed no one... Agents from a global superpower were intimately involved, but it wasn't China."[11]

A key dimension of the media's bias was its parroting of the rioters' claims about police brutality—when the Hong Kong police had often displayed restraint in the face of violent protests and could be compared favorably to U.S. police. (Unlike U.S. police, Hong Kong police do not carry side arms).

A good example of the media bias was a December 2019 *CNN* report on Hong Kong entitled "A Generation Criminalized":

Amidst a backdrop of photos pointing to the brutal suppression of the riots and tally of the number of protesters arrested and hospitalized and rounds of tear gas expended by the police, authors James Griffiths and Jessie Yeung quoted from a protester, Ivan, who said that "we seriously need to win this to say to whoever has the power that you cannot do this, you cannot do this to protesters or people fighting for their lives or their own freedom and values."[12]

Showing which side they were on, the authors lamented "an entire generation criminalized, in a fight for their future which could end up costing them just that."

Left out was the fact that many of the protesters had engaged in criminal activity, along with the hidden hand of the NED.

The Hong Kong riots ultimately failed. Retired Judge Tang says: "Now there is peace in Hong Kong, but there is a proposed U.S. law to devote $300 million to anti-China propaganda." [13]

Belatedly, though, some honest reporting has come out. A CNN story on July 10, 2021, for example, was headlined "Some Hong Kongers are glorifying a man who knifed a cop, showing the city's problems are far from over."[14] It detailed how Hong Kong protesters established a memorial filled with flowers for a man who knifed a cop on July 1ˢᵗ and then committed suicide. The student union of prestigious Hong Kong University passed a motion to say they "appreciated his sacrifice." This is the same university where many of the protesters—heralded as great champions of democracy on CNN and other media a year earlier—came from.

Media Bias, Part II: The Myth of Uyghur Genocide

Besides Hong Kong, the media bias about China has been exemplified by the barrage of stories in mainstream outlets broadcasting the plight of the Uyghurs, many of which echoed U.S. government claims that China was committing genocide.[15]

The genocide claim is unfounded, based on flimsy "evidence" that has been repeatedly debunked. The use of the term concentration camps to describe detention facilities has also been dubious—these facilities function as re-education centers where Uyghurs who were involved in Islamic terrorist activities are provided vocational skills, recreational activities, medical services and a host of other benefits, and allowed to return home regularly.[16]

The U.S. media coverage failed to address the strategic importance of Xinjiang and U.S. support for separatists and Islamic terrorist movements there.

Independent Canadian reporter Daniel Dumbrill reports that the East Turkestan Islamic Movement (ETIM), which has claimed responsibility for attacks in Xinjiang and elsewhere in China, has been identified as a terrorist organization by the governments of China, Kazakhstan, Pakistan, Turkey and the United States.[17]

The U.S. government removed ETIM from its list of terrorist organizations in October 2020 and has since provided funds to it through NED. Following explosive incidents of terrorist violence by ETIM, the Chinese government responded with repression. How much repression, and for how long, are matters of controversy.

When Noam Chomsky was asked in an April 2021 *New York Times* podcast interview whether the situation of the Uyghurs was worse than the people of Gaza, he said "No. The Uyghurs were not having their power plants destroyed, their sewage plants destroyed," and were "not subjected to regular bombing."[18]

The exact number of Uyghurs placed in education camps is not known in the West. China has called the camps a large-scale job training program, as part of its national anti-poverty crusade. On a personal visit to Xinjiang, Dumbrill found that a very small minority of Uyghurs were repressed, and a large portion benefited from job training.[19]

Responding to official U.S. charges of forced labor and genocide, Zhun Xu, an associate professor of economics at John Jay College in New York, says "if [China] has engaged in forced assimilation and eventual erasure of a vulnerable ethnic and religious minority group," there should be a decrease in the Uyghur population and increase in the Han.

But Xinjiang's Uyghur population increased by 24.9 percent from 2010 to 2018, while the Han population in Xinjiang grew by only 2.2 percent. (Cited by Reese Ehrlich, from Zhun Xu's upcoming book, *Sanctions as War.*[20])

Right-wing religious extremist Adrian Zenz, who states he is "led by God" on a "mission against China," is the main source for U.S. government and media criticism of Xinjiang conditions.[21] He is also funded by The Jamestown Foundation, an arch-conservative defense policy think tank in Washington, DC, which was co-founded by William Casey, Reagan's CIA director. Other important sources are the World Uyghur Congress, the International Uyghur Human Rights and Democracy Foundation, and the Uyghur American Association—all of which receive substantial NED funding.

Other sources include the Australian Strategic Policy Institute (ASPI) and the DC-based Center for Strategic and International Studies (CSIS)—both militaristic think tanks funded by U.S. and Western governments and weapons manufacturers. ASPI and CSIS successfully spearheaded a campaign against "forced labor" in Xinjiang, stimulating moves in Congress to ban U.S. imports from Xinjiang. [22]

Professor Kenneth Hammond of New Mexico State University recently explained the two main aspects of Chinese government policy toward ethnic and religious minorities: first, *preservation and respect* for their language and culture and, second, *inclusion and opportunity* through education, health care and job training.[23] Improved health care programs in Xinjiang have contributed to life expectancy increasing there from 31 years in 1949 to 72 currently.[24]

In 1949 there were 54 medical centers in Xinjiang; in 2017 there were more than 7,300 health care facilities and more than 1,600 hospitals. Literacy increased from 10% to more than 90% in the same period.[25] Average income in Xinjiang has increased more than 10% since 2017.[26]

Tens of millions of Chinese people practice the Islamic faith. Of China's 55 officially recognized minority peoples, [27] ten are Sunni Muslim.[28] There are more Islamic mosques in China than the United States. Uyghurs are the second largest group, after the Hui.

Most Uyghurs practice a moderate form of Islam called Sufism, which promotes an ascetic lifestyle and shuns material wants. Sufism is incompatible with radical Islamic funda-mentalism and Wahhabism, extremist beliefs which have been associated with terrorism in recent decades. The overwhelming majority of Uyghurs are not militant or extremist in outlook.[29]

Washington Backs Separatism & Terror to Undermine Belt & Road

Over the past generation Washington and the CIA have provided ongoing support to Uyghur separatist organizations, and terrorist groups such as the Turkistan Islamic Party (TIP), led by Abdul Haq al-Turkistani.[30] The TIP, originally calling itself the East Turkestan Islamic Movement, received direct CIA funding and sponsorship.[31]

Abdul Haq has served on al-Qaeda's executive leadership council. He calls for jihad (holy war) against China to attain the TIP's separatist goals. Prior to the 2008 Summer Olympic Games in Beijing, Abdul Haq ordered the TIP to unleash terrorist attacks against a number of cities in mainland China. Almost all of them were foiled. Following China's clampdown in Xinjiang starting in 2017, no terrorist acts have taken place in the province.

Reports from first-hand delegations to Xinjiang, from countries and organizations including Egypt, Pakistan, Afghanistan, India, Indonesia, Russia, Kazakhstan, Kyrgyzstan, Thailand, Malaysia, the Organization of Islamic Cooperation, and even the World Bank, have testified that neither genocide nor slavery accurately describes the reality of Xinjiang.[32] At two separate convenings of the UN Human Rights Council in 2019 and 2020, letters condemning Chinese conduct in

Xinjiang were outvoted, 22-50 and 27-46—essentially the U.S. and its allies *vs.* non-aligned countries.

Why would the United States back separatism and terror in Xinjiang? *CodePink* points to "a concerted attempt by the U.S. in recent decades to balkanize China by delegitimizing, or creating disruption, in Hong Kong, Taiwan, the South China Sea, Tibet and Xinjiang. Dismembering China has been a long-term goal of the U.S. government since 1949. Now Xinjiang is the linchpin of China's Belt and Road Initiative (BRI), and a rich resource, producing 85% of China's cotton and 25% of its oil."[33]

Xinjiang's largest cities, Urumqi and Kashgar, are main hubs on the BRI's "Silk Road economic belt," with rail links from Kashgar through Pakistan to the Indian Ocean, and from Urumqi through Central Asia to Teheran, Istanbul, Moscow, and Western Europe.

It is the biggest infrastructure project in human history, linking China across Eurasia and parts of Africa—65 countries and more than 4 billion people. This may be why the U.S. considers the BRI a threat. If it could cut Xinjiang away from China, it might stop Belt and Road. (Not too likely…)

Taiwan: the 'Most Dangerous Place on Earth'

Meanwhile in the Taiwan Straits, there is a buildup of war danger. During the Trump years the U.S. broke from recognizing the "one China policy" agreed to by Nixon in 1972, sending cabinet-level officials to meet with Taiwanese leaders, and openly engaging in military cooperation. This continues under Biden, backed by U.S. nuclear-armed warships, just like 1958, when a crisis threatened to escalate into nuclear holocaust.

In May 2021, *The Economist Magazine* called the Taiwan straits the "most dangerous place in earth."

The Biden administration inflamed the situation in August 2021, by approving sale of 40 155mm M109A6 Medium Self-Propelled Howitzer artillery systems to Taiwan in a deal valued at up to $750 million.[34] (A bonanza for the arms industry.)

The progressive forces in the U.S. need to stop the impending war with China before it starts, as CodePink says. "The price of war would be calamitous. We need to aim for peace, not war. China is not our enemy."[35]

Comparing U.S. and Chinese Activity in Africa

There is a stark contrast between U.S. and Chinese political, economic, and security sector activity in Africa. The U.S. Africa Command maintains military presence in fifty African countries, and has staged *coups d'etat* multiple times in the past decade—Libya in 2011, Mali in 2012, 2020 and 2021, Egypt in 2013 and Burkina Faso in 2015. U.S. trade and finance policies and practices in recent decades have amounted to a neo-colonial regime often referred to as a "debt trap" that has left most African countries impoverished. Until the mid-1980s America's closest African ally was apartheid South Africa. The United States and its European allies, principally Britain, France, Portugal and Belgium, have fiercely resisted or sabotaged African decolonization efforts since the end of World War 2.

Kenya's President Uhuru Kenyatta said in 2018 that "We are very keen as a country, and I believe also as a continent, to partner strongly with China." Liberia's Economy Minister Augustus Flomo said "China is a very, very important partner for our development strategy." Both leaders were speaking on the occasion of the 2018 Forum on China-Africa Cooperation, which was attended by nearly all Africa's leaders.[36]

In May 2021 at the United Nations in New York, China's Foreign Minister Wang Yi announced, together with African countries and the African Union (AU), the launch of an Initiative on Partnership for Africa's Development. The emphasis is "to provide greater impetus to Africa's independent and sustainable development." It focuses on response to COVID-19 and post-COVID reconstruction, trade and investment, environmental protection, debt relief, agriculture, agroindustry, sustainable development, infrastructure, energy and transport, scientific and technical cooperation, digitalization and industrialization." It calls for more vaccines for Africa, and to help build African capacity to manufacture vaccines by waiving intellectual property protections for COVID-19 vaccines. As of April 5, 2021, China had donated vaccines to more than 80 countries and exported vaccines to more than 40 countries. As of March 2021, China had shared 48% of domestically-manufactured vaccines with other countries through donations and exports.[37]

The statement said Africa is a stage for international cooperation, not an arena for big-power competition: "this Initiative adheres to multilateralism and is open to all countries and international organizations in the world... under the principle of 'African ownership, equality and openness'."

Chinese foreign direct investment (FDI) in Africa surged from US $75 million in 2003 to US $2.7 billion in 2019. Chinese FDI flows to Africa have exceeded those from the U.S. since 2014, which have been declining since 2010.

China-Africa bilateral trade has been steadily increasing for the past 16 years. The value of China-Africa trade in 2019 was $192 billion. The largest exporter to China from Africa in 2019 was Angola, followed by South Africa and the Republic of Congo. Nigeria bought the most Chinese goods in 2019, followed by South Africa and Egypt.

While China's trade with Africa has surged in the past decade, U.S.-Africa trade has plummeted, from a 2008 high $113.5 billion in imports from Africa to $23.7 billion in 2020. U.S. exports declined from $28.39 billion in 2008 to $22.15 billion in 2020—total trade was about $46 billion, slightly more than one fifth of China's trade with Africa.[38]

Chinese global foreign aid expenditures increased steadily from 2003 to 2015, growing from US $631 million in 2003 to US $3 billion in 2015. Between 2013 and 2018, 45 percent of China's foreign aid went to Africa. For the USA, total global "economic and military assistance" totaled about $50 billion in 2017, of which about $15 billion was military—roughly 30 percent—according to USAID's *Foreign Aid Explorer* website. Total U.S. economic assistance to the top eleven African recipient countries in 2017 was approximately $7.5 billion; military assistance was about $1.5 billion, according to the same source. (Based in Germany, Africom's budget may not be included in U.S. military assistance figures for Africa.)

Africa's debt to U.S. banks and multilateral lending institutions— the World Bank and the International Monetary Fund (IMF)—is another story. "Structural Adjustment Programs," or SAPs, have been the primary mode of the U.S.-Africa financial relationship. These programs forced African countries to pay off debts with *increased* debt in exchange for austerity and privatization measures. African nations have paid over four times the amount of their original debt to World Bank and IMF lenders since 1980. These debt payments bleed Africa of billions of dollars each year.[39]

By contrast, China's economic cooperation includes *concessional loans*, at below commercial interest rates, grants, and interest-free loans. China has *cancelled debt* to Africa's least developed countries.

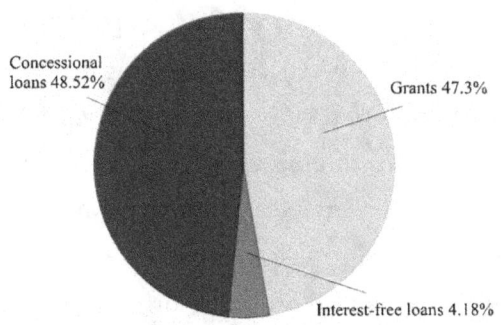

Concessional loans 48.52%

Grants 47.3%

Interest-free loans 4.18%

Chart 1 : China's Foreign Aid in Three Categories, 2013–2018

Xinhua, 10 Jan. 2021/PRC State Council[40]

While China's commercial interest in Africa is clear—it needs mineral resources and oil—it provides significant value in return. Infrastructure projects like sea ports, airports, railroads, highways and digital connectivity grab headlines. Sharing China's own experience in poverty reduction, reversing desertification, and green energy are also important. So are industrial and agricultural assistance programs.

"Chinese are outmaneuvering the U.S. in select countries in Africa," General Stephen Townsend, commander of AFRICOM, told Associated Press late in April. He said the Chinese are "looking for a place where they can rearm and repair warships..."

This has been disputed by Deborah Bräutigam, director of the

China Africa Research Initiative at Johns Hopkins School of Advanced International Studies, who wrote in the *Washington Post* that "many of the things our politicians believe about Chinese engagement are not actually true." She added that China's economic engagements in Africa are not of a predatory nature, but are "very much in line with the economic interests of these African states, providing jobs to locals and improving public infrastructure."[41]

Brautigam's book *Will Africa Feed China?* debunks myths of Chinese "land grabbing" in Africa, according to Amadou Sy of the Brookings Institution's Africa Growth Initiative.[42] Brautigam wrote that "interest in China's role as an overseas agricultural investor in Africa has generated hundreds of newspaper articles and editorials, sensational statements and robust myths – but surprisingly little investigative reporting." She found that out of over 6 million hectares of alleged Chinese land acquisitions, only 252,901 hectares had actually been acquired. In 2021 the UN's Food and Agriculture Organization found that Chinese enterprises working in Africa are making concerted efforts to engage in responsible agriculture.

China's officially stated principles for development cooperation[43] include:

- *Respecting each other as equals*: "When cooperating with other countries for development, no country should interfere in their efforts to find a development path suited to their own national conditions, interfere in their internal affairs, impose its own will on them, attach political strings, or pursue political self-interest."

- *Focusing on development and improving people's lives,* it increases investment in poverty alleviation, disaster relief, education, health care, agriculture, employment, environmental protection, and climate change response, and actively participates in emergency humanitarian relief operations.
- *Providing the means for independent development,* China shares its experience and technologies, and trains local talent and technicians, to empower them to tap their own potential for diversified, independent and sustainable development.
- *Conducting effective cooperation in diverse forms,* including: complete projects, goods and materials, technical cooperation, cooperation in human resources development, South-South Cooperation Assistance Fund (SSCAF), medical teams, outbound volunteers, emergency humanitarian aid, and debt relief.

China is committed to a multilateral approach. By the end of 2019, China had launched 82 projects under the South-South Cooperation Assistance Fund framework in cooperation with 14 international organizations, including the United Nations Development Programme (UNDP), World Food Programme (WFP), World Health Organization (WHO), United Nations Children's Fund (UNICEF), United Nations Population Fund (UNFPA), United Nations High Commissioner for Refugees (UNHCR), International Organization for Migration (IOM), and International Committee of the Red Cross (ICRC). These projects cover agricultural development and food security, poverty reduction, health care for women and children, response to public health emergencies, education and training, post-disaster reconstruc-tion, migrant and refugee protection, and aid for trade. The two largest program areas are agricultural development and food security (37.89%), and poverty reduction (37.71%)

China has also set up funds in the World Trade Organization and the World Customs Organization for building trade capacity and helping developing economies, and particularly the least developed countries, to integrate into the multilateral trading system.

China is not looking for war with the United States. And "China has no intention of building a parallel international economic system, competing with the one led by the U.S. China has been a key benefi-ciary of globalization in the past several decades and has a great stake in continuing that open and integrated international system." The Belt & Road Initiative—of which much of China's engagement with Africa is a part—could "not only significantly increase living standards for 64% of the world population... but also become a new segment of the global supply chain, contributing to world economic growth."[44]

Such a development should be seen as positive, not as a threat.

The real threat today is war over Taiwan. During the Trump years the U.S. broke from recognizing the "one China policy" agreed to by Nixon in 1972, sending cabinet level officials to meet with Taiwanese leaders, and openly engaging in military cooperation. This continues under Biden, backed up with U.S. nuclear-armed war ships, just like 1958, when a crisis threatened to escalate into nuclear holocaust. We need to stop this war before it starts.

"What would happen to the world," retired Judge Julie Tang asks, "if the United States and China were to go to war? The price of war would be calamitous. We need to aim for peace, not war. China is not our enemy."

16

"Democracy and Human Rights": China vs. USA

October 5, 2021

"Democracy is not a special right reserved for any individual country but a right for the people of all countries to enjoy."

—XI JINPING

The leaders of the USA and China faced off at the United Nations General Assembly in September 2021, in a dramatic verbal conflict over peace, democracy, and human values. Biden said "The authoritarians of the world, they seek to proclaim the end of the age of democracy, but they're wrong." He added that the U.S. will "oppose attempts by stronger countries to dominate weaker ones, whether through changes to territory by force, economic coercion, technological exploitation or disinformation... But we're not seeking a new Cold War or a separation of the world into rigid blocs..."[1]

The UN delegates listened as Biden proclaimed the United States "is not at war" for the first time in two decades—weeks after the U.S. withdrawal from Afghanistan. He did not mention continued U.S.

military occupations in Iraq, Syria, and Somalia—all of which have been deemed failures—or U.S. military presence in at least thirteen other African countries and hundreds of bases across the globe.

Biden also offered no explanation for the recent agreement with Australia and the United Kingdom to develop and deploy nuclear submarines in the Indo-Pacific region, or the "Quad" alliance with Japan, South Korea and India to threaten China with war ships and nuclear missiles. The question of U.S. sanctions against targeted enemies across the globe also was not mentioned. Neither were the activities of the National Endowment for Democracy and US Agency for International Development (USAID) to try to control internal affairs in numerous countries, including China.

Xi Jinping responded that "China has never and will never invade or bully others to seek hegemony... A world of peace and development should embrace civilizations of various forms and must accommodate diverse paths to modernization. One country's success does not have to mean another country's failure," Xi continued. "The world is big enough to accommodate common development progress of all countries."

Xi emphasized that "Democracy is not a special right reserved for any individual country but a right for the people of all countries to enjoy."[2]

The U.S. president did not mention his difficulties getting bills through Congress to upgrade the country's infrastructure and provide improved basic services to people—services like health care, child care, housing and education, which are guaranteed in China, often free or at minimal cost. The "Build Back Better" bills are supported by a decisive majority of the U.S. population, but are fiercely opposed by recalcitrant right-wingers in Congress, along with "moderate" Democrats beholden to big oil and big pharma. These bills—dubbed "enormous" and unaffordable by Congressional opponents—pale in cost when compared with the military budget. At $743 billion for *one year,* while the infrastructure and budget reconciliation bills are for *ten* years, the military budget is nearly double their total for each year. (This doesn't include military-related items, such as intelligence and veterans' services, which bring the annual military total up above a trillion dollars.)

An effort to pare off just ten percent of the military budget was crushed in Congress in September 2021—a sign of the political power of the military-industrial complex, which combines with big oil, big pharma, big banks and insurance companies to dominate the U.S. political process. These same forces are helping right-wingers in both Congress and many states to quash voting rights, reversing the historic gains of the mid-20th century Civil Rights movement.

China's Success Against Poverty

While the U.S. economy struggles to recover, levels of inequality reach historic proportions, and the political system is ever more polarized, Xi could point to China's success in helping 800 million people lift themselves out of extreme poverty. A 2021 report by the Tricontinental Research Institute noted that "In 2019, as China entered the last stages of its poverty eradication scheme, UN Secretary General Antonio Guterres said, 'Every time I visit China, I am stunned by the speed of change and progress. You have created one of the most dynamic economies in the world, while helping more than 800 million people to lift themselves out of poverty—the greatest anti-poverty achievement in history'."[3]

China's economic success—growing at an average rate of 9.5 percent per year, growing in GDP size by almost 35 times (according to *China's Great Road,* by John Ross), building railroads, highways, subways, even entire cities, to become the second largest economy in the world—didn't happen without strain. Inequality increased, and some worried that the new "market socialism" was a lot like capitalism. The poverty eradication campaign was essential, just as efforts to restrain big capitalists were as well. These efforts were possible in large part due to the Chinese approach to democracy. At the 2017 CPC National Congress Xi said:

> What we now face is the contradiction between unbalanced and inadequate development and the people's ever-growing needs for a better life... The needs to be met for the people to live better lives are increasingly broad. Not only have their material and cultural needs grown; their demands for democracy, rule of law, fairness and justice, security, and a better environment are increasing.[4]

How China's leaders intervened is an illustration of China's democratic path. A July 2020 report from Harvard University's Ash Center for Democratic Governance and Innovation finds *over 90% of the Chinese people like their government,* and "rate it as more capable and effective than ever before. Interestingly, more marginalized groups in poorer, inland regions are actually comparatively more likely to report increases in satisfaction." It says Chinese people's attitudes "appear to respond to real changes in their material well-being."[5]

This contrasts with people's attitudes in the United States, which are polarized politically, racially, and economically. Public trust in the U.S. government is in crisis. There are very real human rights concerns, with police killings, homelessness and mass incarceration at pandemic proportions. The *NY Times* reported Sept. 30, 2021, that police killings in the U.S. have been undercounted by more than half during the past four decades. Of nearly 31,000 people killed by police during that period, more than 17,000 were unaccounted for in official statistics. Black people were 3.5 times as likely to be killed by the police as white people. Latinx and indigenous people also suffered higher rates of fatal police violence than white people.

Chinese Democracy

The Chinese revolution itself was fundamentally democratic—abolishing feudalistic hierarchy and privilege, equalizing gender differences, and enabling poor workers and farmers to be involved in national administration. The Ash Center study includes an important essay, "Democracy in China: Challenge or Opportunity?" by Yu Keping, director of the China Center for Comparative Politics and Economics: "Western scholars use their democratic standards, such as a multi-party system, universal suffrage, and checks and balances, to evaluate Chinese political development, ... and conclude that Chinese reform is more economic than political." This, he says, is an "unnecessary bias and misunderstanding."[6]

The basics of Chinese democracy are people's congresses at local, provincial and national levels. A *Global Times* report on December 24, 2019, said "according to the State Council, 'Deputies to the people's congresses of cities not divided into districts, municipal districts, counties, autonomous counties, townships, ethnic minority townships and towns are elected directly by their constituencies. Deputies to the NPC [National People's Congress] and the people's congresses of the provinces, autonomous regions, municipalities directly under the Central Government, cities divided into districts, and autonomous prefectures are elected by the people's congresses at the next lower level.' These elections are all competitive."

There are also regular consultations between government officials and the people at all levels. Key principles are "people-oriented government, human rights, private property, rule of law, civil society, harmonious society, government innovation, and good governance," Yu Keping wrote.

The Communist Party of China (CPC) is at the core of all this. Its 95 million members make it a preponderant factor in Chinese society. There are eight non-communist political parties, with which the CPC consults regularly. But CPC members lead society. The guiding slogan is "serve the people." The Tricontinental report on the poverty eradication campaign provides a good example:

> The targeted phase of poverty alleviation required building relationships and trust between the Party and the people in the countryside as well as strengthening Party organization at the grassroots level. Party secretaries [were] assigned to oversee the task of poverty alleviation across five levels of government, from the province, city, county, and township, down to the village... Three million carefully selected cadres were dispatched to poor villages, forming 255,000 teams that

reside there. Living in humble conditions for generally one to three years at a time, the teams worked alongside poor peasants, local officials, and volunteers until each household was lifted out of poverty. In this process, many cadres were unable to return home to visit families for long stretches of time; some fell ill in the harsh natural conditions of rural areas and more than 1,800 Party members and officials lost their lives in the fight against poverty. The first teams were dispatched in 2013; by 2015, all poor villages had a resident team, and every poor household had an assigned cadre to help in the process of... lifting themselves out of poverty. At the end of 2020, the goal of eliminating extreme poverty was reached. [7]

The study says the "cadres and officials who have mobilized in the countryside have been essential in building public support for and confidence in the Party and the government."

China's Response To the Pandemic

The government's effective response to the COVID-19 pandemic continued to build public support. Shortly after Wuhan emerged from the COVID-19 lockdown, York University Professor Cary Woo led a survey of 19,816 people across 31 provinces and administrative regions. Published in the May 5, 2021 *Washington Post*, the study found that 49 percent of respondents became more trusting of the government following its response to the pandemic, and overall trust increased to 98 percent at the national level and 91 percent at the township level. [8]

"The Chinese way of political development," Yu Keping says, "is extremely different from the Western democratic tradition... Consequently, it is almost dead-end to explain the Chinese way of democratic politics through using existing Western democratic theories." Democracy means "govern-ment by the people," the professor says. So "the fundamental criteria to judge whether a country is a 'democracy' or not is government's responsiveness to its citizens... As long as a country has formal institutions to guarantee that government policies can effectively reflect the public's opinions, that citizens can participate in political life, and the incumbent political regime has to respond to people's interests, it can be considered democratic regardless of the particular party systems, election procedures, or power separation mechanisms."

Western Claims Discredited

Former U.S. Secretary of State Mike Pompeo admitted in 2019 that "We lied, we cheated, we stole... It's part of the glory of the American experiment." Pompeo's claims that the Chinese Communist Party is "the greatest danger" to democracy in the world, and that China's to blame for the COVID-19 pandemic have served to discredit the U.S. position rather than strengthen it. Biden, Secretary of State Blinken and most in Congress, to their shame, are continuing Pompeo's infamous campaign. Despite hundreds of millions of U.S. funds to support protests in Hong Kong, that effort has fizzled. Hong Kong ranks in the top three on the 2020 Human Freedom Index, published by the Fraser Institute, a Canadian think tank. The U.S. is in 17th place.[9]

Regarding claims of "genocide" in Xinjiang, Columbia University Professor Jeffrey Sachs, a special advisor to the UN Secretary General, says "The U.S. government has offered no proof, and unless it can, the State Department should withdraw the charge." Webinars sponsored by the U.S. anti-war group CodePink have demolished U.S. anti-China claims. Using lies and false accusations, the U.S. has imposed sanctions and launched an international boycott of products made in Xinjiang. The main result has been to hurt the people of Xinjiang. But the smear campaign has also confused many progressives and so-called "leftists" in the U.S., who have fallen victim to the continued repetition of these lies in the mainstream media.

China has answered the U.S. slander campaign with claims of its own. In late September 2021 it called on the UN Human Rights Council to "work to eliminate the negative impacts of colonialism on people around the world." The statement, issued with 21 other countries, said "Economic exploitation, inequality, racism, violations of indigenous peoples' rights, modern slavery, armed conflicts and damage to cultural heritage are among the legacies of colonial repression."[10] In a separate statement, China "called for nations that have conducted illegal military interventions to pay reparations." Without naming any states, he pointed out that "such action had severe consequences for social and economic development."[11]

"A democratic system is a marriage of universality and particularity," Professor Keping says. "We cannot make arbitrary conclusions that democracy has only one model merely based on the assumption that democracy is a universal value and has common features... The nature of democracy is government by the people or 'people become their own masters,' which is reflected in a series of institutions and mechanisms that guarantee the citizens' democratic rights... Chinese democracy, growing out of Chinese tradition and society, will not only bring good fortune to the Chinese people, but also contribute greatly to the advancement of democratic theory and practice for all mankind." [12]

17

"Yankees Go Home!" Asians Say

[SOURCE: Nathan Keirn/Creative Commons. Wikimedia]

Yankees, Go Home': U.S.-China Rift Rattles South Korea" was the banner headline of the *NY Times* international section October 19.[1] It reported a protest of thousands of South Koreans who fear war between the U.S. and China will impact them. This is just the latest sign of escalating trouble for U.S. war plans in east Asia. In Okinawa, where over 70% of the U.S. military presence in Japan is stationed, protests are constant. Okinawans have voted overwhelmingly, year after year, against the U.S. bases. In a 2019 referendum, over 72% voted against construction of a new U.S. military base, and last month Governor Denny Tamaki was re-elected on a platform opposing the base.

Hideki Yoshikawa, director of the Okinawa Environmental Justice Project, said at a recent Codepink event that "As tensions between China and the U.S. are intensifying, Japan as a client state of the U.S., is taking advantage of this situation trying to push its militarization and the militarization of Okinawa. Unfortunately this fear mongering about 'Chinese threats' is spreading through the Japanese government and major media outlets." In March, the government of Japan declared Okinawa a "combat zone" in the event of a Taiwan contingency. Okinawa is closer geographically to Taiwan than it is to Tokyo, Japan's capital.

The war danger is not Okinawans' only concern. Yoshikawa recently sent a letter signed by over 100 organizations and 40 U.S. state and local elected officials addressed to the U.S. Congress, saying the bases are a constant hell for Okinawan residents.[2] The letter called on the U.S. to honor its 25-year-old promise to close U.S. Marine Corps Futenma Air Station and cancel construction of a new U.S. base at Henoko, Okinawa. Yoshikawa highlighted the massive local opposition to the bases and underscored the importance of upholding the principle of democracy and environmental justice in Okinawa. There is non-stop rage among Okinawans against the intrusive military presence, sexual violence, ecological catastrophe, and settler dispossession by the U.S. military.

Over 55 anti-war, labor, and civil-society organizations in Okinawa and Japan signed the anti-base letter, as well as 45 groups in the U.S. and around the world. Signers among U.S. organizations included Codepink, Asian Pacific American Labor Alliance, DSA International Committee (IC), Center for Biological Diversity, The Red Nation, RootsAction, Empire Files, and World Beyond War. The DSA IC helped organize U.S. signers and has committed to fight to close U.S. foreign military bases and demand reparations for the human and environmental destruction they've caused. Forty DSA affiliated state and municipal elected officials signed to support the letter, including Jabari Brisport, Nikil Saval, Zohran Mamdani, Tiffany Cabán, Ruth Buffalo, David Morales, Julia Salazar, and Tanya Vyhovsky. These organizations and U.S. politicians urged members of Congress to heed calls from Okinawa and support their demands to close these dangerous and destructive U.S. military bases, which only serve the interests of war profiteers.[3]

Jabari Brisport, New York State Senator and DSA representative, shared a message of support in October 2022: "I stand in solidarity with people in Japan and across the world who are opposing construction of this base. U.S. imperialism is in direct opposition to our fight for a more just and equitable world. Our movement *must* be internationalist. There is a wide coalition of progressive forces in Japan who are opposing construction of this base, including socialists, labor unions, anti-war organizers, and local indigenous activists. This project doesn't only affect Okinawa. It impacts us here in New York and across the entire United States. The Biden administration requested $813 *billion* for the next National Defense Authorization Act. That would put total annual military spending at *$1.5 **trillion***. That is an unfathomable amount of money to spend on imperialism and war mongering, instead of caring for our communities at home. This is also about climate justice. Constructing a new base will increase the U.S. military's already out-of-control carbon emissions and destroy a local ecosystem. As it stands, the U.S. military is the world's largest non-state polluter—140 states combined pollute less than the U.S. military."[4]

Constant Fear

"Residents living around Futenma Air Station live in constant fear of objects falling from U.S. military aircraft," the anti-base letter said. "Worse, they have to live in fear of aircraft crashing on them." Noise levels are so bad that "Japanese courts have repeatedly ruled that the plaintiffs have suffered physically and mentally from aircraft noise pollution." Residents are also exposed to cancer-causing chemicals due to accidental spills and discharge of chemicals, which have also poisoned the water, both for drinking and for agriculture. As if all this were not enough, the area is an earthquake zone. Four major quakes with a magnitude of 6 or worse on the Richter scale, have hit the area since 2001—most recently a magnitude 7.2 tremor in 2010.

Veterans For Peace member Doug Lummis, who has lived in Okinawa for many years, recalls that in 2003, then-U.S. Defense Secretary Rumsfeld declared the Futenma Marine Corps Air Station "the most dangerous base in the world." Lummis wrote in 2018 that "Helicopter parts are regularly falling into residential areas." Lummis quotes defenders of the base who say, "Well, it was the Okinawans who built their houses next to the base, of their own will. So the danger is their fault." But, he adds, "the base was originally built right after the Battle of Okinawa [in 1945], when the Okinawan people were being held in concentration camps. The military bulldozed the villages and farmlands that were there, expropriated the land, and built the base."[5]

Part of a Long History

While the U.S. "pivot to Asia" is recent, dating from 2009, its roots can be traced back *at least* to the 19th century. In a recent DSA International Committee webinar, Mark Tseng-Putterman explained that "the U.S. state of permanent war in Asia and the Pacific today is in fact the inevitable product of a centuries-long project of U.S. hegemony in the Pacific."[6] In a major article in *Monthly Review*, he cites "various tactics of empire: from settler colonialism in Hawai'i to colonial war in the Philippines to the formation of an 'open-door' empire in a fabled China market... as the crown jewel of U.S. Pacific manifest destiny." Now we're "in a moment in which the 'Indo-Pacific' reemerges as the primary theater of U.S. militarism, and China in particular emerges as the definitive 'official enemy' around which the project of U.S. Pacific hegemon coheres." He refutes the concept of an "inter-imperial rivalry" between the U.S. and China, which gives false justification of the U.S. militarized posture as "'defensive' in the face of ostensible Chinese belligerence." He says this "lazy condemnation of 'inter-capitalist competition'... obscures the centuries-long project of U.S. Pacific hegemony" that is now being "reconsolidated, operationalized, and expanded" in a hostile Cold War posture aimed at China.[7]

The U.S. now has 375,000 Indo-Pacific Command personnel scattered across hundreds of military bases in the west Pacific. "Endemic sexual violence, ecological catastrophe, and settler dispossession in Hawai'i, Guam, the Mariana Islands and Okinawa continue under a geostrategic discourse that renders places and peoples mere 'island chains' bound in strategic containment of China." The official U.S. purpose for these bases is "protection of U.S. allies from Chinese hegemonic aspirations." The reality is simpler: these are forward operations in a long-term U.S. policy of "containment," and very concrete preparations for war.

Grassroots Opposition To U.S. Bases

The pivot to Asia faces "multiple, overlapping grassroots movements opposing the existential threat continued U.S. militarization poses to local livelihoods, cultural practices, and ecologies." The intense anti-base activism in Okinawa and Korea is matched by Chamorro activists in Guam, whose lives are totally dominated by the U.S. base there, about 2,500 miles east of the Philippines, and roughly equidistant to the Korean Peninsula and the South China Sea. The anti-base fight in Guam[8] has much in common with Puerto Ricans' battle to force closure of the U.S. bombing base on the island of Vieques. Hawaian opposition to U.S. military presence poisoning local water supply also recently culminated in plans to close the Navy's Red Hill military fuel facility.[9] These fights are anti-colonial, just as in the Philippines, where continuous anti-Marcos and anti-U.S. mobilizations forced major bases there to close in the 1990s, though U.S. troops are back today and the struggle continues.

The anti-base mobilizations and activism face constant harassment and repression, from both local authorities and their U.S. backers. Yamashiro Hiroji, head of the Okinawa Peace Research Center, was arrested in October 2016 on trivial offenses, and held in solitary confinement for 152 days—long past the Japanese legal limit of 23 days, in violation of the UN Covenant on Civil and Political Rights. His requests for bail were denied, despite a massive campaign for his release. "During my time in the cells, the interrogation was conducted on an almost daily basis," he said in an interview with *Asia-Pacific Journal.*[10] "Each time I was moved the few meters from my cell to the interrogation room I was handcuffed and a cord fastened around my waist... Each time I was moved I was subject to body search." The

Japanese government made this leader of the anti-base movement an example and a warning to others. But Yamashiro Hiroji's answer is "There will be no stopping the Okinawan resistance."

The prospects for winning a shut-down of U.S. bases in east Asia are challenging, but activists remain committed to organizing for it. On October 27 the Pentagon issued a new National Defense Strategy document highlighting Russia and China as its key rivals.[11] The report said the Pentagon would continue to build up bases and "expand U.S. access" in the western Pacific region. But the rights of local people throughout the region are arrayed against the bases. They make it clear the U.S. role is exactly the opposite of defending human rights and democracy.

Postcript: On April 26, 2023, at the conclusion of far-right South Korean President Yoon's summit with Biden in Washington, the White House announced the U.S. would be docking nuclear-armed submarines in South Korea.[12] The North Korean newspaper *Rodong Sinmun* added that the U.S. "deploys strategic nuclear bombers, nuclear carrier task forces and even strategic nuclear submarines near the territorial waters of the DPRK." (North Korea) "What is more serious," the paper said, was that Biden, at a press conference after the talks, recklessly spoke about "the end of regime" towards the DPRK, and mentioned a "swift, overwhelming and decisive response."[13] The DPRK also denounced recent flights of nuclear-capable B-52 bombers over Korea last month.[14]

The New England Korea Peace Campaign and Massachusetts Peace Action held a protest April 28, in Cambridge, Mass., during Yoon's visit to Harvard. The groups issued a statement that "Since entering office, Yoon's right-wing administration has expanded costly and provocative U.S.-ROK military exercises, heightened tensions with North Korea, rolled back workers' rights,… and has taken many other actions to undermine struggles for peace and justice in South Korea."[15]

The buildup of South Korean forces is part of the U.S. war escalation against China, as well as the DPRK. On April 11, the U.S. and the Philippines began their largest-ever military drills. Known as Balikatan, the drills have about 12,200 U.S. troops and 5,400 Armed Forces of the Philippines members. Balikatan means "shoulder to shoulder" in Tagalog.[16] The Philippines recently agreed to allow the U.S. access to nine more military bases, with four directly facing Taiwan.[17] The Philippines is also increasing military ties with Japan.[18]

18

Biden Travels East
in Clouds of Mistrust

Chinese President Xi Jinping meets with U.S. President Joe Biden in Bali, Indonesia, November 14, 2022. [SOURCE: english.news.cn]

November 20, 2022

U.S. President Joe Biden and Chinese leader Xi Jinping met for more than three hours at the G20 conference November 14 and 15 in Indonesia. They needed to discuss each other's "red lines," Biden said.[1]

The meeting wasn't just about Taiwan, where U.S. war ships cross China's "red lines" constantly. China "is the only country with both the intent to reshape the international order and... the economic, diplomatic, military and technological power to advance that objective," Biden wrote in the new U.S. Defense Strategy document issued in October.[2] That document focused on China and Russia as key "threats" to U.S. hegemony.

Xi warned at the 20th CPC congress in October 2022 that China is "confronted with drastic changes in the international landscape, especially external attempts to blackmail, contain, blockade, and exert maximum pressure on China."[3] But China is committed to deepening and expanding global partnerships, safeguarding the international system with the United Nations at its core and the international order underpinned by international law, and building a human community with a shared future, Xi said.[4]

During the meeting, Biden spoke of what China calls the "Five Noes," which he committed to at last year's summit: not to seek a new Cold War; not to try to change China's system; not to forge alliances against China; not to support "Taiwan independence;" and not to look for conflict with China. Biden added that the U.S. does not seek to halt China's economic development, or to contain China.

"We hope the U.S. can implement President Biden's commitment instead of always saying one thing and doing another," commented the influential Chinese newspaper *Global Times*.[5]

In a November 13 leadup to the G20 conference, *Global Times* editorialized that "the G20 was established due to global financial crises... When the U.S. was hit by a financial crisis, even with the

G7 it couldn't handle it, so there was a real need for it to strengthen coordination and dialogue with emerging countries."[6]

Global Times adds that "the G20 is also a symbol of the transformation from the West having the only say to common governance across the globe… G20 is not an expanded G7… While the latter is just a coterie of rich countries, the former is a sign of multipolarity. The G20 consists of the world's major developed economies and emerging markets, which together account for about 85 percent of the global economy…" It concludes that "the whole world is pinning their hope on G20 to be a catalyst of global economic recovery, especially for developing countries."

The International Monetary Fund's research department director said last month that "a wave of debt crises" are coming in the Global South, and "the global economy is headed for stormy waters." The world faces a "geopolitical realignment" that will be "permanent." He warned "the worst is yet to come," as the depreciation of most currencies against the dollar and rising interest rates make it hard for both governments and companies to service their dollar-denominated debt. The director, PierreOlivier Gourinchas, made these comments in a press briefing in October,[7] reported November 14 by Ben Norton of *Multipolarista* (now called *GeoPolitical Economy*).[8]

The members of the G20 are Argentina, Australia, Brazil, Canada, China, France, Germany, India, Indonesia, Italy, Japan, Republic of Korea, Mexico, Russia, Saudi Arabia, South Africa, Türkey, the United Kingdom, the United States, and the European Union. Several are also members of BRICS: Brazil, Russia, India, China, and South Africa. Argentina, Iran and Saudi Arabia are also candidates for BRICS membership.

Together the BRICS countries comprise well over half the global population, and their combined GDP of $25 Trillion is greater than that of the U.S. at $23 trillion.[9] Saudi Arabia, Iran and Argentina's combined GDPs would add about $2.3 trillion. (If Saudi Arabia follows through with joining BRICS, after welcoming Xi in a recent visit, it could be a game changer.) Other prospective BRICS candidates include Mexico, Indonesia, Nigeria and Türkey, adding their combined GDP of nearly $4 trillion. (The EU, Japan and South Korea have a combined GDP equal to that of the U.S.)

Stops Along the Way

U.S. Treasury Secretary Janet Yellen visited India November 11, enroute to Indonesia for G20. She made it clear the U.S. goal with G20 was to try to reshape the global economic order so "allies depend on one another for the goods and services that power their economies."[10] USAID is providing half a billion dollars to finance a U.S. solar manufacturer's new facility in southern India, specifically to "move away from China," which leads the world in solar technology. Yellen used the canard of "forced labor" in Xinjiang—an evidence-free claim—to smear China.

India "shows little interest in U.S. overtures," the *Times* report says. India refused to join the U.S. campaign against Russia over Ukraine. Its imports from Russia rose 430% since February, mainly due to oil and gas imports from Russia. "There is a layer of apprehension if not outright mistrust in Delhi," said Eswar Prasad, a former IMF official and professor of trade policy at Cornell University.

Biden stopped in Cambodia enroute to Indonesia, to attend the East Asia Summit (EAS) there. EAS includes the 10 members of the

Southeast Asia Treaty Organization (SEATO)[11] plus China, Russia, USA, Japan, South Korea, Australia and New Zealand. Russian Foreign Minister Lavrov represented Russia. He said the U.S. Indo-Pacific strategy ignores "inclusive structures" of regional cooperation and would lead to "the militarization of this region with an obvious focus on containing China, and containing Russian interests in the Asia-Pacific."[12]

The "U.S. better give up attempts to contain China by utilizing Southeast Asian countries," was the headline of a *Global Times* November 3 report by top opinion writer Hu Xijin. It said: "The U.S. has always wished to build an anti-China united front in the South China Sea with Japan, Australia, and Southeast Asian countries.[13]

"Vietnam is a key U.S. target to rope in. But Vietnam is clearly aware that the U.S. wants to use it as a pawn, so Hanoi is vigilant while developing relations with the U.S." Hu wrote that during Vietnamese leader Nguyen Phu Trong's visit following the 20th CPC Congress, "Trong reiterated that Vietnam will not allow any country to establish a military base in Vietnam, or join any military alliance, or use force against any country, or work with one country to oppose another."

A *New York Times* report November 13 said "ASEAN [Association of Southeast Asian Nations] leaders at the EAS conference reiterated their strong ties with Beijing and issued a joint statement with China supporting the One China Policy, opposing independence for Taiwan."[14]

Xi Jinping greets Vietnamese Communist Party general secretary Nguyen Phu Trong Oct. 31, 2022. Trong was Xi's first guest following the CPC's 20th Party Congress. [SOURCE: globaltimes.cn]

"China and ASEAN are each other's largest trading part-ner," a *Global Times* November 12 report said.[15] Indonesia's Jakarta-Bandung high speed railway approached 90 percent completion in October. It is "a flagship project of China-Indonesia cooperation under the Belt and Road Initiative," *Global Times* says.[16] "When fully completed, it will be the first high speed railway in Indonesia and the entire Southeast Asia. This month, the total quantity of freight transported by the China-Laos Railway had exceeded 10 million tons, with the cross-border cargo transportation value hitting $1.7 billion."

"Security Issues"

Biden met in Cambodia with Japanese and South Korean leaders, focusing on "security issues," a week after the U.S. and South Korea launched their largest ever combined military drills, with hundreds of warplanes from both sides staging mock attacks 24 hours a day for most of a week, involving "about 240 warplanes conducting about 1,600 sorties," according to a U.S. Air Force statement.[17] The exercises included the nuclear-powered USS Ronald Reagan carrier group in the first U.S.-South Korea joint military training involving a US aircraft carrier since 2017.[18]

The U.S. has nearly 30,000 troops stationed in South Korea, with another 50,000 in Japan, mainly in Okinawa, with nuclear missiles ready to launch. Anti-base protests are constant.[19] The U.S. is in a "state of permanent war in Asia and the Pacific today," with 375,000 Indo-Pacific Command personnel scattered across hundreds of military bases in the west Pacific, according to Mark Tseng-Putterman, writing in *Monthly Review*.[20]

He refutes the concept of an "inter-imperial rivalry" between the U.S. and China, which gives false justification of the U.S. militarized posture as "'defensive' in the face of ostensible Chinese belligerence." He says this "lazy condemnation of 'inter-capitalist competition'… obscures the centuries-long project of U.S. Pacific hegemony" that is now being "reconsolidated, operationalized, and expanded" in a hostile Cold War posture aimed at China.

Germany and France Seek to Boost Economic Ties With China

German Chancellor Olaf Scholz led a high-level business delegation to China November 4, seeking to boost economic ties, in the midst of major economic difficulties caused by the loss of cheap energy from Russia.[21] Xi told Scholz that as large nations with influence, China and Germany should work together during "times of change and turmoil" for the sake of world peace, according China Central TV (CCTV).

Xi also met French President Macron at the G20. Macron said both France and China are committed to peace, development and economic prosperity in the world, Xinhua reported.[22] The French president added that amid a volatile international landscape, France hopes to continue working with China in the spirit of mutual respect, equality and mutual benefit, increase high-level exchanges and dialogue, and deepen cooperation in areas such as trade, economy, aviation and civilian nuclear energy.

Macron and Xi at G20 [english.news.cn] Scholz and Xi in Beijing Nov. 4 [Aljazeera.com]

Scholz received heavy criticism from German Economy Minister Robert Habeck, and Foreign Minister Annalena Baerbock, who threatened to break up Germany's governing coalition over the Scholz visit. Germany's further right CDU party representative, Norbert Roettgen, said "the chancellor is pursuing a foreign policy which will lead to a loss of trust in Germany among our closest partners." (Which partners?)

Unforgettable Indonesia

The G20's location in Indonesia recalls the 1955 Conference of Non-Aligned Countries, held in Bandung, Indonesia. The Bandung conference drew 29 non-aligned countries, led by Indonesia, India, Egypt and Yugoslavia. Today a majority of the world's countries are members of the UN's Non-Aligned Movement—essentially *all* of Asia, Africa and Latin America.[23] They're the ones who abstained or voted against the NATO countries' vote to condemn Russia this year.

China's then-Foreign Minister Zhou Enlai was an invited observer to the Non-Aligned conference. He narrowly missed an assassination attempt enroute to Bandung.[24] The Taiwanese assassin was flown out of Hong Kong to Taiwan on a CIA-sponsored aircraft. The attempt took place in the wake of the first Taiwan Straits crisis of 1954-55.[25] This was just after the July 1953 armistice in Korea ended open warfare, but left tens of thousands of U.S. troops there. China recently celebrated its decisive role in stopping the U.S. assault in *The Battle at Lake Changjin,*[26] the most expensive film ever produced in China. China remembers all this very well.

In 1965, Ten years after the Bandung conference, the CIA engineered a *coup d'etat* in Indonesia, known as the "Indonesian genocide."[27] An estimated one million people were killed in an effort to destroy the left and popular movements in the country. Indonesia's President Sukarno, who convened the Bandung Conference, was overthrown, replaced by anticommunist General Suharto who ruled Indonesia with an iron fist until the mid-1990s.

The incident is documented in *The Jakarta Method,* by Vincent Bevins. The book goes on to describe subsequent replications of the strategy of mass murder, against left-wing and reform movements in Latin America and elsewhere.

Biden at COP27 Climate Change Conference in Egypt

President Biden touched down in Egypt to speak at the COP27 UN climate talks, on the weekend before continuing to Cambodia and Indonesia. A *New York Times* report November 12 said "he exhorted other nations to follow America's lead and increase their efforts to make swift and deep cuts to the pollution that is driving climate change."[28] He highlighted the Inflation Reduction Act, passed earlier this year, which would impose fines of $1500 per ton of methane gas released into the atmosphere.

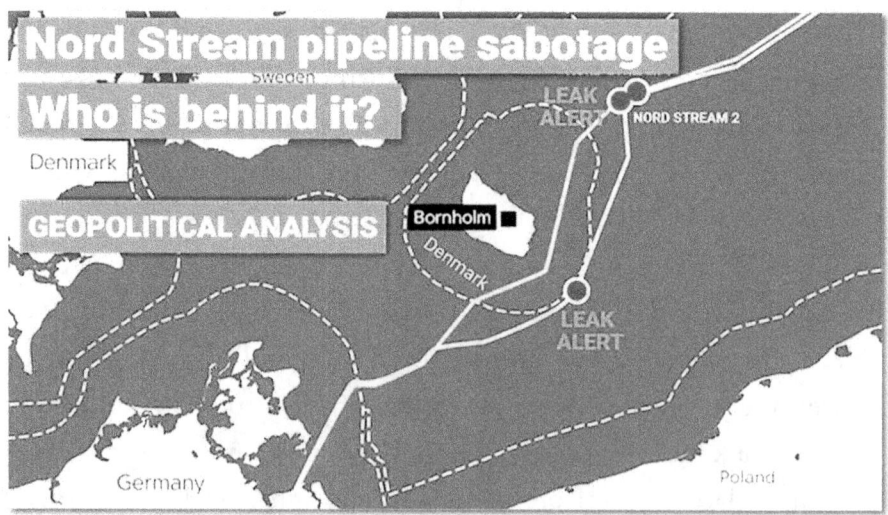

[SOURCE: *youtube.com*]

Methane is a greenhouse gas that "traps about 80 times as much heat as CO_2 (*NYT* 11/12/22)." A proposed EPA regulation would cut emissions by 30% by 2030 and eliminate 36 million tons of methane emissions by 2035, Biden said. It raises a question: *how much methane escaped from the North Sea when the Nordstream pipelines were destroyed?*

A Danish official said Nord Stream gas leaks could emit a CO_2 equivalent of 14.6 million tonnes (32 billion pounds), similar to a third of Denmark's total annual greenhouse gas emissions.[29] Perhaps the EU should impose a $1500 per ton fine of $22 billion on the perpetrator—widely assumed to be the United States.[30]

The U.S. and its allies are blocking calls at COP27 for "loss and damage" funding for countries in the Global South. Rich countries are concerned that it would lead to "unlimited liability," and that determining how much it would cost is difficult. Estimates of financial costs of weather events in low- and lower middle-income countries, just for damages between 1998 and 2017, are *over half a trillion dollars.*[31] Assessing only the immediate damage, these figures do not include long term economic impacts, such as food insecurity or health disorders. It raises another question: how much is due for a century and a half of western industrialization, and six centuries of colonialism and slavery?

There's a trust problem for the U.S. at all these global conferences. Power Shift Africa's founder Mohamed Adow said at the climate conference in Egypt that "Joe Biden comes to COP27 and makes new promises. He's like a salesman selling goods with endless small print."[32] In India, Treasury Secretary Yellen found "a layer of apprehension if not outright mistrust."[33]

In Cambodia, "ASEAN leaders at the EAS conference reiterated their strong ties with Beijing and issued a joint statement with China supporting the One China Policy, opposing independence for Taiwan."[34] And in Indonesia, the U.S. finds the G20 to be "a symbol of the transformation from the West having the only say to common governance across the globe… G20 is not an expanded G7," as *Global Times* wrote.[35] Joe Biden and his team are finding a whole new world out there.

19

"With Us or Against Us" Fails

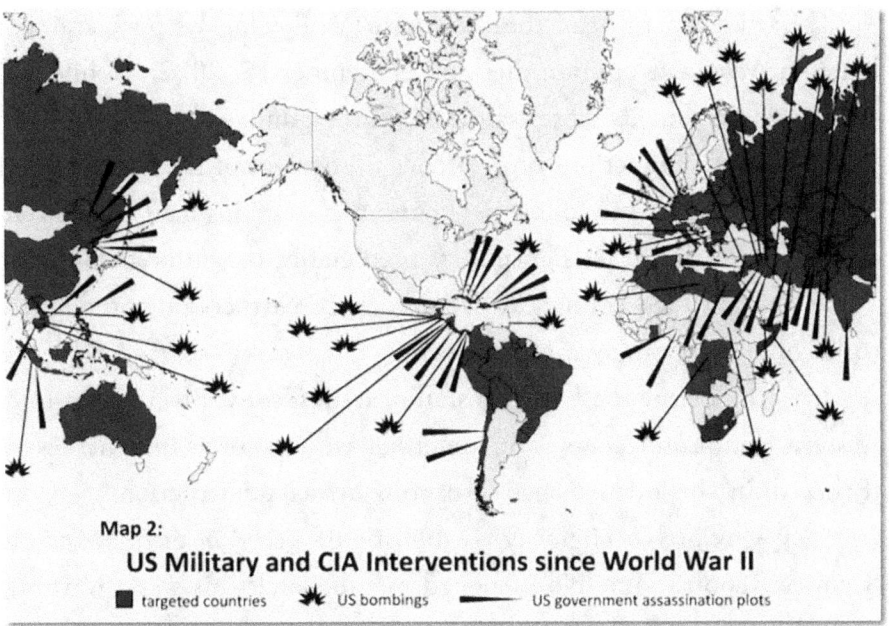

Map 2:
US Military and CIA Interventions since World War II

■ targeted countries ✳ US bombings ▬▬▬ US government assassination plots

[SOURCE: William Blum, *Killing Hope: US Military and CIA Intervention Since World War II, www.killinghope.org]*

March 7, 2023

"You can't be neutral" in NATO's proxy war with Russia, foreign ministers of the U.S., Germany and Ukraine told leaders of Global South countries at the Munich Security Conference February 18.[1] "Neutrality is not an option," said Germany's Foreign Minister

Annalena Baerbock, "because then you are standing on the side of the aggressor." In January Baerbock told the Council of Europe "We are fighting a war against Russia."

U.S. Secretary of State Blinken echoed his German counterpart, stressing "You really can't be neutral."

Why not? What motivates this Mafia style pressure?

"Nearly 90 percent of the World Isn't Following Us on Ukraine," blared a *Newsweek* opinion piece on September 15, 2022. "While the United States and its closest allies in Europe and Asia have imposed tough economic sanctions on Moscow, 87 percent of the world's population has declined to follow us. Economic sanctions have united our adversaries in shared resistance. Less predictably, the outbreak of Cold War II has also led countries that were once partners or non-aligned to become increasingly multi-aligned."[2]

In 2002, before the U.S. invasion of Iraq, George Bush Junior told western European leaders "You are either with us, or against us," even if they didn't believe Iraq had "weapons of mass destruction."

"My Way or No Highway" is the title of a section of the Munich Security Report. Some Non-Aligned members felt this was a warning not to participate in China's Belt and Road Initiative—their preferred "highway." The section cites Chinese President Xi Jinping that "Mechanisms for countering foreign sanctions, interference, and long-arm jurisdiction will be strengthened."

Immediately after the Munich conference, at a summit in Bengaluru, India (*aka* Bangalore), U.S. Treasury Secretary Janet Yellen said G20 countries must condemn Russia for its invasion of Ukraine and they must adhere to US sanctions against Russia.[3] But India, the chair of the G20, demurred. Indian officials said "India is not keen to discuss or back any additional sanctions on Russia during the G20... The existing sanctions on Russia have had a negative impact on the world."[4]

Instead of isolating Russia, the U.S./NATO sanctions are isolating the West against the rest of the world.

"Losing the Trust of the Global South"

French President Macron said at Munich "I am struck by how much we are losing the trust of the Global South." Macron's "we" refers to the NATO countries, especially the G7. He added that "The west has been losing the Global South and hasn't done enough to respond to the charge of double standards, including by not helping poor countries fast enough with Covid vaccines."[5] U.S. Vice President Kamala Harris observed glumly that "many countries sit on the fence."[6]

Colombia's new Vice President Francia Márquez, speaking at a Munich panel on "defending the UN Charter and the Rules-Based International Order," said "We don't want to go on discussing who will be the winner or the loser of a war. We are all losers, and, in the end, it is humankind that loses everything."[7]

"Our focus is on resolving the problem... not on shifting blame," said Namibia's Prime Minister Saara Kuugongelwa-Amadhila. "We are promoting a peaceful resolution of that conflict" in Ukraine. "The money used to buy weapons could be better utilized to promote development in Ukraine, in Africa, in Asia, in other places, in Europe itself, where many people are experiencing hardships."[8]

China's Top Diplomat Weighs In

China's top diplomat, State Counselor Wang Yi, stole the show at Munich. He told the delegates "it is imperative to return to the Minsk

II agreement… as quickly as possible."[9] That would mean a ceasefire and autonomy for the Donbas, and getting NATO out of Ukraine. Wang said Minsk II "is a binding instrument negotiated by the parties concerned and endorsed by the UN Security Council." He said "Russia and the EU both support Minsk II," and claimed U.S. Secretary of State Blinken had expressed U.S. support "in a recent phone call." He called for "the relevant parties [to] sit down together" to work out a roadmap and timetable for implementation of the agreement.

Wang announced China's 12-point plan for peace in Ukraine. It calls for "abandoning the Cold War mentality, saying "All parties should… prevent bloc confrontation, and work together for peace and stability" by promoting talks for peace, and "help parties to the conflict open the door to a political settlement as soon as possible." It says "Nuclear proliferation must be prevented and nuclear crisis avoided" and concludes that "China opposes unilateral sanctions unauthorized by the UN Security Council."[10]

Blinken responded by changing the subject, saying China "is considering providing lethal support" to Russia, "and we've made very clear to them that that would cause a serious problem for us and in our relationship."[11] Joe Biden dismissed China's plan: "I've seen nothing in the plan that would indicate there is something that would be beneficial to anyone[12] other than Russia if the Chinese plan were followed."[13]

Ukraine's President Zelensky indicated he was willing to consider aspects of the Chinese proposal, according to a February 24 *Guardian* report.[14] He said he planned to meet President Xi Jinping and said it would be "useful" to both countries and global security.

Following the Munich conference Wang Yi flew to Moscow. He

told Russian President Putin "our relations are always not directed at third countries and, of course, they are not subject to pressure from third parties, since we have a very strong foundation—from the economy, politics, and culture."[15]

On February 21, 2023 China issued its "Global Security Initiative" Concept Paper—a broad statement of principles "calling on countries to adapt to the profoundly changing international landscape in the spirit of solidarity, and address the complex and intertwined security challenges with a win-win mindset." At its center the document says "War and sanctions are no fundamental solution to disputes; only dialogue and consultation are effective in resolving differences... Major countries must uphold justice, fulfill their due responsibilities, support consultation on an equal footing, and facilitate talks for peace."[16]

China's former ambassador to the U.S., Qin Gang, who is now Foreign Minister, introduced the Concept Paper saying "we urge relevant countries to immediately stop adding fuel to the fire, stop blaming China and stop provoking the situation by using references like 'Ukraine today, Taiwan tomorrow'."[17] Chinese Foreign Ministry spokesperson Mao Ning said "China issued its position paper on the political settlement of the crisis, whereas the U.S. imposed sanctions on Chinese and other foreign companies. Who is promoting peace and de-escalation, and who is fueling the tension and making the world more unstable? The answer is fairly obvious."

"U.S. Hegemony and Its Perils" – China Takes the Gloves Off

As if to clarify it doesn't always have to be polite and diplomatic, China's foreign ministry issued a frank and forceful document which is a detailed indictment that "the United States has acted... to interfere in the internal affairs of other countries, pursue, maintain and abuse hegemony, advance subversion and infiltration, and willfully wage wars, bringing harm to the international community."[18] The document traces U.S. interference in other countries from the Monroe Doctrine of 1823, including the 61-year blockade of Cuba, and a succession of "color revolutions" over the past two decades, the plot to intervene in Venezuela, attacks on UN agencies for their support of Palestine, forcing an "Indo-Pacific Strategy" with "exclusive clubs like the Five Eyes, the Quad and AUKUS, and forcing regional countries to take sides."

"The U.S. arbitrarily passes judgment on democracy in other countries, and fabricates a false narrative of 'democracy versus authoritarianism,' the document says. It mentions the failed 2021 "Summit for Democracy," which "drew criticism and opposition from many countries for making a mockery of the spirit of democracy and dividing the world." Another such summit planned for March 2023, "remains unwelcome and will again find no support."

The document quotes former U.S. President Jimmy Carter that "the United States is undoubtedly the most warlike nation in the history of the world." It cites a Tufts University report, "The Military Intervention Project: A new Dataset on U.S. Military Interventions, 1776-2019," which says the United States undertook nearly 400 military interventions globally in those years. "Since 2001, the wars and military operations launched by the United States in the name of fighting terrorism have claimed over 900,000 lives with some 335,000 of them civilians, injured millions and displaced tens of millions... So far, the United States... has imposed economic sanctions on nearly 40 countries across the world, including Cuba, China, Russia, the DPRK,

Iran and Venezuela, affecting nearly half of the world's population. 'The United States of America' has turned itself into 'the United States of Sanctions.' And 'long-arm jurisdiction' has been reduced to nothing but a tool for the United States to use its means of state power to suppress economic competitors."

The document concludes that "The United States must… critically examine what it has done, let go of its arrogance and prejudice, and quit its hegemonic, domineering and bullying practices."

Anniversary Speeches – Brave Talk & Grim Realities

After a dramatic February 20, 2023 visit to Kyiv, U.S. President Biden flew to Warsaw for his February 21 speech on the first anniversary of the Ukraine Conflict. He warned of "hard and bitter days ahead" as Russia's invasion of Ukraine nears the one-year mark, but vowed that no matter what, the United States and allies "will not waver" in supporting Ukraine. "NATO will not be divided, and we will not tire," Biden declared bravely.[19]

However, the *Washington Post's* "Today's WorldView" reporter Ishaan Tharoor says "An awkward tension lies beneath the West's support for Ukraine." He writes that "for all of the bravura on show last week, with Biden journeying to Kyiv and Warsaw, it's still uncertain that a united West won't blink first."[20]

French President Emmanuel Macron and German Chancellor Olaf Scholz privately told Ukrainian President Volodymyr Zelensky earlier… that Ukraine cannot win the war against Russia and it should begin peace talks with Moscow this year, the *Wall Street Journal* reported. "The public rhetoric masks deepening private doubts among politicians in the UK, France and Germany that Ukraine will be able to expel the Russians from eastern Ukraine and Crimea…, and a belief that the West can only help sustain the war effort for so long."[21]

Former senior British diplomat Alastair Crooke asks ominously: "Can we imagine the U.S. throwing up its hands and conceding Russian victory? 'No'. NATO might disintegrate in the face of such spectacular failure. Will Biden become desperate? And, as many suspect, gamble by doubling-down into a worsening situation?" Crooke asks "Can Biden be trusted (again) to not be reckless in the wake of his erratic decision to blow up the gas lifeline of close NATO ally, Germany? No, it's not just one instance of recklessness (Nord Stream) at issue, but that of multiple misjudgments, giving rise to mounting Deep State anger directed at Biden, and more particularly at his close team of neocons with their immature political judgments."[22]

Speaking to a UN Security Council special session on Seymour Hersh's exposé of the U.S. destruction of the Nord Stream pipelines last September, former CIA analyst Ray McGovern said "no one wants to go back 20 years to [former U.S. Secretary of State] Colin Powell's speech before this Security Council. We all know about that." [Powell embarrassed himself by officially lying to the UN.] McGovern commented that those U.S. government spokespeople who are smearing Hersh, "don't have a good record for credibility."[23]

Columbia University Professor Jeffrey Sachs also spoke at the Security Council session: "As the destruction of the Nord Stream pipelines on 26 September 2022 constitutes an act of international terrorism and represents a threat to peace, it is the Council's responsibility to take up the question of who might have carried out the act, help bring the perpetrator to justice, pursue compensation for the damaged parties and prevent such actions from recurring in the future."[24]

China's UN Ambassador Zhang Jun testified that "Recently, we have come across a lot of… relevant information concerning the Nord Stream incident, which is alarming… Faced with such detailed materials and comprehensive evidence, a simple statement of 'utterly false and complete fiction' is obviously not enough to answer the many questions and concerns raised around the world. Finding a way to dodge today's meeting does not mean that truth can be concealed. We expect convincing explanations from relevant parties. Such a request is entirely legitimate and reasonable."[25]

Putin: NATO's Goal is Strategic Defeat of Russia

In Moscow, Russian President Putin delivered a remarkably philosophical—and upbeat—speech. He said "This is a time of radical, irreversible change in the entire world, of crucial historical events that will determine the future…"[26] Analyst Pepe Escobar, writing in *The Cradle,* paraphrases Putin that "Ukraine, part of Russian civilization, now happens to be occupied by western civilization, which Putin said 'became hostile to us.' So the acute phase of what is essentially a war by proxy of the west against Russia takes place over the body of Russian civilization."[27]

Escobar says Putin emphasized that "Ukraine is being used as a tool and testing ground by the West against Russia… The more long-range weapons are sent to Ukraine, the longer we have to push the threat away from our borders."

So this war will be long—and painful, Escobar concludes. "Putin remarked on how 'our relations with the west have degraded, and this is entirely the fault of the United States;' how NATO's goal is to inflict a 'strategic defeat' on Russia."

Escobar reports that the U.S. ambassador was summoned to the Ministry of Foreign Affairs right after Putin's address. Russian Foreign Minister Lavrov demanded a detailed explanation of the destruction of the Nord Stream 1 and 2 pipelines, and a halt to U.S. interference in an independent inquiry to identify the responsible parties. He added that Washington must remove all U.S. and NATO military forces and equipment from Ukraine.

Antiwar Forces Mobilize

A major antiwar mobilization took place in Washington, DC, and other cities for March 18, on the 20th anniversary of the U.S. invasion of Iraq, demanding "Peace in Ukraine—Say NO to Endless U.S. Wars" and "Fund People's Needs, Not the War Machine."[28] The call said "since 2003, the U.S. has engaged in sanctions (economic war) on more than 40 countries. These targets of U.S. economic warfare include the people of Cuba, Zimbabwe, Venezuela, Ethiopia, Eritrea, Iran and many other nations. Even in the wake of the worst disasters, like the recent deadly earthquake, Washington keeps its cruel sanctions in place against Syria."

The call says the Biden administration is "determined to escalate the Ukraine war. The real goal of the massive arming and training of Ukrainian forces has nothing to do with the interests of Ukrainian, Russian or American people. The aim instead is to 'weaken Russia' as stated by the U.S. Secretary of Defense himself, even at the risk of a catastrophic nuclear war that could end life on Earth. It adds that "A U.S. General commanding 50,000 troops in the Pacific also issued a letter to his sub-commanders in recent days informing them that he believes that the United States will be at war with China within two years."

Key demands include:

- Peace in Ukraine—No weapons, no money for the Ukraine War
- Abolish NATO—End U.S. militarism & sanctions!
- Fund people's needs, not the war machine!
- No war with China!
- End U.S. aid to racist apartheid Israel!
- Fight racism & bigotry not war!
- U.S. hands off Haiti!
- End AFRICOM!

In Europe, massive protests were held during February in Berlin, Germany, over providing weapons to Ukraine in its war against Russia. Thousands took to the streets holding banners and posters saying 'negotiate and not escalate' and 'not our war.' Demonstrations also took place in London, Paris and other French cities: Bordeaux, Rennes and Montpellier; also in Brussels, Belgium, Prague, and numerous cities in Italy: Rome, Florence, Milan and Genoa, against Western sanctions imposed on Russia. The protesters demanded that the Italian government stop supplying Kyiv with weapons.

V

What Makes the War Machine So Monstrous?

20

Dr. Strangelove Is No Longer Satire

March 1, 2023

Expansion of U.S. weapons supplies to Ukraine makes nuclear war more conceivable

W e are fighting a war against Russia," German Foreign Minister Annalena Baerbock told the Council of Europe on January 24. The next day German Chancellor Olaf Scholz and U.S. President Joe Biden announced plans to send high-powered tanks to Ukraine, in a major escalation of the conflict.

"Germany has really stepped up," Biden said, "and the chancellor has been a strong, strong voice for unity…and for the level of effort we're going to continue."

Biden said nothing about destruction of the Nord Stream pipelines in September 2022, considered by many as a direct attack on its European "ally." Other voices were not so united. Croatian President Zoran Milanovic commented at the Council of Europe meeting that "The German FM said we must be united because we are at war with Russia. I did not know that. Maybe Germany is at war with Russia again, then good luck to them, maybe it will turn out better than 70 years ago."

World-renowned economist Jeffrey Sachs declared on January 25 that "We are at the brink of a disaster…first and foremost because of the United States, which is a major provocateur of this war, and a major threat to peace." He made an impassioned plea to "get us off this reckless war between Russia and NATO, which is escalating by the day. The Doomsday Clock was moved to 90 seconds to midnight at the same time as the U.S. and Germany agreed to send new highly advanced tanks to Ukraine, in a guaranteed reckless escalation that brings us closer to nuclear war."[1]

Sachs said the conflict goes back more than 30 years to 1990, when the U.S. began to "pursue its unipolar agenda, moving its systems further east, with the idea of surrounding Russia."

"Passing Germany the Poisoned Chalice"

A leader of Germany's Left Party (Die Linke), Sevim Dagdelen said "This is obviously about passing Germany the poisoned chalice. Berlin is to be sent into the line of fire, to conclusively destroy German-Russian relations and turn them into open war for others' benefit."[2] Dagdelen is the spokesperson for her party in the German Parliament's Committee on Foreign Affairs.

Dagdelen's view echoes economist Michael Hudson, who says the U.S. war against Russia is actually waged against Europe, to keep the European Union (EU) subordinated to U.S. capital. Hudson says the sanctions against Russia and China aim to prevent America's allies from opening up more trade and investment with Russia and China, to "keep them firmly within America's own economic orbit."[3] European industry has been shutting down recently as energy prices soar due to sanctions.

The German Left Party leader said delivering German tanks to Ukraine would "entail the greatest security threat to face the German population since the Second World War." She added that "many Russians, especially those who lost loved ones in [WWII]...will see in these weapons a renewed German military campaign against their country."

A large majority of Germans and other Europeans share these concerns. In a December 2022 poll by Project Europe, more than two-thirds of respondents in the 27 countries of the EU think the conflict is "worrisome."[4]

Across Europe, more than 80% want negotiations, not continued war, the poll said. European public opinion reflects the impact of sanctions against Russia, which have had a "boomerang" effect, with skyrocketing inflation leading to near-depression conditions. Street protests and strikes across Europe have had an impact, as people pressure their leaders to stop doing Washington's bidding.

Former Prime Minister Boris Johnson, Washington's loudest "poodle" in London, was toppled by the crisis, along with Italy's ex-Prime Minister Mario Draghi; and French President Macron lost his majority in the French National Assembly.

In the United States, people are more divided: A survey completed in late November 2022 by the Chicago Council on Global Affairs found the U.S. public split 48% to 47% on whether Washington should "support Ukraine as long as it takes," or "urge Ukraine to settle for peace as soon as possible."[5]

It is a changing trend: The percentage supporting "as long as it takes" went down ten points from 58% in July 2022; and the "settle for peace" percentage rose from 38% in the same period. During that time there were anti-war protests in dozens of cities and towns across the country. More recently the protests intensified—spreading to more than 90 localities, as major national coalitions joined forces around Martin Luther King's birthday weekend.

Mission Creep: How the U.S. Role Has Escalated

A January 28, 2022 article in *Responsible Statecraft* by Branko Marcetic says "NATO and the United States are creeping closer to the catastrophic scenario President Joe Biden said 'we must strive to prevent'— direct conflict between the United States and Russia… NATO arms transfers have now escalated well beyond what governments had worried just months ago could draw the alliance into direct war with Russia, with the U.S. and European governments now sending armored vehicles and… preparing to send tanks."[6]

The article adds that "[d]espite stressing at the start of the war that 'our forces are not and will not be engaged in the conflict,' current and former intelligence officials…[said] 'there is a much larger presence of both CIA and U.S. special operations personnel' in Ukraine than there was when Russia invaded, conducting 'clandestine American operations' in the country that 'are now far more extensive'."[7]

Responsible Statecraft cites a January 18 report in the *New York Times* that U.S. officials are "strongly considering giving Ukraine the green light to attack Crimea, even while acknowledging the risk of nuclear retaliation that such a move would carry. Fears of such an escalation 'have dimmed,' U.S. officials told the paper."[8]

Russia's Deputy Foreign Minister Sergei Ryabkov is quoted in *Newsweek* saying that "We have repeatedly warned the U.S. about the consequences that may follow if the U.S. continues to flood Ukraine with weapons. It effectively puts itself in a state close to what can be described as a party to the conflict."[9]

A "Spanner in the Works"

German Left Party leader Dagdelen says "we must do all we can to put a spanner in the works"—that is, do something that prevents this plan from succeeding (*Cambridge Dictionary* explanation). "If the German tanks are delivered, the door will be open for more weapons. Calls for combat aircraft have already been voiced…The next thing will be missiles, followed, when that does not work either, by our own soldiers. But a gambler's mentality, which responds to losses by raising the stakes and eventually betting everything on one play, is a bad guide for any society."

Dagdelen adds: "The tank deliveries are today what war loans were in 1914. They lead directly to participation in the war. They cannot be considered in isolation from their purpose—that is, victory in NATO's proxy war against Russia in Ukraine. But consideration must also be given to the Russian response. In the end, after all, Western tanks would practically invoke the use of nuclear weapons—against Germany first...

"Why is it in Washington's interest to send the Germans, of all people, into Russia's line of fire?...Germany, it appears, is supposed to draw Russia's counterfire...The United States would thus have achieved one of its long-term strategic objectives, namely to prevent cooperation between Germany and Russia forever."[10]

It is a reminder of the explosion of the Nord Stream pipelines in September 2022, which served as a guarantee, at least for now, that Europe cannot depend on Russian gas. All evidence about who did it has disappeared. But months before, Biden assured reporters the U.S. "has the capacity" to do it. [11]

Russian President Vladimir Putin sent a message to ordinary Germans during his visit to Volgograd—formerly Stalingrad—on February 2, the 80th anniversary of the Soviet Union's historic and decisive 1943 victory against Nazi Germany in the Battle of Stalingrad. Russia's official news agency Tass reported that Putin said "they remember it in Germany, that German anti-fascists became the first victims of the German fascism, Nazism. And it is very good that such memory remains in ordinary citizens. Unfortunately, modern elites seem to be losing it."[12]

He noted that an "ordinary citizen of the Federal Republic of Germany treats Russia and the heroes that defeated Nazism with respect."

The RAND Corporation, which functions as the Pentagon's planning agency, released a January 2023 study entitled "Avoiding a Long War," which concludes that "the consequences of a long war—ranging from persistent elevated escalation risks to economic damage—far outweigh the possible benefits."[13]

This is not the view of NATO Secretary General Jens Stoltenberg, who declared on January 5 that "weapons are, in fact, the way to peace."[14] Victoria Nuland, along with her bosses, Biden and Secretary of State Antony Blinken, tend to see things more like Stoltenberg than their RAND advisers. "They don't see the world the way sane people do," commented Margaret Kimberley, of *Black Agenda Report*, in a February 1, 2023 article. "They have made the Ukraine conflict an existential crisis, and then decide they have no choice but to engage in dangerous actions… The idea of peaceful coexistence is anathema to Nuland, Biden, and Blinken. Blown up pipelines are seen as proof of victory to people who thought they could make dangerous and irrational obsessions come true."[15]

"Dr. Strangelove Is No Longer Satire"

Roger Harris, of the U.S. Peace Council and the Sanctions Kill campaign, says "The world was fortunate that the Cuban Missile Crisis ended with both sides willing to seek accommodation rather than victory. In contrast, the currently raging and indeed escalating Ukraine War could be the prelude to World War III because neither side appears to have an exit strategy; one by choice, the other because its back is to the wall."[16]

"The U.S.'s intent," Harris further wrote, "is victory by 'overextending and unbalancing' Russia," as a 2019 RAND paper suggested. Harris cites analyst Rick Sterling that "this was the playbook for the U.S. to provoke Russia into the current conflict. Bombers have been repositioned within striking range of key Russian strategic targets, additional tactical nuclear weapons deployed, and U.S./NATO war exercises have been held on Russia's borders."[17]

Harris adds that "Now the prevailing propaganda from Washington is that nuclear war can be 'won.'[18] Dr. Strangelove is no longer satire. This planning to fight a nuclear war[19] as if it were not an existential threat is institutionalized insanity." He cites Robert Kagan, spouse of U.S. Under Secretary of State Victoria Nuland, asking: "Can America learn to use its power?"[20] He says Kagan "argues in favor of a vigorous nuclear confrontation with Russia on the grounds that Putin will most likely back down."

Whether Russia will "back down" or not is debatable. But back in December 2021, Russian initiatives might have prevented hostilities and made the region more secure with a reduced likelihood of war. Following are the proposals Russia made then:[21]

- Russia and the U.S. shall not use the territory of other countries to prepare or conduct attacks against the other.
- Neither party shall deploy short- or intermediate-range missiles abroad or in areas where these weapons could reach targets inside the other's territory.
- Neither party shall deploy nuclear weapons abroad, and any such weapons already deployed must be returned.

- Both parties shall eliminate any infrastructure for deploying nuclear weapons outside their own territories.
- Neither party shall conduct military exercises with scenarios involving the use of nuclear weapons.
- Neither party shall train military or civilian personnel from non-nuclear countries to use nuclear weapons.

When Russia proposed these measures in December 2021, they were called "non-starters" by the U.S. Now the question is whether there is anyone in Washington, DC, who could convince the Biden administration to reconsider. That is what Jeffrey Sachs is demanding.

Events in Munich and Moscow since Blinken's late January 2022 off-the-cuff suggestion of talks without anything concrete clarify that the U.S. is really offering *nothing* for peace. Instead it continues to escalate the war while attempting to project blame onto both Russia and China.

21

Why It's So Hard to Stop
the U.S. War Machine

American Exception: Empire and the Deep State, by Aaron Good
American Exceptionalism and American Innocence: A People's History of Fake News, by
Robert Sirvent and Danny Haiphong

September 14, 2022

Credibility is low these days for the U.S. government, politicians and the mainstream media. Sorting through news reports for reliable fact and analysis would make George Orwell weep. Jeffrey Sachs, director of the UN Sustainable Development Center, decries the fact that "the world is on the edge of nuclear catastrophe" due to "the failure of Western political leaders to be forthright about the causes of the escalating global conflicts." ("Forthright" means honest.)

Oliver Stone and Peter Kuznick, co-authors of *The Untold History of the United States,* praise Aaron Good's *American Exception* as "something we might call untold social science," digging deep into "the pernicious impact of intelligence and security forces and their role in undermining [U.S.] integrity as a country."

American *exception* and *exceptionalism* are different things—interrelated but distinct. For the first, we can recall the concept of a "state of exception," when a government leader suspends normal laws and governs by decree. *Exceptionalism,* on the other hand, is the "normal" justification for all manner of power mongering and conquest, from the "manifest destiny" *(ie, divine right)* to relieve the indigenous people of North America of their land and lives, to the "right" to wage U.S. military occupation and constant wars across the globe to protect "democracy and human rights," always for the good of all, no matter how bad it may seem. A working definition of "manifest destiny" is that European settlers were "sent from heaven" to "civilize" inferior people, and if they resist, heaven's hosts are justified to subdue them.

Sirvent and Haiphong focus on "the American nation's roots in slavery, genocide, and corporate theft." They show how the dominant narratives of American exceptionalism and innocence cause many Americans "to forget, distort, or excuse the crimes of the nation." They ask: "why does the U.S. military have free rein to dictate how other nations conduct themselves, while other countries aren't allowed to critique the U.S. for the very same actions? And if the U.S. really cared about protecting our 'freedom,' why is nothing done to alleviate the declining living standards of ordinary Americans?"

The ideologies of American exceptionalism and innocence, the authors say, "have inoculated the U.S. population from making the connection between the death imposed by modern day U.S. capitalism at home and the misery the U.S. military reigns on nations abroad." The authors highlight how this plays out for the working class soldiers who are pushed by the poverty draft to join the military. They are "constantly thanked for their 'service' while the victims of war are stripped of their humanity... Wars are effectively sanitized as heroic operations that defend the 'freedom' and 'democracy' of all. Soldiers... are celebrated for supposedly protecting the interests of Americans from the inferior nations and peoples seeking to harm them." The authors explain that "inferiority has been a mark placed on communists, nationalists, and most recently 'terrorists' to justify the plunder, power and profit" derived from U.S. military expansionism. "U.S. troops represent 'whiteness' in the form of heroism as opposed to the 'threat' posed by darker nations and peoples."

In contrast to the corporate-sponsored "Concert for Valor" on Veterans Day in 2014, Sirvent and Haiphong cite former Army Ranger Rory Fanning's pointed questions: "Is anyone going to dedicate a song to Chelsea Manning, or John Kiriakou, or Edward Snowden—two of them languishing in prison and one in exile—for their service to the

American people? Will the Concert for Valor raise anyone's awareness when it comes to the fact that... veterans lack proper medical attention, particularly for mental health issues, or that there is a veteran suicide every 80 minutes in this country?" Fanning cites "the approximately 50,000 war resisters who have joined the military since 2001." In most cases they entered the military with their eyes wide open, ready to "serve their country, defend democracy and human rights," and kill the enemy. They came out disillusioned and angry. Fanning thinks "the potential for veterans who come back to become positive influences in the fight against exploitation and oppression is really high." Meanwhile the U.S. government prosecutes whistle blowers and hopes to put Julian Assange on trial for "espionage" for having publicized the truth about the war machine.

Examining Origins

Aaron Good digs deep to find the roots of the problem. He highlights the "Guardian elite" (a term introduced by Lance DeHaven-Smith)—"high-ranking officials who are privy to state secrets, who decide what the public may and may not know, and who plan and authorize covert operations, foreign and domestic surveillance, and other espionage and intelligence activities." This elite "polices—largely in secret—the political class and the mass public. They serve to allow the state to overcome three potential impediments to the exigencies of empire, namely: America's moral code, global meta-norms, and the rule of law... *Exceptionism*—the institutionalized suspension of legal restraints—protects them from facing legal consequences stemming from their illicit clandestine activities."

Good traces back the legitimacy or illegitimacy of the modern state's monopoly on violence to the protection rackets, but on a global scale, as in "the trans-Atlantic slave trade, the Opium Wars, and overt imperialism like colonialism." Good says "it is noteworthy that Henry Cabot Lodge, the man perhaps most responsible for steering the U.S. into the Spanish-American war, was descended from Boston Brahmins who had made vast fortunes in the opium trade." He was a loud proponent of the U.S. "open door" policy, designed for the emerging U.S. empire to stand shoulder-to-shoulder with imperial Britain, Germany and France in dominating China for a century following the opium wars of the mid-1800s. Lodge opposed U.S. entry to the League of Nations, but his son, Henry Cabot Lodge, Jr., was U.S. ambassador to the UN from 1953 to 1960, and to South Vietnam from 1963 to 1967.

Lodge Junior worked closely with CIA operatives in planning the coup against Ngo Dinh Diem, the U.S. puppet leader of South Vietnam, who was assassinated on November 2, 1963. Three weeks later JFK was assassinated in Dallas. There had been a tug-of-war over the Vietnamese coup plot, between Lodge and JFK's top military advisors, Defense Secretary Robert McNamara and General Maxwell Taylor. All this followed Kennedy's famous "Strategy of Peace speech" at American University on June 10, 1963, which caused alarm on the right and among hawks in the military and CIA. After Kennedy was gone, Good notes that "the CIA under President Johnson would reverse several Kennedy era policies in several third world countries, most notably Brazil, Congo and Indonesia."

CIA-backed Coups and Slaughters on Three Continents

In Brazil a U.S.-backed military coup overthrew the progressive government of President João Goulart,[1] installing a military regime aligned to U.S. interests, which lasted 21 years, until 1985.[2] Meanwhile the CIA was very busy across South America, helping to overthrow Salvador Allende's Popular Unity government in Chile in 1973, fostering the "dirty war" against Argentina's left in the mid-1970s, as part of Operation Condor which the CIA described as "a cooperative effort by the intelligence/security services of several South American countries to combat terrorism and subversion." The operation included Argentina, Chile, Uruguay, Paraguay, Bolivia, Brazil, Ecuador and Peru. The results were 50,000+ killed; 30,000 "disappeared," and 400,000 arrested and imprisoned.

In Indonesia, the story is detailed in *The Jakarta Method* by Vincent Bevins. In 1965, the U.S. CIA helped the Indonesian military kill more than a million innocent civilians. This largely unpublicized slaughter inspired copycat terror programs in other countries. It was widely overlooked, but served as a model for CIA's secret interventions elsewhere.

In the Congo—Africa's second largest country geographically, with a population of more than 100 million—the CIA was involved in the 1961 assassination of Prime Minister Patrice Lumumba, and helped foster a four-year civil war killing tens if not hundreds of thousands. Lumumba's followers founded a state, the People's Republic of the Congo, with its capital in the northeastern city of Stanleyville, supported by the Soviet Union and China, as well as Tanzania and Cuba. Che Guevara led a group of 100 Cuban advisors there. The CIA supported the government of Prime Minister Joseph Mobuto, who seized power and set up his own state of exception in 1965, with U.S. backing. In 1971, Mobutu renamed the state Zaire.[3] He was deposed in 1997, in an insurrection led by the *Lumumbist* forces of

Laurent-Désiré Kabila, who became president of the restored Democratic Republic of the Congo. Since then the Congo has been a scene
of ongoing struggle between left and right both internally and inter-
nationally. Two rebel movements, along with Rwandan and Ugandan
troops and U.S. backing, attacked the DRC army in 1998. Angolan,
Zimbabwean, and Namibian militaries helped the *Lumumbist* side,
which had supported their liberation efforts in the 1970s and '80s.
The *Lumumbists* won, but conflict continues to the present day.

Meanwhile across the rest of Africa and Latin America there were
assassinations, attempts, and tragic deaths of liberation leaders. Amilcar
Cabral of Guinea-Bissau was assassinated in Conakry, Guinea at the
age of 48 by political rivals. Samora Machel of Mozambique died in a
mysterious airplane crash in 1986 near the South African border. Both
Kwame Nkrumah, president of Ghana, and Agostinho Neto, founder
of the MPLA and president of Angola, died relatively young of pan-
creatic cancer. Fidel Castro has the distinction of surviving countless
CIA assassination attempts. Venezuelan leader Hugo Chavez was not
so fortunate. Chavez himself speculated that he had been poisoned.[4]
His successor, Nicolas Maduro, called it an assassination.[5] Chinese
Foreign Minister Zhou Enlai was nearly assassinated when he was en
route to the Bandung conference of non-aligned nations in 1955.[6]

A "Tripartite State"

Good traces the origins of the modern "deep state" to the Wall
Street-dominated Council on Foreign Relations, which conducted the
State Department's *War and Peace Studies Project* prior to U.S. entry
into World War 2. The study was largely financed by the Rockefeller
Foundation, which Good says "represented an enormous accumulation

of wealth acquired via Standard Oil's longtime monopoly control of the U.S. petroleum industry." He cites a number of "fateful instances in which top-down power was brought to bear in the making of history during this period"—the War and Peace Studies Project itself, "Pauley's coup," by which Henry Wallace, FDR's choice for vice president was defeated by illegal maneuvers at the 1944 Democratic convention, the dropping of the atomic bombs, and the National Security Act of 1947.

Wallace had rebutted CFR member and media tycoon Henry Luce's bombastic "American Century" vision by calling for a "Century of the Common Man"—a vision "calling for a worldwide 'people's revolution,' toward which end the U.S. and USSR would work together, championing the cause of labor unions, women, African Americans, and the victims of European colonialism," as cited in *The Untold History of the United States,* by Oliver Stone and Peter Kuznick. Wallace had effectively won the vice presidential nomination at the 1944 convention, but the Democratic Party's Treasurer, Edwin Pauley, a California oil millionaire, hatched a conspiracy which he called "Pauley's Coup," together with major party bosses to choose Truman instead. (Kuznick tells the story in a 2013 Real News Network interview, "Untold History: The Coup Against Wallace and What Might Have Been."[7])

What followed was the bombing of Hiroshima and Nagasaki and the launch of the Cold War anti-communist crusade with the National Security Act of 1947, which created the Joint Chiefs of Staff, the National Security Council, and the CIA. Good says "the CIA was willed into being through the efforts and influence of the upper strata of corporate America... Notably, it was a Wall Street lawyer who penned the 'elastic clause' in the National Security Act. Shortly thereafter, the passage came to be interpreted as giving the CIA authority to carry out all manner of illegal covert operations—or 'other duties' in the Act's oblique language." The lawyers in question were the Dulles brothers: Allen Dulles, who became CIA director, and John Foster Dulles, Secretary of State under Eisenhower.

"Very early on, CIA elements began establishing illicit self-funding operations… Specifically, the CIA's Office of Policy Coordination (OPC) collaborated with opium-trafficking Kuomintang (KMT) officers in Burma and Thailand, ostensibly so the proceeds could fund the KMT's … effort to retake mainland China." The legendary "Flying Tigers" Civil Air Transport line became the CIA's principal drug running operation, changing its name to Air America in 1959. Air America's slogan was "Anything, Anywhere, Anytime, Professionally." Its aircraft flew many types of cargo to countries such as Vietnam, Laos, and Cambodia, from bases in Thailand, Taiwan, Japan, Burma and China itself. Historian Alfred W. McCoy's book, *The Politics of Heroin in Southeast Asia*, stated that the CIA was knowingly involved in the trade of heroin in the Golden Triangle[8]—a term coined by the CIA.

While colluding with the KMT in the drug trade, the CIA also worked diligently to foster separatism and break up China—in Tibet, Xinjiang, Hong Kong and Taiwan—setting up long-term operations with the National Endowment for Democracy (NED), the U.S. Agency for International Development (USAID), and numerous non-governmental organizations.[9] Former CIA Director and Trump Secretary of State admitted in 2019 that "We lied, we cheated, we stole… It's part of the glory of the American experiment." USAID Director Samantha Power has chimed in to say U.S. policymakers "have been consistently reluctant to condemn mass atrocities as genocide or to take responsibility for leading an international military intervention." Pompeo and Power have led the evidence-free campaign against Chinese "human rights violations" in China. They don't mention U.S. violations of human rights.

Mainstream Media and the Deep State

Good emphasizes that "the mainstream media must be considered part of the deep state." He tells the story of Katherine Graham, former publisher of the *Washington Post,* who in 1988 spoke at CIA headquarters, "asserting that 'We live in a dirty and dangerous world,' and that there were 'some things the general public does not need to know and shouldn't.' She also stated that 'official secrecy is necessary to preserve liberty'." The *Post* was "one of the chief newspapers that attacked the work of Gary Webb," of the *San Jose Mercury,* in the 1990s. "Webb's articles revealed the CIA protection of Contra-cocaine traffickers whose profligate operations fueled the Los Angeles crack epidemic that began in the 1980s." Good says "Though a CIA Inspector General report would later confirm and expand upon Webb's central allegations, his career and life were essentially ruined by the counterattack of the CIA and its media allies." Webb's death was described as suicide.

The deaths of countless ordinary soldiers, veterans and street people from heroin and cocaine overdoses may not *all* be directly traceable to CIA operations, but some definitely can. And the whole episode provides an ironic backdrop to the so-called "war on drugs" waged across Latin America and the streets of the U.S., and the resulting mass incarceration of tens of thousands of smalltime dealers, and whole populations south of the border.

Good says "the *security state* that emerged after World War II was informed by logics of secrecy, hierarchy, and authoritarianism..." He says the notion of "a supranational deep state component of a tripartite state" helps explain "the decisive power wielded by elites whose interests dominate the security state, the public state, and the economy—and thus society at large." Good clarifies that "the institutions that comprise the deep state are not uniformly obscured. Some are formally organized and transparent," like the Council on Foreign Relations. "Other entities like the Safari Club or the Bilderberg group... are largely opaque." He provides details of the Safari Club—a group of satellite intelligence agencies in governments allied with the U.S., such as those of Saudi Arabia, Egypt, the Shah's Iran, and Morocco. "The most common account of the Safari Club maintains that it was created... in response to the post-Watergate scrutiny of intelligence operations." Others argue it began earlier, "in the mid-1970s as a search for new proxies following the debacle that was U.S.-South African intervention into the Angolan civil war." (It's an adventure in itself to follow Good's footnotes. He cites Joseph Trento's *Prelude to Terror: The Rogue CIA and the Legacy of America's Private Intelligence Network,* and John Prados' and Arturo Jimenez-Bacardi's "The Rockefeller Commission, the White House and CIA Assassination Plots."[10])

Good writes that "U.S. *Exceptionism* is also key to understanding Watergate, since the crimes of the Nixon administration were decidedly minor relative to the various scandals and state crimes that have been documented and/or suspected. Good tells a fascinating story of a *tete-a-tete* between Nixon and CIA director Richard Helms, in which Helms refused the president's request for information about the 1962

Bay of Pigs debacle and the 1963 assassination of JFK. According to the story, Nixon "fires" Helms and then appoints him ambassador to Iran, which led to the mobilization of the Safari Club as a CIA proxy, and ultimately to the Iran hostage crisis of 1979. Meanwhile, according to Good, the CIA deployed the Watergate Plumbers in the "damningly well-documented burgling of Dan Ellsberg's psychiatrist," and "the disastrous second Watergate break-in." Good says that "as with Kennedy, Nixon was undone by his failure to either counter or accommodate powerful factions of the American deep state."

The horror stories in *American Exception* go on and on. It recalls the CIA role in toppling the governments of Iran in 1953, and Guatemala in 1954; its intervention in Italian and French elections following World War 2 to prevent leftist victories; and the use of around $175 million to establish and fund Japan's Liberal Democratic Party. The LDP has "dominated Japanese politics for decades, making Japan into a de facto one-party state, firmly pro-U.S. and anti-neutrality." It also tells of post-WW2 use of Marshall Plan funds to "support Nightingale, a Nazi-created guerilla army in Ukraine which during the war had carried out thousands of murders." Good adds that "in Europe, NATO's Operation Gladio created 'stay behind' armies to resist Soviet occupation... Gladio assets were used to carry out false flag terror as part of a 'strategy of tension' designed to move countries politically to the right." That strategy of tension can be seen in Ukraine today.

In Syria, Good writes, "the U.S. and its allies have been similarly deceptive and lawless. Jeffrey Sachs summarizes: 'While the Syrian War is often described as a civil war, it was in fact a war of regime change led by the U.S. and Saudi Arabia under a U.S. presidential directive called Timber Sycamore.' This U.S.-orchestrated operation has killed around 500,000 people and displaced more than 10 million Syrians." Good details the role of the so-called "White Helmets"—a supposedly "humanitarian" operation that is really "a devious deep state propaganda operation to legitimate the illegal overthrow of the Syrian government by al Qaeda-dominated proxy forces." The millions of displaced Syrians, along with similar numbers from U.S. military fiascos in Iraq and Afghanistan have created a massive humanitarian crisis in western Europe, now multiplied exponentially by refugees from Ukraine. It raises the question of how long the U.S. can continue to brand itself as the world's defender of "democracy and human rights."

Looking for solutions—and comfort—in the face of these grim realities, we can return to Sirvent and Haiphong's book, which is intended, they say, "to be a tool to help rebuild the U.S. antiwar movement currently on life support. Heroic efforts of groups such as the Black Alliance for Peace and Veterans For Peace have kept the spirit of anti-imperialism alive in a period where it seems like American exceptionalism has won the day." Sirvent and Haiphong highlight "the connection between U.S. militarism and movements against racism such as Black Lives Matter." They add that "social movements cannot be relegated to a single issue if they are to be successful." So they call for linking demands against militarism to "the demand to scale back the mass incarceration dragnet in the U.S.;" that environmental justice advocates should emphasize that "one of the biggest polluters in the world is the U.S. military;" and that "fights for $15 an hour and a union" should "target the U.S. military for its role in forcing other countries to enact free-market policies that emphasize low wages;" and that the movement to preserve public education oppose the targeting of poverty stricken schools for military recruitment."

Finally, they say "our struggles for collective liberation must always reject the 'fake news' of a benevolent, freedom-loving United States."

22

Empire's Debt Trap: How to Resist Gluttonous Greed

America's response to its declining industrial and economic power is to tighten its control over Europe by force and sanctions. The result? A new Iron Curtain.

August 10, 2022

Michael Hudson has become famous in recent years. The *Financial Times* credited him with forecasting the 2008 financial crash and its aftermath. His "magnum opus," *Super Imperialism,* now in its third edition, was the first explanation of how going off the gold standard in 1972 allowed the U.S. to force other nations to pay for its wars, while becoming indebted to U.S. banks and financial institutions.[1]

Now, in *The Destiny of Civilization: Finance Capitalism, Industrial Capitalism or Socialism,* Hudson provides a series of lectures on neoliberalism to Chinese economic planners, meant as a contribution to ongoing Chinese debates about the direction of the super-successful Chinese economy. (This level of trust is shared by few other U.S. economists, notably Jeffrey Sachs and Joseph Stiglitz.) Hudson explains how Washington's aggressive neoliberalism, bolstered by military force, is backfiring. In one of his many articles in recent months, Hudson says:[2]

> The U.S./NATO confrontation with Russia in Ukraine is achieving just the opposite of America's aim of preventing China, Russia and their allies from acting independently of U.S. control over their trade and investment policy. Naming China as America's main long-term adversary, the Biden Administration's plan was to split Russia away from China and then cripple China's own military and economic viability.

But the effect of American diplomacy has been to drive Russia and China together, joining with Iran, India and other allies. For the first time since the Bandung Conference of Non-Aligned Nations in 1955, a critical mass is able to be mutually self-sufficient to start the process of achieving independence from Dollar Diplomacy.

Neoliberalism itself is fairly simple: "the government that governs least governs best," as Ronald Reagan said. The Reagan Revolution slashed taxes for the rich, deregulated basic industry and the banks, gutted environmental, consumer and workplace safety rules, cut back social welfare programs, privatized or contracted out public functions, and emphasized globalization.

Free trade agreements led to factory jobs disappearing overseas. In its wake, the Reagan Revolution left a rust belt of abandoned factories, millions of "discouraged workers" no longer counted in unemployment figures, skyrocketing household debt, and an explosion of homelessness.

Chile was the Latin American laboratory for neoliberalism, after General Augusto Pinochet's 1973 coup, orchestrated by Nixon and Kissinger, which overthrew the socialist government of President Salvador Allende. Pinochet crushed Allende's popular economic policies, privatized most public services, slashed the work force, and brought in the "Chicago Boys," led by economist Milton Friedman, to implement an economic strategy in tune with U.S. mining corporations and banks.

Hudson identifies Friedrich Hayek's *The Road to Serfdom* as Friedman's inspiration. Hayek warned of "the danger of tyranny that inevitably results from government control of economic decision-making through central planning." He scorned progressive taxation and pushed for "a race to the bottom" for wages and public spending.

He got an echo from Margaret Thatcher, the UK Prime Minister during Reagan's time, who famously quipped "there is no such thing as society, there is only the market." Hudson shows how this philosophy and the scorched earth policies it inspired have been the true road to serfdom in the west and everywhere else—at least everywhere Washington can impose the debt regime that strangles prosperity, with military force to back it up.

The FIRE sector—finance, insurance and real estate—has displaced industrialism as driver of the U.S. economy in recent decades, Hudson explains. That sector's business plan is to "roll back the 20th century's democratic reforms and lead economies down the road to serfdom and debt peonage... Neoliberal policy sees democratic laws as intruding on liberty if they oblige business to take the common weal into account, *e.g.,* by holding corporations liable for damages that they cause."

U.S.-Style "Democracy"

The concept of democracy has been twisted: "Democracy as managed by the Donor Class is a set of patronage relationships governed by wealth at the top." So "what is euphemized as U.S.-style 'democracy' is a financial oligarchy privatizing basic infrastructure, health and education.

"The alternative is what President Biden calls 'autocracy,' a hostile label for governments strong enough to block a global rent-seeking oligarchy from taking control. China is deemed autocratic for providing basic needs at subsidized prices instead of charging whatever the market can bear... U.S. and other Western officials define military coups as democratic if they are sponsored by the United States in the hope of promoting neoliberal policies."

In the case of Venezuela, Hudson comments on Trump's pirate-like 2018 confiscation of Venezuela's gold reserves held in London, and placing them at the disposal of the puppet Juan Guaidó. "This was defined as being democratic," Hudson says, "because the regime change promised to introduce the neoliberal 'free market' that is deemed to be the essence of America's definition of democracy for today's world."

The Carter administration staged a similar theft in November 1979, when it "paralyzed Iran's bank deposits in New York after the Shah was overthrown.... That was viewed as an exceptional one-time action as far as all other financial markets were concerned. But now that the United States is the self-proclaimed 'exceptional nation,' such confiscations are becoming a new norm in U.S. diplomacy. Nobody yet knows what happened to Libya's gold reserves that Muammar Gadhafi had intended to be used to back an African alternative to the dollar. And Afghanistan's gold and other reserves were simply taken by Washington as payment for the cost of 'freeing' that country...

"But when the Biden Administration and its NATO allies made a march larger asset grab of some $300 billion of Russia's foreign bank reserves and currency holdings in March 2022, it made official a radical new epoch in Dollar Diplomacy." Now "the U.S. confiscations have accelerated the end of the U.S. Treasury-bill standard that has governed world finance since the United States went off gold in 1971."

In the case of western Europe, Hudson explains how the U.S. used its post-WW2 dominant financial position to impose dependency on its former allies. After the 1944 Bretton Woods Conference, the U.S. leant enormous sums to the UK and France, as well as Italy and West Germany. "Neither the World Bank's reconstruction loans nor the IMF's balance-of-payments stabilization loans were sufficient to meet the financial needs of European recovery. France lost 60 percent of its gold and foreign exchange reserves during 1946-47... The effect was to concentrate in U.S. Government hands most of the major decisions as to how much, to which countries and on what conditions international loans would be extended."

The Price of "Friendship"

"Chronic austerity is now also being imposed on Eurozone members, making the euro a satellite currency of the dollar." Hudson says "this year's proxy war in Ukraine and imposition of anti-Russian sanctions is a perfect illustration of Henry Kissinger's quip: 'It may be dangerous to be America's enemy, but to be America's friend is fatal'."[3]

In the current conflict, "Now that NATO and the Eurozone have expanded eastward to include the Baltic states and Poland, the result has been to block the EU politicians in Brussels from following policies at odds with U.S. plans, particularly in relation to Russia, China and other countries the United states treats as adversaries or potential rivals... Countries that do not approve of the combination of U.S. military policies and U.S. takeover of their economic assets face a dilemma: If they do not recycle their dollar inflows in U.S. capital markets, their currencies will rise, threatening to price their exports out of world markets."

This intense pressure to conform to "Dollar Diplomacy" has a new and special blowback: "the path of least resistance taken by Russia, China and some other payments-surplus nations is to *de-dollarize.*" Enter gold, of which China, Russia, and their BRICS allies are among the world's largest producers. Hudson says "gold's use to settle payments deficits is likely to be the smoothest route in any transition to an alternative currency bloc." Such a transition is considered an "existential threat" in Washington. So far, however, its efforts to break up Russia, or to roll back China's revolution, have shown bleak prospects.

A Depression Is Coming

Hudson warns a "long depression" is coming, as inflation in western Europe and the U.S. accelerates. "To Wall Street and its backers," Hudson says, "the solution to any price inflation is to reduce wages and public social spending," that is, "to push the economy into recession in order to reduce hiring. Rising unemployment will oblige labor to compete for jobs that pay less and less as the economy slows." He adds that "public discussion of today's inflation is framed in a way that avoids blaming [it] on the Biden Administration's New Cold War sanctions on Russian oil, gas and agriculture, or on oil companies and other sectors using these sanctions as an excuse to charge monopoly prices…

"The entire blame for inflation is placed on wage earners," Hudson says, "and the response is to make them the victims of the coming austerity, as if their wages are responsible for bidding up oil prices, food prices and other prices resulting from the crisis. The reality is that they are too debt-strapped to be spendthrifts."

The global effects of the crisis are even more serious. Hudson notes that JP Morgan Chase head Jamie Dimon recently warned Wall Street investors that the sanctions will cause a global "economic hurricane." And the IMF's Managing Director Kristalina Georgieva warned that, "To put it simply, we are facing a crisis on top of a crisis." The Covid pandemic has been capped by inflation, with the war in Ukraine making matters "much worse, and threatening to increase inequality," adding that "the economic consequences from the war" are "hitting the world's most vulnerable people…"

Hudson raises a shocking question: "when it comes to global famine, was a more covert and even larger strategy at work? It is now looking like the major aim of the U.S. war in Ukraine all along was merely to serve as a catalyst, an excuse to impose sanctions that would disrupt the world's food and energy trade, and to manage this crisis in a way that would afford U.S. diplomats an opportunity to not only lock in Western Europe but to confront Global South countries with the choice 'Your loyalty and neoliberal dependency or your life'—and, in the process, to 'thin out' the world's non-white populations…" Basic survival hangs in the balance for more than half the world's people.

An Implicit Russian and Chinese Counterplan

"What is needed for the world's non-U.S./NATO population to survive is a new world trade and financial system," Hudson says. "More people will die of the Western sanctions than will have died on the Ukrainian battlefield. Financial and trade sanctions are as destructive as military attack." So Global South countries "need to reject the sanctions and reorient trade to Russia, China, India, Iran and their fellow members of the Shanghai Cooperation Organization."

A debt moratorium—really a debt *repudiation*—must be declared. And the World Bank and IMF must be replaced with "a genuine Bank for Economic Acceleration" and "a replacement for the IMF that is free of austerity junk economics and does not subsidize U.S. client oligarchies or currency raids of countries resisting U.S. privatization and financialization takeovers." Hudson adds that Global South countries should join "a military alliance as an alternative to NATO, to avoid being turned into another Afghanistan, another Libya, another Iraq or Syria or Ukraine."

Hudson's book derived from lectures to people involved in China's economic strategy circles, who invited him largely to hear his opinions about neoliberalism and its risks, and how to avoid them. His basic thesis was that:

> "The tensions between the wealthy and the rest of society have always been mediated by governments... All economies are mixed economies, and the key to understanding any economy, and to designing any national income accounting format, needs to begin with the government's relation to the private sector... Public

policy invariably backs either the wealthy layer at the top or the economy at large. Any pretense by a government to be steering a 'middle course' is rarely anything other than a cover for public policies perpetuating a status quo favoring the wealthy, who always have used their wealth to influence and control governments and public policy."

In a clear comment on Western capitalist countries, Hudson says "political democracies have not shown themselves to be very effective in resisting the tendency to turn into financialized oligarchies. Avoiding that fate requires a strong central power not captured by the propertied financial classes. Throughout history, that was achieved only by palace rulers (in the Bronze Age Near East) or today in socialist economies."

As if to eliminate any doubt about his central message, Hudson stipulates that "keeping the money and credit system in government hands is China's great advantage over Western financialized economies." He adds a set of keys China has used to "avoid the American financial disease":

1. Instead of privatizing natural monopolies and key infrastructure, China has kept its "commanding heights" in the public domain, headed by banking as the most important public utility.

2. China has pursued an "Economy of High Wages policy by providing high-quality education and health standards to make its labor more productive."

3. As a socialist economy, China uses government regulation strong enough to prevent an independent financial oligarchy from emerging. (Still to be achieved is a progressive tax policy falling mainly on *rentier* income, headed by land rent.)

4. China and Russia are creating an alternative international payments system to avoid using the U.S. dollar and SWIFT bank-payments system. The policy of de-dollarizing their monetary systems, foreign trade and investment includes securing their own self-sufficiency in food production, technology and other basic needs.

5. U.S. diplomats and politicians accuse nations that put in place public restrictions against monopoly and related rent-seeking of being autocratic and authoritarian if they defend their economies against privatization and the associated American attempt at financial takeover," Hudson observes. He cites U.S. Secretary of State Blinken saying "The Chinese and Russian governments, among others, are making the argument in public and in private that the United States is in decline so it's better to cast your lot with their authoritarian visions of the world than our democratic one."

6. Chinese President Xi Jinping expressed his view on this issue: "At present, income inequality is a prominent issue around the globe. The rich and the poor in some countries are polarized with the collapse of the middle class. This has led to social disintegration, political polarization, and rampant populism… Our country must resolutely guard against polarization, drive common prosperity, and maintain social harmony and stability."

7. Hudson also quotes Russian President Vladimir Putin, who said "this is basically a crisis of approaches and principles that determine the very existence of humans on Earth," and despite claims in recent decades "that the role of the state was outdated and outgoing," only strong nation-states can resist the economic carve-up and immiseration of the planet."

8. Hudson concludes by saying "America's response to its declining industrial and economic power at home has been to tighten its control over Europe and other client economies by military force and political sanctions. The result is a new Iron Curtain aiming to block these allies from expanding their trade and investment with the Russian and Chinese economies in the rising Eurasian core. Forcing nations to choose which geopolitical block they will belong to is driving many out of the dollarized trade and investment orbit with remarkable speed."

9. It is likely that an end to Dollar Dominance in the world foreshadows a general disintegration of capitalism's last great empire. The question of how to avoid a turn to fascism at home is not addressed, except to observe that the efforts of Bernie Sanders *et al* have been blocked, suggesting that stronger medicine is needed.

23

Neoliberalism Has Been Far from "Liberal"

[SOURCE: LA PROGRESSIVE]

Review by Dee Knight in LA Progressive

April 26, 2022

Reagan's neoliberalism: slashing taxes for the rich, deregulating basic indus-try and the banks, gutting environmental, consumer and workplace safety rules, cutting back social welfare programs, privatizing or contracting out public functions, and emphasizing globalization.

The term "neoliberal" can be confusing. In the United States, "liberalism" has meant less harsh social and economic policies than either "conservative" or "moderate" ones. For example, FDR was a liberal while his successor Truman was more conservative. JFK was more liberal than moderate conservative Eisenhower. Barack Obama was more liberal than arch-conservative Bush. And so on.

Neoliberalism differs from these *political* labels. It's an economic policy dating back to the 18th and 19th centuries, the period of classical economic liberalism. Think Adam Smith and *laissez faire,* letting the "invisible hand" of the market prevail: "the government that governs least governs best." Ronald Reagan said things like that. He launched the Reagan Revolution—slashing taxes for the rich, deregulating basic industry and the banks, gutting environmental, consumer and workplace safety rules, cutting back social welfare programs, privatizing or contracting out public functions, and emphasizing globalization. Free trade agreements led to factory jobs disappearing overseas.

Reagan said this would benefit everyone, that is, everyone who was already rich. Neoliberalism felt like a return to the Roaring Twenties for the investor class. The top tax rate in 1950 was 91 percent for the top income bracket. The Economic Recovery Tax Act of 1981 slashed the highest rate to 50 percent.[1] The Tax Reform Act of 1986 dropped it to 28 percent. Under Obama it rose to 43.4 percent. Trump pushed it down to 40.8 percent. Meanwhile wages and profits grew at about the same rate from the end of WW2 to the mid-1960s. From 2000-2007 profits were growing more than 13 times faster than wages.

But the Vietnam war's end, and a global oil crunch hit profits hard in the 1970s. The overall rate of corporate profit plunged from nearly 18 percent in 1965 to a dismal eight percent in 1982. Both inflation and unemployment skyrocketed in the seventies, causing a big business panic.

"The smoothly functioning 'mixed economy' promised by regulated capitalism had stopped functioning smoothly," Kotz observed. And its remedy for fixing economic problems—Keynesian demand management—was not able to solve the problems. The Keynesian system had prevailed since the time of FDR, but it was insufficient for the "stagflation" of the 1970s.

When Ronald Reagan took office in 1981, the Business Roundtable rallied around his economic program. "The business community feels strongly that all four parts of the economic recovery plan [decreases in social spending, tax cuts, regulatory reduction, and tight monetary policy] are essential, interrelated, and must be acted upon."

Rate of Profit in the U.S. Nonfinancial Corporate Business Sector

David Kotz graphic

To punctuate the change, Reagan crushed the Air Traffic Controllers union, PATCO, firing more than 11,000 of its 13,000 members when they struck for better work conditions and pay. The move sent shock waves through the labor movement, and stimulated business to crack down on unions across industry nationwide.

Born in Chile

Neoliberalism was introduced in Chile, after General Augusto Pinochet's 1973 coup, orchestrated by Nixon and Kissinger, which overthrew the socialist government of President Salvador Allende. As Vijay Prashad wrote, "Pinochet brought in a group of free-market economists called the Chicago Boys to hastily give U.S.-based multinational companies the best deal possible (particularly for Chilean copper)."[2] The deal slashed taxes and privatized most public services, including pensions, all backed by brute force. The leading economic theorist of this deal was University of Chicago economist Milton Friedman. For the U.S., Friedman believed "monetary policy was so incredibly crucial to a healthy economy that he publicly blamed the Federal Reserve for causing the Great Depression."[3]

The Third World debt crisis in the 1980s and the demise of the USSR in 1991 fostered neoliberalism everywhere. The International Monetary Fund (IMF) had a field day, "pushing austerity regimes upon societies that had no capacity to tolerate public sector cuts as a condition to access financing," Prashad wrote. Strapped with unpayable debt, leaders in "Third World" countries surrendered to IMF policies *en masse*.

In 1989, when Venezuelan President Carlos Andrés Pérez adopted an IMF package with deep cuts in fuel subsidies and other austerity measures, the result was a mass uprising, the *Caracazo*. That inspired a young military officer, Hugo Chávez, to enter political life. Revolted by the violence Pérez used to impose the austerity program, Chávez fought against it, winning the presidency in 1999.

Chávez condemned neoliberalism as a policy of mass starvation. He sparked a continent-wide "pink tide" of countries in the region winning anti-neoliberalism leaders in the years that followed: Haiti in 2000, Brazil in 2002, Argentina in 2003, Uruguay in 2004, Bolivia in 2005, Honduras in 2005, Ecuador in 2006, Nicaragua in 2006, Guatemala in 2007, Paraguay in 2008, El Salvador in 2009.

The U.S., especially the CIA, teamed up with local oligarchies in nearly all these countries to turn back the pink tide: an attempted coup against Chávez in 2002, and against his successor Maduro in 2020; successful coups in Haiti in 2004 and Honduras in 2009; "lawfare" (using the legal establishment as a weapon) leading to impeachments in Paraguay in 2012 and Brazil in 2016; a "self-coup" in Ecuador by President Lenin Moreno in 2017; and a *temporarily* successful coup against Bolivia's President Evo Morales in 2019.

Prashad says "the combination of the U.S. illegal war on Iraq in 2003, the global financial crisis of 2007–08, and the general fragility of U.S. global power provided the international context" for the rise of the Pink Tide.

Unsustainability Builds To a Crisis

Kotz provides a more technical analysis. He identifies three trends that built to a crescendo and a crash in 2008: rising levels of household and financial sector debt; toxic financial assets spread throughout the banking system; and growing excess productive capacity as consumer spending power ebbed.

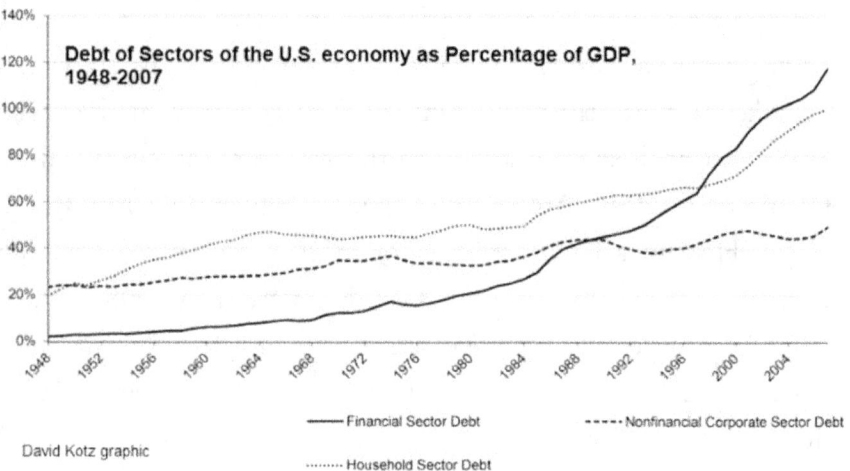

Debt of Sectors of the U.S. economy as Percentage of GDP, 1948-2007

David Kotz graphic

——— Financial Sector Debt   - - - - Nonfinancial Corporate Sector Debt

·········· Household Sector Debt

Household debt—mainly mortgages and credit cards—had grown slowly since the end of WW2. In the 1980s, the price of housing shot up, while wages plummeted. Families began using home equity like credit cards. And banks "leveraged" equity to invest on credit. A huge "credit bubble" formed, which "popped" in 2008.

The top five investment banks had asked the Securities Exchange Commission (SEC) for an exemption to a rule that limited investment banks' borrowing. They got the exemption. But as one commissioner remarked, "If anything goes wrong it's going to be an awfully big mess."

The ensuing "mess" was the collapse of the global capitalist financial system—the most severe of any recession since the Great Depression of the 1930s (apart from the postwar readjustment in

1945–46). "During the first twelve months of the recession," Kotz writes, "both global output and global trade contracted more rapidly than they had during the first twelve months of the Great Depression of the 1930s."

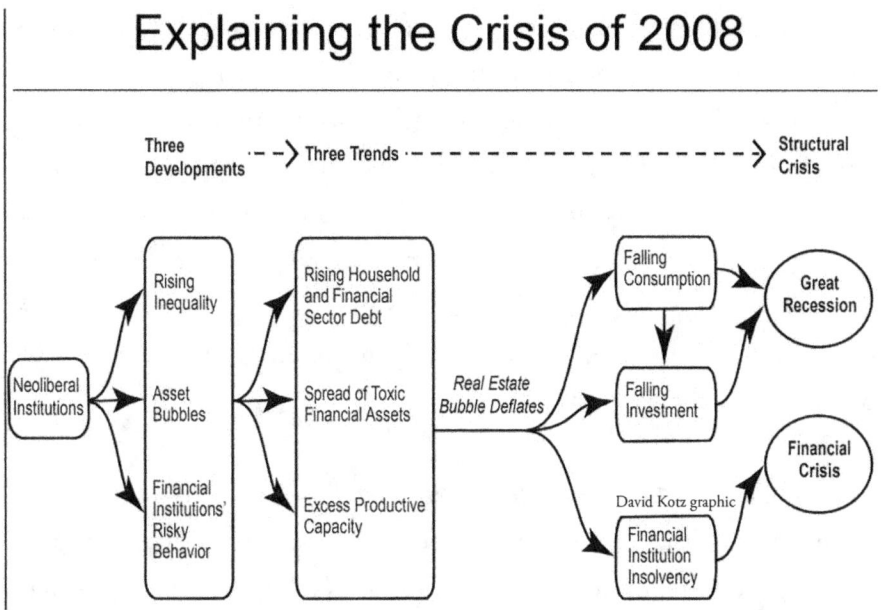

Kotz adds that "the astonishing near-collapse of the major financial institutions and one of the most famous industrial giants (GM), followed by an unprecedented government bailout, had a profound effect on society…" In September and October 2008, more than 450,000 jobs disappeared *each month;* then 700,000 per month in November and December.

"The economy seemed to be falling off a cliff," Kotz wrote. "For decades the public had been told that free-market capitalism was a self-regulating system that delivered the goods. The old days of government intervention in the economy were over… Now the economy seemed to be collapsing, and the government was rescuing the largest banks and other financial institutions." But not the people.

"Suggestions even appeared in the mainstream media," Kotz notes, "that the economic crisis showed Karl Marx had been right after all about capitalism's self-destructive tendencies, although…of course Marx had long ago been proven wrong about socialism."

The sole exception globally to generalized crisis with inadequate government response was China, which launched a massive infrastructure investment program in November 2008, amounting to about 7% of China's GDP each year for two years. The U.S. government response was less than a third of China's program relative to U.S. GDP. As a result, "China's economy quickly resumed growth at 9 to 10% per year," Kotz observed.

Sluggish Recovery – End of an Era?

"Normally," Kotz writes, "a particularly deep recession is followed by a vigorous rebound… This recovery has been far from normal." The details are grim and fairly well-known: nagging unemployment and underemployment lasting for years, along with drastically lower median family income. But not for everyone: "from 2009 to 2012, 95% of the real family income gains in the U.S. economy went to the richest 1%, leaving only 5% of income gains for the other 99% of families." No wonder Occupy Wall Street happened in 2011!

None of this resulted in re-thinking neoliberalism among the political class. In fact, the reverse happened, as Republicans took over Congress in 2010, "with the new 'Tea Party' movement pushing… to renounce 'big government'." Austerity became de facto economic policy at home and abroad. In Europe, Greece, Ireland and Spain descended into stagnation. Kotz writes that "as the crisis—and the bank bailout—unfolded, millions of people became outraged at the banks... The bankers and been saved from the consequences of their folly by the taxpayers."

Ironically, there's a silver lining: "austerity may be nearing the end of its period of dominance," Kotz writes. "It appears the neoliberal form of capitalism has exhausted its ability to function... It is justified to regard the crisis that began in 2008 as the structural crisis of neoliberal capitalism." And so "there is reason to expect that some kind of major economic change lies ahead."

Possible Future Paths

Kotz identifies "four possible future directions of change (or absence of change)":

- continuation of neoliberalism, perhaps with some adjustments;
- a new regulated form of capitalism, with business still in charge;
- a form of regulated capitalism based on capital-labor compromise;
- replacement of capitalism by an alternative socialist system.

Just one of these alternatives really interests us. Kotz says "the possibility that socialism will again come to represent a viable alternative future, even in the United States, should not be discounted," for several reasons:

- First, "since the crisis began in 2008, the worst sides of capitalism have been on vivid display, as millions lost their jobs and millions faced the loss of their homes... while corporate profits and the income of the richest 1% have soared.

- Second, "in some Latin American countries..., new attempts to build a "Twenty-First Century Socialism" have emerged, in Venezuela and Bolivia... The idea has lived on as the egalitarian alternative when capitalism inflicts unbearable hardships on people."

- Third, "even in the United States a larger-than-expected percentage of the population has a favorable view of socialism... Among respondents under age thirty, the results [of a survey] were 37% for capitalism, 33% for socialism, and 30% undecided." (Recent polls have been even more favorable to socialism.)

- Fourth, "the sudden outbreak of the Occupy Wall Street movement... was the first significant avowedly anti-capitalist protest movement in the United States within memory. Its demonstrations took place in at least 150 U.S. cities and towns (as well as abroad)... showing the existence of a potential mass base for a radical movement against capitalism in the United States."

And Vijay Prashad says "there is now a changed context across the region, namely a more engaged China. China's interest in expanding the Belt and Road Initiative (BRI) across Latin America has provided new sources of investment and financing for development in the region. It is widely accepted in Latin America that the BRI project is an antidote to Washington's largely discredited IMF project and agenda of neoliberal austerity.

"With little original capital to invest in Latin America, the United States has mainly its military and diplomatic power to use against the arrival of Chinese investment." This will make it much harder for the U.S. and the IMF to force austerity on the people of Latin America.

Next up is a struggle for 21st Century Socialism here at home. Some people are reading Martha Harnecker's *A World To Build: New Paths Towards 21st Century Socialism.* That book focuses mainly on Venezuela. Harnecker says: "for Chavez, the art of politics was to make the impossible possible, not by sheer will power, but by taking the existing reality as one's starting point and working to build favorable conditions and a correlation of social forces capable of changing that reality."

So can it happen here? Time will tell.

24

Sanctions: A Wrecking Ball
in a World Economy

December 9, 2022

The Sanctions the U.S. government imposes on other countries are often called "a substitute for war," or "just short of war." That's not true. They're war—a key element in the "hybrid war" waged against most of Eurasia, much of Africa, and part of Latin America. Joe Biden says he doesn't want World War III, but look again. Regime change war *through sanctions* is ongoing *now,* against Russia, China, Cuba, Venezuela, Nicaragua, Zimbabwe, and more than three dozen countries, who together make up about a third of the world population.

The first slide in the Sanctions Kill slide show, available with a full script from SanctionsKill.org[1] lists 38 sanctioned countries:

Afghanistan, Belarus, Bosnia & Herzegovina, Central African Republic, China, Democratic Republic of Congo, Cuba, Cyprus, Eritrea, Ethiopia, Guinea, Guinea-Bissau, Haiti, Iran, Iraq, Democratic Republic of Korea, Laos, Lebanon, Liberia, Libya, Mali, Moldova, Montenegro, Myanmar, Nicaragua, Palestine, Paraguay, Russia, Serbia, Somalia, South Sudan, Sudan, Tunisia, Turkey, Uganda, Venezuela, Yemen, and Zimbabwe. *(List as of September 2022.)*

U.S. sanctions on these countries are indeed a "wrecking ball," as this crucially important anthology demonstrates well. But they're also a *boomerang* that is devastating Europe, and rapidly surging into the lives of people at home. High prices for gasoline, food and other necessities are the tip of an iceberg, or the headwinds of a hurricane. Much worse is headed our way. We need this book to understand what's coming and get ready. We need the explanations and background, to *really understand* what's happening, and we need the "Sanctions Kill Toolkit"—with its excellent script and full-color slides—to spread the word.

As the slideshow says, U.S.-imposed sanctions are basically *economic* warfare, used to strangle countries that don't kowtow to U.S. dictates. They devastate economies by cutting off access to credit and trade, investment, and much more. That may sound like the sanctions are aimed mainly at governments and businesses in target countries. But they strangle people, too—crippling food production and distribution, cutting off medicine and medical supplies, energy and transportation.

Embargoing Cuba, for Example

The U.S. embargo of Cuba is a good example. Imposed in 1962 following the revolution that brought Fidel Castro to power, the embargo is designed to isolate Cuba, and "make its economy scream," so the people there might rise up and overthrow their government. The United States not only bars trade or financial transactions by U.S. companies but also punishes other countries and companies that trade with Cuba. Cubans are famous for keeping classic 1950s American cars running. That's a tribute to Cuban ingenuity, but it doesn't change the fact that for over six decades the economic blockade has deprived Cuba of nearly a trillion dollars. That's conservative, of course, since the damage to people's lives is incalculable.

Economic sanctions can be more effective than bombs at destroying a country's basic infrastructure—electrical grids, water treatment and distribution systems, transportation hubs, and communication networks—by blocking access to fuel, raw materials, and replacement parts. This causes droughts, famines, disease, and poverty, resulting in the death of millions.

The UN General Assembly voted this year 185 to 2 against the U.S. embargo of Cuba, as it has repeatedly each year for several decades. The U.S. and Israel provide the "No" votes and ignore the votes of the majority. This highlights another point—*Sanctions are illegal:* they violate the UN Charter, the Fourth Geneva Convention and the Genocide Convention, the Nuremberg Charter, the WHO Constitution, the Universal Declaration of Human Rights... and the Supremacy Clause of the U.S. Constitution, which says treaty law is the law of the land. The U.S. has approved all these charters and conventions as treaties.

Strangling Nicaragua, Venezuela, Zimbabwe and Haiti

Ajamu Baraka of the *Black Agenda Report* highlights Nicaragua, the second poorest nation in the Americas, where universal healthcare and education are guaranteed to the population as a human right, unlike in the U.S. Congress has passed not one but *two* acts of anti-Nicaragua sanctions: the NICA and RENACER Acts. Together they're designed to strangle and isolate Nicaragua despite the fact it's recognized as the safest country in Central America, and even though it's poor it has the best land reform in the region and is nearly self-sufficient in food.

Baraka asks: Why do Nicaragua, Cuba and Venezuela pose such an existential threat to the U.S.? Why are they able to unite both major U.S. political parties against them? He cites two factors. First, the power of their example in attempting to build independent, self-determining projects that center the material needs and interests of the people over those of capital. Second, the U.S. policy of "full spectrum dominance," that is, there shall be no variance from its hegemonic rule.

The same is true for Zimbabwe, a landlocked country just north of South Africa, which instituted a land reform program that took back property seized by British colonists centuries ago. Zimbabwe's crime was violating the human rights of the colonizers. Zimbabweans won their independence in 1980, but over 80 percent of the arable land was still held by settlers who were less than five percent of the population. The government of Robert Mugabe returned most of it to Zimbabweans who had fought for it. The U.S. responded by designating Zimbabwe as "a threat to national security," and has used sanctions to strangle it.

Haiti is also targeted for punishment. Its crime might be that its people finally elected a democratic leader, Jean-Bertrand Aristide, instead of the dictators and puppets the U.S. had imposed on them for decades. It wasn't enough for the U.S. to merely kidnap Aristide in 2004 to get him out of power. The Haitian people have continued to protest and rebel against the starvation policies and dictatorial rulers imposed on them by the U.S. The U.S. uses sanctions as part of its toolkit of permanent control. But there's another side to the story. While we often hear "Haiti is the poorest country in the hemisphere," it is also "the most exploited manufacturing hub in the Americas," and is being touted as the "manufacturing Taiwan of the Caribbean," according to Tamanisha John of Black Agenda Report.[2]

Notably, the report says U.S. corporations use Taiwan to supply military and security gear to Haiti to suppress protests. Now the Biden administration is calling for yet another intervention of foreign troops for Haiti "to alleviate the humanitarian crisis" there.[3] As of early December, *Counter-punch* reported the UN Security Council had not approved the proposal, due to concerns voiced by the governments of Russia and China.[4] On the ground in Haiti, there have been major demonstrations against new intervention of foreign troops. The best would be for the "Core Group" of the U.S., France and Canada to pay reparations and then take their knees off Haiti's neck.

Using Russia to Hit 'An Awful Lot of Countries'

When announcing sanctions against Russia, President Joe Biden said in Brussels March 24, 2022 at a NATO press conference: "The price of the sanctions is not just imposed upon Russia. It's imposed upon an awful lot of countries as well, including European countries and our country as well." We should remember this. As Sara Flounders writes in the book's introduction, "The U.S.-NATO sanctions against Russia are creating unprecedented inflation—the highest in 40 years—supply chain chaos and sharply higher costs of energy for industries, transport and homes."

Flounders adds: "Washington is demanding that countries act against their own economic interests and enforce sanctions… in which they had no voice or prior notice."

How could Biden get the EU and NATO partners to go along? He issued an ultimatum: "You have two options. Start a Third World War; go to war with Russia, physically. Or, two, make sure the country… ends up paying a price." Biden said: "I know these sanctions are the broadest sanctions in history," but he added in an interview that his "goal from the very beginning" was to keep NATO and the EU "on the same page." (*Fox News*, Feb. 26) So in essence, Flounders writes, "the U.S., through its command of NATO, is holding all of Europe hostage in order to reestablish its economic dominance and expand its military might on the continent."

Can it work, or is Biden going too far, and can he really keep the U.S. NATO allies "on the same page"? So far, it's the western European economies that are suffering a major crisis with industries shutting down and people freezing in their homes for lack of energy. Crushing inflation is threatening to bring on a major recession. Meanwhile the freezing—and outright theft—of hundreds of billions of Russian assets, and cutting it off from SWIFT and western banks, has caused Russia to forge new and better economic ties with its major Asian partners, China and India. "Russia is self-sufficient in grains, meats, other proteins and in energy," Flounders writes. "Its trade with China,

India, Brazil and Iran ensures its industry will not collapse for lack of spare parts."

The Boomerang, and Resistance in the Global South

This is the sanctions' boomerang. While the "European countries and our country as well" (as Biden said) are facing high inflation and economic crisis, other countries are cutting loose from the grip of the U.S. dollar. As Brazil's Lula said, even before he won the presidency in October, "to be freed of the dollar... we are going to create a currency in Latin America, because we can't keep depending on the dollar." (*Popular-resistance.org*, May 6) Meanwhile Russia is selling gas, oil, and fertilizer for rubles, rupees and Chinese renminbi. Both Iran and Saudi Arabia are joining in this trade, and both have applied for membership in the BRICS trading alliance, which is set to expand dramatically. As this happens, the U.S. stranglehold on the world economy will gradually be loosened or broken.

China can be considered the key to success in resisting U.S. and EU sanctions. Despite intense and constant economic warfare against it from the U.S.—including a blizzard of sanctions—China has fortified itself and largely defeated the sanctions, by beating the U.S. in the trade game. Now the vast majority of countries in the world trade more with China than the U.S. And through the Belt and Road Initiative, BRICS, and the Shanghai Cooperation Organization, China has shielded itself—and most of its trading partners—from the U.S. dollar stranglehold. While it is still a developing country, China runs its own economy. Health care, education, and the general well-being of Chinese people don't depend on the whims of the U.S., the World

Bank and International Monetary Fund. And China can now help other countries.

China's message is "Developing countries should jointly fight the consequences of Western sanctions against Russia," said the Chinese publication *Global Times* on May 6. "Developing countries, including China, India, Indonesia, Brazil and others that have refused to take sides over Western sanctions against Russia, need to consider ways to strengthen their economic coordination to weather the consequent shocks brought about by the West."

This is the beginning of the end for the U.S. sanctions regime, which is indeed a wrecking ball on the world economy.

VI

Looking Backward
to See Ahead

25

Dissenting Soldiers Challenge the War Machine

[SOURCE: Jonathan McIntosh/Creative Commons]

September 28, 2022

This review of Paths of Dissent *relates the experience of soldiers who have spoken out on their experience of the 'forever wars.'*

People who have seen active duty in the U.S. "forever wars" are more and more speaking out. One of them, West Pointer Eric Edstrom, said in *Paths of Dissent,* the "War on Terror strip-mined my soul. My time in Afghanistan, from May 2009 to June 2010, was defined by the horror of watching good people getting mutilated and dying terrible deaths. It was filled with intense moral anguish... It strained my relationships, destroyed my notion of patriotism, eroded my support for American foreign policy... and made me deeply sad."

Moral injury has been a killer. Edstrom says "suicide has been deadlier than combat for the military. There have been over thirty thousand suicides among U.S. service members and veterans of the post-9/11 wars"—nearly five times the roughly seven thousand service members killed in them. Right after 9/11, Edstrom asked himself "what will I do about it? My answer then was to join the military. My answer now is different: dissent."

Jonathan Hutto was a student leader and president of the Howard University Student Association before graduating in 2003. His plans to become a teacher fell through. "A navy recruiter spotted me... promising me 'a new lease on life.' When he got to the part about the Navy repaying student loans, I began to listen..."

Hutto was a reluctant recruit. "My unwillingness to serve as cannon fodder connected directly to the tradition of Black resistance to the Vietnam War." He said he found that "despite the military's supposed inclusivity..., it offers no escape from racism and white nationalism. And this racism is directly connected to the acts of aggression and even war crimes committed by the U.S. military overseas."

Aboard the aircraft carrier USS *Theodore Roosevelt,* Hutto encountered overt racism at all levels, including name calling, a hangman's noose, and intense punishment when he took his concerns up the chain of command. After he'd had enough, he went AWOL and headed to Washington, DC. He contacted civil rights icon John Lewis, "who represented the Georgia congressional district where my parents resided." He also reached out to David Cortwright, author of *Soldiers In Revolt,* the landmark history of GI resistance during the Vietnam War. Cortwright had become a professor of peace studies at Notre Dame University and president of the Fourth Freedom Forum. He helped Hutto prepare to fight back. Together they made history, as Hutto developed an *Appeal for Redress from the War in Iraq,* which gathered thousands of signatures from GIs around the globe and caused a major stir in the halls of Washington and in national media. (Read the full story in *Antiwar Soldier: How to Dissent Within the Ranks of the Military.*)

Joy Damiani "needed money for school; a recruiter got me." He got her home phone number from a community college list and asked what she wanted to study." When she said "journalism" he told her "I can get you a journalism job in the army!" She thought "that couldn't possibly be journalism," but she went for it, and got a journalism MOS. She called it "a propaganda of omission... We painted only the pictures the generals wanted the troops to see... our team's task was to tell the story of victory."

In Iraq, Joy said, "the more I saw the more I realized what the government was doing to its soldiers; I thought we couldn't possibly be doing anything good for anyone else. I became very bitter." After her discharge, "people thanked me for my service; I felt sick." She thought "I'm dying on the inside because you're not paying attention." She became aware "the U.S. government has been running a gaslighting operation on the U.S. people. It says we're united when we're not. We're not a democracy, we're an oligarchy… No money to keep people alive but plenty for killing people."

About a year after returning from her final deployment, Joy chanced to meet Sonia, another woman vet, who asked "have you ever heard of Iraq Veterans Against the War?" As "neurons exploded" in her head, Joy asked "There's a group?" A few nights later Sonia brought her a pile of papers. "Words jumped off the printed pages—*illegal… unjust… occupation*—that I'd rarely heard other soldiers say out loud." After a few years she said "it finally sank in for me: we are a nation founded on genocide and slavery. We can't claim the moral high ground." Once she got involved in activism, she had a community of other traumatized veterans. "But it's a hard community—people are always killing themselves." Still, she says "I can never not be a veteran—that's your identity forever. You're going to think of that experience every day until you die. It's hard walking around in this brain."

When asked what can be done to reduce the trauma, she answers "abolish the military. There's no way to stop the trauma—we are all suffering because of this oligarchy we live under. Get out into the streets and…! Every time I go out to protest, the riot cops are out, and the soldiers are out. I see confused teenagers like me, attacking us—we're all on each other's side… We have to be individual revolutionaries. We have to realize the system isn't broken, that's how it was designed to work. It's always been control the many by the few. It's basically a war on poor people—it's always been that way. I would be more comforted if I heard more people talking about it."

Joy Damiani has become a songwriter and performer, and has a new book coming out, *If You Ain't Cheatin', You Ain't Tryin' and other lessons I learned in the Army.* A recent hit song is "It's alright to not be OK."[1]

While growing up in Indiana, Vincent Emanuele "watched and rewatched *Rambo, Commando, Navy Seals, Missing in Action,* and every other war movie in the hypermilitarized American culture. He "didn't know the first thing about resistance,... didn't know anything about the modern antiwar movement." He learned quickly during his first deployment to Iraq, which ended in 2005. Following a second deployment in 2014, he realized the "Iraqi resistance fighters were always going to control their country—no matter how long U.S. forces stayed, no matter how brutal our attacks became. The Iraqis were fighting for their families, their land, their pride, their dignity. American troops were only in it for healthcare, college money, steady housing, or ideological nonsense. Almost none of us actually believed the people we encountered posed a threat to our homeland. And those who did believe that were absolutely out of their minds, as history has shown."

Emanuele landed in a two-month VA inpatient drug and alcohol rehab program. "The doctors tried their best to convince the command that I should stay home, but my commanding officers disagreed and forced me to return... Back home, my father and uncle started writing letters to every Senate and House Armed Services Committee member. Soon after, letters, phone calls, and inquiries poured into our unit's commanding officers." Still, Marine commanders and NCOs "talked to me about 'the mission' and 'American freedom' and all the rest." Emanuele "kept repeating 'I will not go to the armory, and I will not board an airplane.' They were going to have to drag my unconscious body to Iraq if they wanted me to deploy a third time." But "eventually the command acquiesced and offered me a 'general discharge under honorable conditions.'... They would rather lose a seasoned gunner than allow me the opportunity to bring down unit morale."

There's a lesson here. Emanuele tells of traveling most of the country with IVAW from 2006 to 2008. He gave antiwar speeches at union halls, religious services, universities, community centers, town halls, libraries, street corners, parks, and protests. He was interviewed "by every media outlet under the sun, culminating in the 2008 Winter Soldier hearings, when hundreds of veterans converged on Silver Springs, Maryland, for several days of testimony about U.S. war crimes, sexual assaults in the military, drug abuse, and much more. Later that year, about a dozen of us officially testified before the United States Congress."

Emanuele has remained very active, writing, speaking and organizing both locally with PARC (*Politics Art Roots Culture Media²*), Organized & United Residents of Michigan City, Indiana, and nationally with Veterans For Peace.

Kevin Tillman is Pat Tillman's brother. Both became professional athletes—Kevin with the baseball Cleveland Indians franchise, and Pat with the NFL's Arizona Cardinals. They enlisted together in the wake of 9/11, seeing action in both Iraq and Afghanistan. Pat never made it home. He was killed by "friendly fire," a story related by fellow veteran Rory Fanning in *Worth Fighting For: An Army Ranger's Journey*. Kevin says "belligerent U.S. foreign policy not only creates victims in other countries while getting our soldiers killed and injured but inevitably reverberates at home—with violence and corruption replacing political process and the rule of law; with reality subverted by false narratives; with a flourishing of fear, ignorance, and hate. War dissenters understand this, historically and conceptually. That's why war dissent is reasonable, necessary, and morally sound. In some cases, depending on your ethical framework, it is even obligatory."

Tillman acknowledges that "if the dissenter has the power to sway public opinion, or provides damning evidence against the U.S. administration, then the price to be paid can be very real. Such people can find themselves classified as 'enemies of the state.' This can mean government-backed discrediting campaigns, harassment, and imprisonment." He mentions whistleblowers Daniel Ellsberg, Chelsea Manning and Daniel Hale, and Wikileaks founder Julian Assange, who has languished in a British prison awaiting extradition to the U.S. on espionage charges for publishing information about U.S. war crimes in Iraq.

"All evidence suggests that we as a nation remain a long way off from fixing our foreign policy," Tillman says. "We are likely to keep reading courageous, clarifying, and insightful pieces of war dissent while American soldiers die, vulnerable nations get destroyed, and the moral rot spreads at home." But he thinks "in the long term… sustained progress can and will be made, and war dissent will reach critical mass both in America and around the globe—tipping the scales in favor of peace, diplomacy, and accountability… Until then, let us hope war dissenters continue their courageous work of providing transparency, honesty, and optimism to us all."

26

The Socialist Antiwar Tradition: Leading the Fight Against War and Imperialism

Commons.wikipedia.org/Debs-Canton-1918

"I am opposed to every war but one. I am for that war with heart and soul, and that is the worldwide war of the social revolution."

— EUGENE DEBS, 1918

May 3, 2021

Socialists in the U.S. have a proud tradition of anti-war and anti-imperialist action. It's time to revive that tradition and end the endless wars.

As a generation of endless war continues to grind on, it is time for socialists to make a meaningful political intervention. As internationalists loyal to the world's working class, we are challenged not merely to avoid falling for official lies, but to actively organize our class to stop the war machine and prevent further slaughter.

Socialists in the U.S. have a proud—and sometimes tragic—tradition of anti-war and anti-imperialist action. It found perhaps its highest expression in the Socialist Party's (SP) heroic opposition to World War I, including Eugene Debs' imprisonment and the nearly forgotten Green Corn Rebellion of August 1917.[1] The SP, the Industrial Workers of the World (IWW) and other radicals suffered intense state repression for their opposition, but Socialist leader Eugene Debs garnered nearly a million votes running for president from prison in 1920.

The U.S. socialist movement was a mass force in the first decades of the twentieth century. Total circulation of the socialist press exceeded two million copies. About 1,200 socialists held public offices in 343 municipalities across the country, including 79 mayors in 24 states. In Oklahoma, the SP had 1,500 locals with 57,000 members, many of whom were also members of the Working Class Union, a secret society that often resorted to night riding, barn burning, and dynamite.[2] They defied fierce repression by the Wilson administration, typified by the so-called Espionage Act, which is still in force and was used to convict and imprison anti-war whistleblower Chelsea Manning.

The lesson from that time is the importance of combining legal electoral work with mass organizing and resistance, fighting repression, and staying united. The left and right wings in the SP tended to split in the face of repression, leading to imprisonment, demoralization, and the ultimate decline of the party.

Across the Atlantic, socialist parties in various European countries abandoned their promise to stay united against the war, and instead joined their respective national governments and marched off to slaughter. For the most part, only the Russian Social Democratic Labor Party, the Italian Socialist Party, and certain factions of the German Social Democratic Party held firm. Each of these valiantly resisted the war, and were positioned to lead revolutionary uprisings at its conclusion. But the socialists' failure to prevent or stop the war was a key factor in the deaths of millions and the devastation of Europe.

SDS, SNCC, and the Anti-Vietnam War Movement

There was no meaningful left-wing opposition to World War II. There was no mass opposition to the Korean War either. But in the 1960s, opposition to the Vietnam war galvanized a new generation of socialists and radicals. Students for a Democratic Society (SDS) formed coalitions with a variety of socialist groups as well as civil rights organizations to build a massive anti-war crescendo that shook the foundations of the country. Of course, such opposition did not go unpunished. The federal government's counterintelligence program (COINTELPRO) intensified the repression of anti-war and civil rights activists. The Black Panthers and their allies were largely crushed, and the National Guard killed students at the Jackson State and Kent State campuses, delivering a clear message to all. Despite the repression, the transformative movement of the sixties had numerous currents, and the socialist currents played a historic role in a variety of ways.

SDS, in alliance with the Student Nonviolent Coordinating Committee (SNCC), led the first large Vietnam era anti-war demonstration, mobilizing 25,000 to protest in Washington, DC in April 1965. The SDS-SNCC alliance was inspired by resistance against both the draft and the brutally racist attacks on freedom riders and voter registration activists in the South. The alliance was transformative. It changed the focus from earlier, pacifist-led actions which tended to emphasize the threat of nuclear war more than U.S. aggression in Vietnam. This new movement, given wide resonance by the leadership of the Rev. Dr. Martin Luther King, Jr., mushroomed to encompass thousands of local, regional and national mobilizations involving millions of people.

President Lyndon Johnson's large-scale deployments of combat troops to Vietnam stimulated militant resistance. Anti-draft activity on campuses became widespread, as burning draft cards gave way to attacks on draft boards and military ROTC (Reserve Officer Training Corps) centers on campuses. In some places, these hated symbols of the U.S. war machine were actually burned to the ground.

Alongside such tactics, socialist organizers looked for ways to reach out to the soldiers themselves, the actual working-class people who were being forced to fight. GI "coffee houses" sprang up near many military bases across the country. Soldiers and sailors created their own underground newspapers, which educated soldiers in the ranks about their rights and encouraged them to join off-base anti-war activities. Some activists—often socialists—made the conscious decision to join the military to organize against the war, and in one case launched an anti-war union in the ranks, the American Servicemen's Union (ASU).

Meanwhile SNCC, the Black Panther Party, and others encouraged African-American soldiers to fight for their rights in the military, where segregation and racist abuse had always been dominant. The ASU's newspaper, *The Bond*, and other anti-war literature circulated widely among the troops in the war theater. These developments led gradually to open rebellion, even mutiny, which became a material factor in ending the war, together with the relentless resistance of the Vietnamese national liberation forces.

In May 1971, another approach emerged: non-violent direct action aimed at "shutting it down." Following two weeks of non-stop mass protests in Washington, as L.A. Kauffman put it in her book *Direct Action*, these protests ranged "from a half-million-person march to large-scale sit-ins outside the Selective Service, Justice Department, and other government agencies, some 25,000 young people set out to... disrupt the basic functioning of the federal government through nonviolent action."[3] Repression was fast and intense—thousands of military troops helped the DC police round up everyone suspected of participating in the protest. White House aide Jeb Magruder later noted that the protest had "shaken" Nixon and his staff, while CIA director Richard Helms called it "a very damaging kind of event," and "one of the things that was putting increasing pressure on the administration to try and find some way to get out of the war."

Veterans Lead the Way

Combat veterans returning from the war also became lightning rods for intensified anti-war activity. These new working-class anti-war voices were natural allies of socialists trying to reach and mobilize civilian workers against the war. Veterans' demands for jobs, benefits, and improved care for their wounds and traumas tended to concretize the war's negative impact on working people, while dramatizing the war's criminal character. At least half a million veterans returned to civilian life with punitive "less than honorable" discharges which added to their difficulty reintegrating into a society already torn asunder by war.

Anti-war veterans became the natural allies of war resisters—draft resisters and military deserters, as well as civilian anti-war activists—fighting for amnesty. Their joint message was that the war should never have happened, that it was a crime and the politicians who foisted it on the country and the world were the criminals. Their call for amnesty was a clear signal for the future: it's right to refuse to fight in illegal, imperialist wars of aggression.

The massive character of the anti-war movement gradually penetrated all sectors of U.S. society, including the pro-Cold War leadership of the AFL-CIO unions. The union leadership—which through the 1930s and World War II included many socialists and communists—had been effectively purged and terrorized in the "Red Scare" witch hunts of the 1950s. Conservative union leaders, including AFL-CIO president George Meany, were among the most vocal supporters of the war effort. Images of construction workers bashing anti-war protesters' heads became common fare in the mainstream media. But socialists and other anti-war activists never gave up on reaching out to union workers. And some union leaders never caved in, notably the United Electrical Workers (UE) and the International Longshore Workers Union (ILWU), as well as more mainstream unions like the United Auto Workers (UAW) and the American Federation of State, County, and Municipal Employees (AFSCME). Over time Labor Against the

War and other groups were able to develop anti-war and progressive activism in the unions.

The anti-war movement evolved into a genuine social rebellion across U.S. society. This rebellion fed into the women's liberation and LGBTQ liberation movements, both of which faced vicious reactions and media vilification. Socialists were among the first to legitimize the liberationist character of these movements, recognizing them as major new forces in the broad effort to transform capitalist society. This didn't happen smoothly or easily. The progressive movement had tended to reflect the patriarchal character of the broader society, and women and gay people often had to call out hypocrisy and discrimination among their friends and allies. But these efforts resulted in early victories, ultimately leading to a stronger and more united movement for change.

All of these new voices and social actors could be seen in the composition of the delegations to the 1972 Democratic National Convention, a kind of *de facto* "rainbow coalition" that supported the anti-war candidacy of George McGovern. It was exhilarating, but it was an illusion: Richard Nixon successfully mobilized his "silent majority" against it. The lesson was not that the rainbow did not exist. The illusion was locating itself in the Democratic Party. The real rainbow coalition emerged in the streets of Chicago, led by Fred Hampton and the Black Panthers, and later by Jesse Jackson.

Anti-Imperialism in the Reagan Era and After

The Vietnam era anti-war movement and its allies were a major component of the massive opposition to President Ronald Reagan's interventions in Central America and elsewhere in the 1980s. This opposition took on an anti-imperialist character through its solidarity with the *Frente Sandinista de Liberación Nacional* (Sandinista Front for National Liberation, FSLN) of Nicaragua, the *Frente Farabundo Martí para la Liberación Nacional* (Farabundo Marti National Liberation Front, FMLN) of El Salvador, the Palestinian Liberation Organization (PLO), and the freedom struggles in South Africa and former Portuguese colonies in Angola, Mozambique and Guinea-Bissau.

Reagan came to power in 1981 determined to put an end to the so-called "Vietnam syndrome." In the wake of the Sandinista and Iranian revolutions of 1979, he called for a "spiritual renewal" of the country that translated into military buildup and intensified support for anti-communism in Central America. A new anti-war coalition, the People's Anti-War Mobilization, staged an answer, with more than 100,000 people marching in Washington and major actions in other cities, against Reagan's military buildup and adventures in Central America. While this new movement ultimately did not expand further, there were continuous anti-war and anti-imperialist activities during the Reagan years, including solidarity efforts with the FSLN and FMLN in Central America, and a large anti-apartheid movement in support of the African National Congress (ANC) of South Africa.

In 1984 the ILWU Local 10 shut down the port of San Francisco rather than unload cargo from apartheid South Africa. It won the support of thousands in the Bay Area who rallied in solidarity. This movement succeeded in crippling U.S. government and corporate support for the racist apartheid regime. It forced Congress to pass the 1986 Comprehensive Anti-Apartheid Act, and then override Reagan's veto. The South African government ultimately had to release ANC leader Nelson Mandela from prison after 27 years, and he became South Africa's first post-apartheid president in 1994.

The U.S. wars and sanctions against Iraq in the 1990s stimulated an anti-war resurgence, as did the belligerent response to the 9/11 terrorist attacks. In 2002 and 2003, a crescendo of ever larger mass protests opposed George W. Bush's war buildup against Iraq. At least 100,000 protested in Washington in October 2002, and millions more marched all over the country and around the world. By mid-February 2003, a *New York Times* front-page report read "there are two superpowers on the planet: the United States and worldwide public opinion." Socialists played a key role in these mobilizations by making them anti-imperialist, anti-racist, and international in scope, while organizing on a broad basis to encompass all social sectors. The lull that took hold with Bush's and Obama's wars, has only recently begun to lift. The drumbeats against Venezuela and Iran have awakened a renewed determination to stop and prevent the never-ending U.S. "regime change" interventions. The 2019 coup in Bolivia—officially hailed by the government in Washington and by corporate media as a "victory for democracy"—opened the way for broad opposition to the U.S. imperialist interventions in Latin America and across the globe.

Beyond the Endless Wars

The endless wars of our age have tended to numb the American population, including progressives, to their devastating toll and impact. This presents an opportunity—and obligation—for socialists to intervene. While attention is rightly focused on such pressing concerns and interests of our working class as Medicare for All and a Green New Deal, we need to be aware that only by ending the wars and dismantling the U.S. war machine, including demobilization of nearly a thousand forward bases across the globe, will it be possible to get these desperately needed social programs.

We should not pretend that a Green New Deal can happen without sidelining the fossil fuel industry and dramatically shrinking the military. Despite official efforts to make the public believe the war machine is "defending human rights and democracy around the world," we can and must convince people that its main reason to exist is for U.S. control of oil reserves across the globe. Thus, the good news: demobilizing the fossil fuel industry and the military are really two sides of one coin.

The obvious lesson is that peace and social transformation go together: we can't have one without the other. And that is precisely the socialist vision the people of this country, and the world, so desperately need. Bernie Sanders actually said it: "the real challenge of our time is to see how we can... stop aggression and keep our people safe. Because if we are not successful right now, then I think all this world has to look forward to in the future for our children is war, and more war, and more war... as if we haven't had enough war already."

VII

From Genocide in Gaza, To Global War?

27

From Genocide to Global War?

January 14, 2024

As the International Court of Justice heard the case for genocide against Israel, its onslaught against the Palestinians threatened to mushroom into a global war. Israel is unlikely to convince the court that it has been a victim of "terrorism" after 75 years continuously terrorizing the original inhabitants of the Holy Land, and after "grass mowing" attacks[1] on Gaza almost every other year since 2008. Unsuccessful in eradicating the Palestinian resistance in Gaza, in spite of the awesome toll of its bombing campaign, Israel has already resorted to provocative targeted assassinations in Lebanon, Syria and Iran. Netanyahu, whose political fortunes seem to depend on "many more months of war,"[2] seems to hope to drag the U.S. into a regional war.

Will the U.S. take the bait? "Endless war" was the nightmare promise of Donald Rumsfeld and George Bush back in 2001, following the attacks on the World Trade Center that year. The world has lived that nightmare ever since, in Afghanistan, Iraq, Syria, Libya, the former Yugoslavia, Yemen, Ukraine,… and at home. The nightmare threatens to morph into global catastrophe, as Israel's U.S.-backed genocidal slaughter against Gaza hits the brink of regional war in West

Asia. It could easily become global, involving both Russia and China. Such a war, even if it did not blow up the world, would destroy the global economy the U.S. and its allies want to dominate.

While Biden and Blinken "caution" Israel about civilian casualties and international law, they rush endless tons of munitions to keep the slaughter going. As 2023 ended, Israel has begun withdrawing ground troops from northern Gaza. The onslaught failed to eradicate the resistance, but succeeded in crushing tens of thousands of civilians, mainly women and children, and demolishing homes, hospitals, schools and Gaza's entire civilian infrastructure.

How has all this happened? According to Biden, Blinken and Netanyahu, it's the fault of their enemies: "terrorists" in Palestine and "dictators" in Russia and China. But is that true?

A deep fog of lies and false propaganda has been a major strategic weapon of war for the U.S. war makers and their allies. *"We lied, we cheated, we stole… It's part of the glory of the American experiment,"* declared former U.S. Secretary of State Michael Pompeo in May 2019, bragging to a college audience in Texas. That unusual admission reflects the *bipartisan* official U.S. approach to maintaining global hegemony.

The lie machine and the war machine are linked: the military-industrial complex and AIPAC (American-Israeli Political Action Committee) are among the largest political donors to politicians in Washington. Together with the major oil corporations, the largest banks and big business as a whole, they forge conformity to the official narrative, especially in time of war. They largely control the mainstream media.

The Big Lie is the weapon of choice for Biden and his *neo-cons* in waging the proxy war in Ukraine against Russia, in support for

Israel's genocide in Palestine, in the hybrid war against China — and in a wider war in West Asia. In each case the path to peace must first break through the official big lies.

Sensational Lies Uncritically Parroted

"Israel tried desperately to control the narrative in a series of fabrications that immediately unraveled," wrote *Electronic Intifada*. "Sensational lies about rape and beheaded babies[3] were quietly retracted despite being uncritically parroted by mainstream western media."[4] Biden repeated the Israeli narrative *verbatim,* even after it was debunked.

The biggest lie is about terror and terrorism. Zionist Israel has waged permanent terror against the Palestinians since 1948, always with massive and lavish support from the U.S. and its allies. Just as Nelson Mandela and the African National Congress were called terrorists by the apartheid rulers of South Africa, with U.S. support, the Palestinians are considered terrorists because they reject the Israeli theft of their land, and have fought against terrible odds to get it back. Hamas and the rest of the Palestinian resistance are called terrorists because they lead this fight. The real terror is on the other side, as both the U.S. and Israel use brute force to protect their theft, and to maintain the racist repression and expulsion of the land's original inhabitants.

In the case of the conflict in Ukraine, the U.S. has spent billions over decades to transform that country into an effective battering ram against Russia, culminating in the 2014 coup that brought Ukrainian fascists to power. It then backed these fascists in attacks against Russian speakers in eastern and southern Ukraine, while "NATO-izing" the Ukrainian military and bludgeoning its European NATO allies to support the effort. When Russia stepped in to stop these attacks, Biden raised a hysterical hue and cry about the need to protect "Ukrainian democracy" and oppose "Russian aggression." The war that ensued has gone bad for the U.S. and NATO, because it was false from the start. The U.S. backed an actor and former comedian as Ukraine's president, and pumped him up as a latter day Churchill who could "fight to the last Ukrainian." Biden still calls it a success — a sign of difficulty distinguishing his own propaganda from reality.

About China, the war planners and DC politicians are frustrated. They wanted it to be their "war of choice," following the "pivot to Asia" announced in 2011. Breaking with the One China policy agreed to in the 1970s, they are trying to foment separatism in Taiwan, and use it to weaken and divide China. They tried the same earlier with Hong Kong, and with Tibet in previous decades. They have hoped to stop China's rise by weakening it however possible. Michael Pompeo's rants about "genocide" in China's far-western province of Xinjiang were part of the effort. But the results have been illusory, as China continues to rise, and sticks with its policy of common prosperity for a shared future.

Deceit is Not Enough

Deceit is combined with a war against "disinformation," designed to suppress anything but the official narrative. "The relentless Western narrative that the West is noble while Russia and China are evil is simple-minded and extraordinarily dangerous," Columbia University Professor Jeffrey Sachs has said. "It is an attempt to manipulate public opinion...."[5]

Dissent is met with repression. Students for Justice in Palestine and similar groups have been banned at numerous universities. Presidents of Ivy League schools were forced to resign in an AIPAC-sponsored campaign to suppress anti-Zionist activists by smearing them as "antisemitic."

Then there's the case of Julian Assange, who is now facing extradition from England to the U.S., after years of torture. He is charged with "espionage" because he publicized information about U.S. crimes in Iraq, and faces up to 175 years in prison (a virtual death penalty) for practicing honest journalism. If the U.S. cared about honest journalism, Assange would get a prize. But he is barely mentioned in the mainstream media.

The rise of social media has helped break the grip of the official information monopoly. Even though Jeffrey Sachs has said he can't even get an antiwar "op-ed" published in the New York Times or Washington Post, he has become famous on YouTube. So have "turn coat" intelligence analysts like Scott Ritter, Ray McGovern, and others.

The Palestinian resistance movement itself has been a major force in breaking through the media smokescreen. The sight of Israel's saturation bombing of homes, hospitals and schools in Gaza has brought millions into the streets, just as scenes of Vietnamese children running away naked from napalm attacks ignited a storm of antiwar protest decades ago. They have inspired non-Zionist Jews everywhere to say "not in our name," and expose the lie that opposing U.S.-backed Israeli genocide is somehow "antisemitic."

Scenarios for "End-Game"

At the start of 2024, after three months of war in Gaza, and nearly two years in Ukraine, "postwar plans" became news items. Blinken took off on another major Middle East tour, stating "goals"[6] of increased humanitarian assistance to Gaza, steps to protect Palestinian civilians and allow them to return to their homes, and plans to "soften" Israel's bombing attacks. But the U.S. continues to send tons of bombs and other munitions to Israel. If they really want to "soften" Israel's bombing attacks, they could stop sending the bombs. Before Blinken took off on his "peace tour," protesters arrived at his Virginia residence and splashed fake blood on his government vehicle and held signs branding him a war criminal.[7]

Blinken "intends to tackle the thorny topics of plans for governing Gaza and prospects for reaching a political solution between Israel and the Palestinians once this conflict is over," the New York Times report said. But Netanyahu says he is "proud" to have blocked a Palestinian state during his multiple turns as prime minister since the 1990s.[8] And Israel continues the ethnic cleansing of Gaza, and its plans for Israelis to re-occupy the enclave.

The U.S. officially wants a "revamped and revitalized" Palestinian Authority to govern Gaza after the war, viewing it as a path toward a two-state solution.[9] That would involve "crushing" Hamas and its Palestinian Resistance allies first. But many question "whether resolving to destroy such a deeply entrenched organization was ever realistic," the Times reports.[10]

Palestinians "are open to any proposal for a final and complete ceasefire in the Gaza Strip but are opposed to administrations imposed by Israel or the U.S.," said Hamas leader Osama Hamdan at a Beirut press conference Dec. 28.[11]

Following the January 2 targeted Israeli assassination of a top Hamas leader in Beirut, Hezbollah leader Hassan Nasrallah warned Israel against waging war on Lebanon. "If the enemy thinks of waging a war on Lebanon, we will fight without restraint, without rules, without limits and without restrictions," Nasrallah said.[12] The Yemenis have said the same.[13]

Regarding a wider regional war, there is an internal debate in the State Department.[14] "Hawks" led by Victoria Nuland oppose Blinken's "moderate" stand. The hawks tend to prevail in such debates. "From Lebanon to the Red Sea, a Broader Conflict With Iran Looms" was the lead headline in the NY Times on January 7.[15] "Iran is posing a new challenge to the West," the article says, "this time with Russia and China on its side." *Translation: a regional war could become a global war.*

Support to Ukraine Has Begun to Erode

Meanwhile on the Ukraine front, the Russians are winning. U.S. leaders are groping to deal with it. "The political willingness to continue providing military and economic support to Ukraine has begun to erode in both the United States and Europe," say top U.S. foreign policy leaders Richard Haass and Charles Kupchan, writing in *Foreign Affairs* Nov. 17, 2023. "The time has come for Washington to lead efforts to forge a new policy that sets attainable goals…" They cite "the enormous human and economic costs of the war and the reality that Russia has succeeded…"[16]

The conflict in Gaza has "grabbed the world's attention, relegating the war in Ukraine to the back burner. The issue is not only that

Washington is distracted; the U.S. military has only finite resources, and U.S. defense industrial base has far too limited production capacity. The United States is stretched thin as it supports two partners engaged in hot wars…"

In an earlier *Foreign Affairs* article (April 13, 2023), the same authors said "the United States must prepare for potential military action in Asia… and the Middle East." They add that "the war is imposing high costs on the global economy," and "economic duress is triggering political unrest" and "is also polarizing the international system."

The solution they offer is "a ceasefire in place." A ceasefire, they add, "would save lives, allow economic reconstruction to get underway, and enable Ukraine to devote incoming Western arms to investing in its long-term security rather than to quickly expending weaponry on a deadlocked battlefield." So the proposal is *not for a complete ceasefire:* "Ukraine could continue using long-range weapons, naval assets, and covert operations to strike at Russian positions in rear areas and in Crimea, raising the costs of continuing occupation."

The *Foreign Affairs* leaders admit it's "likely that Moscow would spurn a cease-fire proposal." That's a good bet. In realistic terms, the Ukrainian forces — and their NATO backers — are exhausted. Russian forces are establishing security for Russian speakers in eastern and southern Ukraine, and defending their self-determination. In effect they are implementing the Minsk accords, which all parties agreed to years ago. Meanwhile the sanctions only stimulated Russia to align itself economically with India and China, and the rest of the Global South. The main victim of the sanctions was the western European economy.

A Fantasy World

Western leaders, like the *Foreign Affairs* writers, continue to live in a fantasy world where they are on top. Their current proposal is modeled on the armed truce in Korea, established seven decades ago. That truce was meant to maintain intense pressure on China, which had helped the Koreans resist the U.S. onslaught. A lot has changed in seven decades. Most importantly, China is no longer exhausted from a century of humiliation and three decades of revolutionary war. Its leader, Xi Jinping, has reaffirmed China's close friendship with Russia. China has presented a peace plan to the West to resolve the Ukraine crisis. French President Macron, German Chancellor Scholz and European Commission President Van der Leyen all visited Beijing to secure economic ties with China. Europe trades more with China than the U.S.

The Chinese newspaper *Global Times* reported that "after concluding his visit to China, Macron emphasized that 'the great risk' Europe faces is that it 'gets caught up in crises that are not ours, which prevents it from building its strategic autonomy... The paradox would be that, overcome with panic, we believe we are just America's followers'."[17] The *Global Times* report says "Macron is warning Europe not to go so far on this issue and risk damaging Europe's own interests. Macron's stressing the need for Europe's strategic autonomy was a result of a sober awakening from the U.S.' selfish policies on Europe, especially since the Russia-Ukraine crisis, and also from being emboldened by his 'very successful' visit to China, during which he saw China's good will toward France and the huge potential of cooperation with China."

Following the European visits to China, Brazil's President Lula Da

Silva was China's next state visitor. The *New York Times* report was headlined "Brazil's Lula Meets Xi in China as They Seek Path to Peace in Ukraine."[18] Their joint statement said negotiation is "the only viable way out of the crisis in Ukraine." They want China's peace plan to be the basis for talks. The *Times* report said U.S. and *some* European officials "have been critical" of China's plan, "because China has not suggested that Russian forces must withdraw from occupied Ukrainian territory." Lula also wants other countries, like South Africa, India and Indonesia, to help mediate the conflict. They also have not signed on to isolating Russia.

As part of his visit to China, Lula helped inaugurate his political ally Dilma Rousseff as president of the New Development Bank set up by the BRICS nations. Rousseff was Brazil's president from 2011 to 2016, when she was impeached in a "soft coup" backed by the U.S. At the inauguration ceremony Lula said "Why should every country have to be tied to the dollar for trade?.... Who decided the dollar would be the (world's) currency?"[19] He added that "No bank should be asphyxiating countries' economies the way the IMF is doing now with Argentina, or the way they did with Brazil for a long time and every third-world country...."

Lula's comments are a signal of the changed environment in the world. He also called for China's territorial integrity to be respected with regard to Taiwan, as Macron had done.

Just before hosting these high level visits from France, the EU and Brazil, China hosted the leaders of Iran and Saudi Arabia, scoring possibly the most significant peace agreement of this century so far. No military guarantees were needed to convince Iran and Saudi Arabia to abandon hostilities. Instead the parties agreed to peace on the basis of cooperation in attractive trade deals with China. It's a new approach, part of China's Global Security Initiative Concept.

There is no guarantee that a similar approach could work for peace between Russia and Ukraine, or Russia and the EU and NATO. In all these cases the main obstacle is the United States, which does not want peace based on mutual cooperation. But the U.S. may not have a choice, either in the Ukraine conflict, or in western Asia, or against China itself.

A New Movement

The role of popular protest in all this is significant. Digging out the truth and spreading it is not enough. People are hitting the streets in protest and in serious efforts to stop the war machine. Yara Shoufani of the Palestine Youth Movement said it's "a major watershed moment where the Palestinian Youth Movement has been a part of a movement in North America and Britain to shut down industry and organize mass mobilizations across the world and across North America and Europe."[20] It goes further, she suggests. "We're building a broad coalition of national liberation struggles, of working class struggles, of left struggles; and Arab and Palestinian and Muslim communities are coming together." Now, she says, "we have work to do to channel this moment into serious political organization. And I think what we're seeing is actually the beginning of that."

The Palestinians are leading the way. Their resistance, with massive global support, in the face of attempted genocide has exposed the moral and political bankruptcy of both Israel and its U.S. sponsor. The apparent unity of the apartheid settler state is beginning to crack. While the Israelis want to expand their assault on Gaza to a regional war — and force the United States to come to their rescue — they're betting on a time-worn balance of forces that is no longer valid. Now both Israel and the U.S. are isolated globally. The people who live in historic Palestine, of all religions, will gradually conclude that peaceful coexistence is possible, and is much safer than apartheid.

The Stakes are High

What if the U.S. war machine can be stopped, and the U.S. disarmed? It may seem like a distant hope now, but the progression of current events could change that. The neocons in Washington are gambling big-time with their proxy war against Russia, support of Israeli genocide in Gaza, and their escalating threats against China. What if they lose?

The Palestinians refuse to retreat, and are frustrating Israel's effort to "crush" their resistance. Russia is determined not to lose, because if it were to lose it would be broken up, like Yugoslavia and the USSR. And defeating China is not likely to be any easier for the U.S. than its adventures in Korea and Vietnam, probably much harder.

The U.S. war on Vietnam caused severe damage to the U.S. economy, ultimately leading to the end of the Gold Standard in 1971. The shift to the dollar standard—sometimes called the *petrodollar* standard—has worked well for the U.S. since then. But things are changing fast. Economist Michael Hudson says: "The U.S./NATO confrontation with Russia in Ukraine is achieving just the opposite of America's aim of preventing China, Russia and their allies from acting independently of U.S. control over their trade and investment policy. Naming China as America's main long-term adversary, the Biden Administration's plan was to split Russia away from China and then cripple China's own military and economic viability."[21]

Instead the alliance between Russia and China has become stronger, and has attracted support from an increasing number of countries throughout the world. The U.S. managed to bludgeon its European allies to go along with war, even against their own interests, but for how long? The boomerang effect of sanctions against Russia has led to economic crisis and social instability in Europe, threatening "NATO unity."

Meanwhile the effect of the savage sanctions and the proxy war "has been to drive Russia and China together, joining with Iran, India and other allies," Hudson says. "For the first time since the Bandung Conference of Non-Aligned Nations in 1955, a critical mass is able to be mutually self-sufficient to start the process of achieving independence from Dollar Diplomacy."

China's central bank has taken a series of steps to accelerate the global drive toward de-dollarization,[22] challenging the hegemony of the greenback.[23]

With the sudden emergence of "de-dollarization," the U.S. economic grip on the world will diminish fairly fast. As that happens, the U.S. is sure to become even more recklessly aggressive, but it is not likely to win militarily against either Russia or China—or successfully fight a regional war in West Asia. The U.S. is over-extended globally, and a majority of its people are tired of war, to say the least. Instead, we may begin to see possibilities of a "post-U.S.-imperialism" world. It may involve passing through intensified dangers of fascism, like the fascism the U.S. has imposed in Ukraine and elsewhere. But those dangers could be mitigated by economic and political collapse at the top of U.S. society. Glimpses of this can already be seen with the disarray in Washington, and the beginning of a banking crisis. This disarray could offer opportunities for positive change.

What Could Positive Change Look Like?

Fighting against fascism can galvanize ordinary people to organize and fight back. Ajamu Baraka, co-founder of the Black Alliance for Peace, says "the Left in the U.S. must organize an authentic radical opposition to the ruling class and have a clear political program rooted in a people-centered human rights framework..."[24]

"We need to revive the antiwar movement," Baraka said. "We need to demand that the resources transferred from people's needs to the military must cease... We need to place the plight of the people at the center. We need to re-center self-determination, social justice and equality to develop effectively... We have to struggle for minimum programs of unity among the authentic left."

This is a virtual call for a *united front against imperialism and fascism.* Easier said than done, of course, but such a call is a crucial first step. Just starting the process of building such a united front—through joint actions, conferences and other unity-building activities in dozens of localities and regional centers—could trigger a chain reaction of groups coming together as well as many people joining the effort. It could recall the popular crescendo Dr. King aroused as he organized rallies and marches in the 1960s. In his historic 1967 speech at Riverside Church, a year before he was assassinated, King said:

> *Our only hope today lies in our ability to recapture the revolutionary spirit and go out in a sometimes hostile world declaring eternal hostility to poverty, racism and militarism.*

The "sometimes hostile world" King mentioned was real. It killed him. A united front will also encounter hostility—repression, reaction, infiltration, police violence and fascist mobs—as well as vilification by politicians and mass media. It will need to organize to counter all this. Voices across the country have already been calling for unified efforts against both war and fascism. Immigrant groups have had to reach out for help against repression wherever they are. They and their support groups are likely to become part of a united front.

This type of organizing can also stimulate a broader "people's democratic front" focusing on peace and democratic rights, as well as providing legal support and protection. These two fronts together can grow to include a large percentage of the general population— unions, churches, community organizations and a wide variety of social groups. Such a mushrooming progressive coalition could turn the tide of militarism and fascist and racist reaction that has already shown itself. It would provide an answer to the noxious narratives of politicians and mass media that make it *seem* that "everyone" is for war, racism and reaction. And it would offer a vehicle for an escalated battle for peace as well as economic and democratic rights.

Baraka says "the system is no longer able to shield the reality of the profound gaps in wealth and income, the suffering and immiseration of the working class and the poor.... People know the crisis that caused the crash of 2008 was never really overcome. It's increasingly hard to convince people they're getting either a fair deal or straight answers."

Biden's "justification" of Israel's slaughter in Palestine has exposed his hysterical denunciations of Russia's "aggression" against Ukraine as pure hypocrisy. As U.S. bombs and tanks crush Palestinians and sacrifice Ukrainians, people start to make connections.

About democracy, Baraka says "there's no democracy here. We need to expand the concept of democracy—dismantle the duopoly, win ranked choice voting, ban PACs, push for democratic reforms…

"The capitalists are providing opportunities for us, if we can see them. They saw what happened with the George Floyd protests, and they were shaken to the core by it.

"The working class, organized and unorganized, remains pivotal. They're on the move: dozens and dozens of wildcat strikes, and the emergence of new formations. They're putting pressure on the official union leadership. And there's hope from the South. In South America there are very effective social movements that have seized nominal state power in various places. That represents hope: We're seeing movements leading the way towards a transformation of power."

A Major Turning Point

"The Ukraine conflict promises to constitute a major turning point," says Radhika Desai, author of *Capitalism, Coronavirus and War: A Geopolitical Economy.*[25] She writes:

> The conflict that the West calls Russia's invasion of Ukraine, and Moscow its special military operation for Ukraine's demilitarization and denazification, is not a conflict between Ukraine and Russia. It is a phase in the hybrid war that the United States has been waging for over a century against any country that chooses an economic path other than subordination to itself or

the broader capitalist world... In this war, Ukraine is the terrain, and a pawn—one that can be and is being sacrificed....

Desai says "this more than century-long project has reached a tipping point where U.S. actions are not merely failures, they are counter-productive, accelerating the shift in the world's center of gravity away from itself and the West towards socialist China." But this does not mean China will be the "successor" to U.S. hegemony. "China will certainly overtake the United States as the largest economy in the world, but it will still remain one among other weighty economies."

The bottom line is the U.S. will no longer be able to control the world. As its empire collapses new possibilities will emerge across the globe and here at home. It's a reminder of what happened when Dorothy landed in the mythical land of Oz, in the 1939 film, *The Wizard of Oz*. When a very ordinary—that is, working class—girl is caught in a storm and swept away, she inadvertently lands on a "wicked witch" who has terrorized everyone in the land of Oz. She inadvertently kills the witch. The people come out dancing and singing: *"Ding Dong, the witch is dead!"*

People in real life will come out dancing and singing if we can kill the witch that rules and oppresses us. Radhika Desai concludes her book with the programmatic statement "Through Pluripolarity toward Socialism: A Manifesto,"[26] issued in 2021, during the "storm" of global pandemic and war. It has been signed by thousands of people around the world, individuals, organizations, and national leaders.

"We must oppose the U.S.-sponsored imperialist New Cold War

and build an ambitious multilateral international governance," the Manifesto says. "We must replace [imperialistic domination] with common values and principles to tackle common challenges... International governance needs to reflect the world's objective and developing *pluripolarity*. The original ideals of the United Nations Charter and the principles of peaceful coexistence advocated by the Non-Aligned Movement are excellent foundations for further constructing alternatives to institutions of U.S. and Western dominance."

Saying all this doesn't make it so. Getting there, as the saying goes, is "half the fun," and is our current challenge. It's a long march, of course, but there really are no short cuts. In many parts of the world the process has already begun. In some Latin American countries neoliberal and proto-fascist regimes have been replaced. The CIA has fought back with coups in Bolivia and Peru, but the most recent coup in Bolivia was reversed. There have been more than 190 coups and revolutions in Bolivia since its independence in 1825.[27] So Bolivia holds the record, but there have been innumerable coups throughout the Americas in the past two centuries. In most cases, the coup's purpose was to restore capitalist control after local people moved to reclaim their national patrimony.

Pedro Castillo, the president of Peru who was deposed in December 2022, had condemned foreign companies for "pillaging" his country.[28] He wanted to renegotiate contracts to ensure 70 percent of all proceeds from mining would go to the state, to fund social programs.[29] "Let's be clear," Castillo said, "these decades of betrayal, corruption, and cynicism are the symptoms of this neoliberal system dedicated exclusively to the exploitation of our people and natural resources for the benefit of a few scoundrels."[30] He declared, "We are rescuing the resources of the country for all Peruvians."[31] His goal: "We want our natural resources to directly benefit the people."[32]

The U.S. ambassador in Peru, Lisa Kenna, is a CIA veteran who supported the December 2022 parliamentary coup that overthrew Castillo.[33] One day before the December 7 coup, the former CIA officer-turned-U.S.-ambassador met with Peru's defense minister, who then told the country's powerful military to turn against President Castillo.[34] After the coup, Kenna met with Peru's mining and energy ministers to discuss "investments." Europe is now importing Peruvian Liquid Natural Gas to replace what it lost when the Nordstream pipeline blew up.

Leaders of Peru's neighbors in the rest of Latin America have condemned the coup. In 2019, following the U.S.-backed coup in Bolivia, electric car magnate Elon Musk twittered: "We will coup whoever we want—deal with it!" In Venezuela and Nicaragua and Cuba, the people and their revolutionary governments "deal with it" by defending their sovereignty. Many people in the U.S. and everywhere are dealing with it by "changing sides" in support of the victims.

The day of reckoning is likely to come sooner than expected, as a result of the extremely bad gamble the U.S. neocons are taking against Russia, China, and the people of Palestine. For many, that day cannot come soon enough.

As U.S. hegemony wanes, new possibilities will emerge across the globe and here at home. The maniacs in Washington may try to do what they've done before, using extreme measures to hold back change. But popular forces in this country and around the world can and must intervene to protect our interests and make change happen.

A new multipolar world is dawning that will replace the old imperialist order with peace, and common prosperity for a shared future. It is the destiny of today's generation to hasten its arrival.

2024 and Beyond

The 2024 electoral season began with greater uncertainty than ever. Fear and loathing are normal reactions to disenfranchising "choices" between continued endless war and open appeals to fascism in the name of "peace." The enormous profits made by military contractors, energy companies, AIPAC and big pharma now monopolize the electoral process, draining it of all but the illusion of democracy.

People need to find ways to register a genuine vote for peace and social justice. The moment is ripe for a new political response that could lead to a united fight against war, racism and fascism. Major obstacles remain to be overcome. The grip of war propaganda continues to confuse and disorient the majority of people, especially in the United States. But the same economic devastation the war and sanctions have brought to Europe has come home in high prices, lost jobs, increased insecurity and homelessness. A new great recession (or depression) encroaches week by week.

The genocidal slaughter against the people of Palestine has ignited a massive global protest movement, with millions in the streets everywhere. The U.S. and Israel are isolated globally.

Dollar dominance is fading fast across the world, so that U.S. super-profits are no longer guaranteed. Bankers are plagued by the specter of massive debt default at home and abroad—at both household and government levels.

Meanwhile China's peace efforts, based on mutual cooperation instead of weapons and war threats, have already brought countries together for common prosperity where only war seemed possible before. China has led efforts to mediate the Ukraine conflict on a realistic basis—realistic in the sense of providing justice and security for the Donbas, Crimea and the rest of Russia, as well as the rest of Ukraine. The same can happen for Palestine and West Asia, as China has proposed.

China's approach to peace has been working. Mutually beneficial trade has opened the way to better lives in nearly 150 countries across the globe that were previously mired in endless colonial and neocolonial debt. At home Chinese people are guaranteed health and economic wellbeing, and actually have *more* say in government policies than people in the West. The leaders of the United States are determined to stop China's rise. That's like trying to stop the sun from rising. A better plan is to pull back from war and threats of war, in favor of peace.

People in the United States and western Europe could have a better life if we can stop the U.S./NATO war machine. That would take the world back from the threat of nuclear war. And it could lead to true prosperity everywhere. But we have to fight for it. We need to stop business as usual and refocus the country on peace and justice—redirect the war economy to meet people's needs; stop building weapons and invest in a liveable future, based on social equality and common prosperity. We can make it happen.

ABOUT THE AUTHOR

Dee **Knight** is on the Advisory Council of Friends of Socialist China, and a member of DSA's International Committee Working Group on China. He's the author of *Befriending China: People-To-People Peacemaking*, and *My Whirlwind Lives: Navigating Decades of Storms*. He was part of national organizing efforts to oppose U.S. invasion of Iraq, resulting in protest actions of millions of people in the United States and across the globe. His writing appears at **DeeKnight.blog** and at **RealPathtoPeace.com**.

During the years of the U.S. war against Vietnam, Dee Knight was an editor of *Amex-Canada*, the newsletter of American exiles and expatriates who went to Canada in resistance to that war. He lived in Toronto, Canada, from 1968 to 1974. *Amex-Canada* helped organize American war resisters and their allies, including antiwar veterans, to sustain the resistance. In 1973 Knight helped to launch the National Council for Universal Unconditional Amnesty, which waged a campaign to end government repression of war resisters and active-duty U.S. soldiers.

Much of this history is covered in Knight's political memoir, *My Whirlwind Lives: Navigating Decades of Storms,* published in 2022.

Knight's writing has appeared in *LA Progressive, Hollywood Progressive, Veterans For Peace News, Courage To Resist, Workers World, Covert*

Action Magazine, and *CounterPunch.* Some of these articles are online at DeeKnight.blog.

In 1975 Knight witnessed the "Carnation Revolution" led by Portugal's Armed Forces Movement and People's Power organizations. His reports appeared in *The Guardian.* He helped found the American Portuguese Overseas Information Organization (APOIO), a group of journalists in defense of the Portuguese revolution. In the 1980s, Knight worked as a technical consultant to the Sandinista newspaper *Barricada,* and other Nicaraguan publishing efforts. In the 1990s, he was a publishing consultant for the United Nations Development Programme in New York.

During the buildup to the U.S. invasion of Iraq in the early 2000s, Knight was part of national organizing efforts to oppose that war. Those efforts resulted in protest actions of millions of people in the United States and across the globe.

In the mid-1960s Knight studied at University of San Francisco and San Francisco State College. He completed a B.A. in English at York University. In 1996 he completed a Master's Degree at New York University. He worked as a teacher of English and Social Studies in South Bronx alternative high schools for several years. Knight was born in the state of Idaho, and grew up in eastern Oregon. In 1969 he received the Oregon Peace Educators award.

INDEX

20th CPC Congress, 171
100,000 protested, 264

Aaron Good, 202, 203, 205
Abdul Haq al-Turkistani, 140
Adam Smith, 228
Adrian Zenz, 138
Afghanistan, xliii, xlvi, 35, 36, 50, 60, 64, 67, 81, 94, 96, 98, 125, 140, 149, 214, 220, 223, 239, 249, 254
AFL-CIO, 261
Africa, xlii, 39, 43, 46, 49, 63, 67, 83, 94, 98, 141, 142, 143, 144, 145, 146, 148, 169, 175, 181, 207, 208, 238, 264
African Union, 46, 83, 143
AFRICOM, 43, 145, 189
AFSCME, 261
Agence France Presse, 59
Agostinho Neto, 208
Ajamu Baraka, xi, 63, 241, 282
Alexander Mercouris, 79
Allen Dulles, 210
Alliance of Democracies Foundation, 132

Amazon Labor Union, 116
Ambassador Zhang Jun, 187
American Exceptionalism, iii, 202
American Servicemen's Union, xlvii, 259
Amex-Canada, 291
Amilcar Cabral, 208
Amnesty, 291
Amy Goodman, 105
Anatol Lieven, 55
ANC, 63, 263
Angola, 144, 208, 263
Annalena Baerbock, 174, 180, 194
ANSWER, xi, xliii, 42, 94, 95, 112
Appeal for Redress, 251
April 4, 1967 speech, xliv
Argentina, 169, 170, 207, 231
Ash Center for Democratic Governance and Innovation, 133, 152
Asia, xlii, xlvi, xlvii, xlix, 49, 56, 94, 111, 116, 128, 129, 132, 141, 159, 162, 164, 165, 171, 172, 173, 175, 180, 181, 210
ASPI, 139
Australia, v, 126, 132, 150, 169, 171
Austria, 133

Azov, xliii, 70, 71

Babi Yar, 68
Banderistas, 69
Bandung conference, 175, 208
Barack Obama, 121, 132, 228
Beijing, v, 85, 135, 140, 171, 174, 177
Belgium, 133, 142, 189
Belgrade, 60
Belt and Road, 62, 132, 140, 141, 172, 180, 236, 244
Belt and Road Initiative, 132, 141, 172, 180, 236, 244
Bernice King, 105
Bernie Sanders, 125, 134, 226, 265
Biden, xiv, xli, xliv, xlv, xlvi, xlviii, xlix, 38, 43, 45, 48, 54, 61, 67, 69, 73, 76, 80, 93, 95, 97, 102, 119, 124, 132, 134, 141, 148, 156, 161, 167, 170, 172, 176, 182, 185, 194, 217, 238, 242, 243, 244, 271, 280
Big Lie, xlv, li, 75, 77, 87, 271
Bilderberg, 212
Bill Clinton, 121
Black Agenda Report, xi, xlviii, 42, 50, 63, 76, 199, 241, 242
Black Alliance for Peace, xi, 42, 94, 116, 214, 282
Black Lives Matter, 103, 214
Black Panther Party, 260
Black Political Empowerment Project, 107
Black Sea, xxiv, 47, 53, 54, 78

Blinken, xli, 41, 95, 156, 180, 182, 199, 201, 225
Bolivia, 50, 94, 207, 231, 236, 264, 286, 287
Boomerang, 244
Boris Johnson, 79, 113, 196
Brazil, 50, 83, 85, 169, 206, 231, 244, 245
BreakThrough News, xliii, 95
BRI, 141, 236
Brian Becker, xi, xliii, 94, 97
BRICS, 85, 169, 170, 221, 244
Bronx Anti-War Coalition, 115
Brussels, 59, 62, 189, 221, 242
Bucha, 71, 72, 73
Build Back Better, 82, 124, 125, 150
Burkina Faso, 142
Bush Junior, xlv, 180

Canada, xi, 54, 82, 94, 133, 169, 242, 291
Capitalism, Coronavirus and War, 284
Carlos Andrés Pérez, 230
Carter, 120, 184, 219
Ceasefire, 39, 81
Central America, 94, 241, 262, 263
Century of the Common Man, 209
CGTN, 120, 122
Che Guevara, 207
Chelsea Manning, xlv, 36, 204, 255, 257
Chiang Kai Shek, 128
Chicago Council on Global Affairs, 111, 196

China, iii, xiv, xli, l, 38, 43, 57, 61, 74, 80, 83, 85, 90, 110, 195, 201, 206, 207, 210, 217, 219, 221, 234, 236, 272, 280, 285, 287

Chinese Women's Justice Coalition, 112

CIA, 43, 50, 60, 68, 90, 97, 127, 135, 139, 140, 175, 179, 186, 197, 206, 231, 260, 286

CIO, 109, 261

Civil Rights, xliv, 104, 151

Claudia Cruz, 93

CodePink, xi, 42, 64, 95, 106, 110, 112, 130, 141, 142, 157

COINTELPRO, 258

Colin Powell, 121, 186

Congo, 83, 144, 206, 207, 239

Core Group, 242

Cornell West, 105

Costs of War, 64, 124

Council of Europe, 180, 194

Council on Foreign Relations, 208, 212

Covert Action Magazine, xii, xxvii, 53, 75, 291

COVID19, 39

Credibility Gulch, 66

Crimea, xli, xlviii, 40, 48, 51, 53, 54, 69, 70, 95, 186, 197

CSIS, 139

Cuba, 75, 94, 115, 184, 188, 207, 238

Cuba Sí Coalition, 116

Cyril Ramaphosa, 63

Dan Cohen, 60

Dan Ellsberg, 213

Daniel Hale, 255

Danny Haiphong, iii, 50, 202

David Cortwright, 251

David Kotz, 231

Democracy Now, 105

Democratic National Convention, 262

Denmark, 133, 177

Depression, 221, 233

Dick Cheney, 76, 86, 101

Dismember Russia, 86

Dollar Diplomacy, 217, 220, 221, 281

Donbas, xli, xlviii, 38, 40, 47, 51, 53, 55, 60, 69, 73, 78, 81, 85, 95, 99, 122, 182

Donbas People's Republic, 53

Donetsk, 40, 45, 53, 54, 55, 79

Douglas MacArthur, 128

Douglas MacGregor, xi, xlix

Dr. Strangelove, xiv, 193, 199, 200

East Asia Summit, 170

East Turkestan Islamic Movement, 137

Ecuador, 50, 207, 231

Edward Snowden, 204

Egypt, 140, 142, 144, 175, 212

Eisenhower, 129, 210, 228

Ellen Taylor, 49, 85, 99, 100

Elon Musk, 287

El Salvador, 231, 263

Eritrea, 188, 239

Espionage Act, 257

Ethiopia, 83, 188, 239

ETIM, 137

Eugene Debs, 98, 256, 257

Eugene Puryear, xliii, 95
Eurasia, 84, 122, 141, 238
European Commission, 122
European Council on Foreign Affairs, 57, 132
European Union, 59, 69, 89, 169, 195

Fidel Castro, 208, 240
Finland, 79, 89
FIRE sector, 218
FMLN, 263
Foreign Affairs, 47, 134, 188, 195
Forum on China-Africa Cooperation, 143
France, 41, 56, 62, 80, 83, 113, 132, 142, 169, 173, 185, 206, 220, 242
Fraser Human Freedoms Index, 135
Fred Hampton, 98
Freedom Road Socialist Organization, 116
Friedrich Hayek, 218
FSLN, 263

G7, 59, 132, 169, 178, 181
G20, 167, 168, 169, 170, 174, 178, 180
Gary Webb, 211
General Milley, 95
General Valery Zaluzhny, xlix
Geopolitical Economy, iii, xi, 284
George Floyd, 284
George H.W. Bush, xlv
George McGovern, 262
George W. Bush, 121, 264

Germany, 55, 62, 78, 80, 83, 86, 95, 99, 132, 144, 169, 173, 179, 185, 189, 194, 198, 206, 220
Ghana, 208
Global Security Initiative, 183
Global South, ix, 81, 83, 169, 177, 179, 181, 222, 244
Global Times, 41, 62, 129, 153, 168, 169, 171, 245
Grand Chessboard, xxiv, 76
Great Depression, 230, 232
Greece, 132, 133, 235
Green Corn Rebellion, 257
Green New Deal, xliv, 264
Guatemala, 213, 231
Guinea-Bissau, 208, 239, 263
Gulf of Tonkin, 75, 120, 121

Haiti, 43, 50, 116, 189, 231, 239, 241
Haiti Liberté, 116
Harry Truman, 121
Hawaii, xlvii
Hegemony, 183
Henry Cabot Lodge, 206
Henry Wallace, 209
Hideki Yoshikawa, 111, 160
Honduras, 50, 231
Hong Kong, 127, 135, 141, 156, 175, 210
Hudson Institute, 90
Hugo Chavez, 208
Hugo Chávez, 50, 231

I.F. Stone, 128

ILWU, 261, 263
IMF, 144, 170, 220, 222, 230, 237
India, 38, 83, 85, 127, 132, 140, 150, 169, 170, 175, 177, 180, 217, 223, 243, 245, 281
Indonesia, 132, 140, 167, 169, 172, 175, 178, 206, 245
Inflation, 176
Inflation Reduction Act, 176
Innovation and Competition Act, 134
International Action Center, xliii, 42, 94
International Monetary Fund, 144, 169, 230, 245
International Uyghur Human Rights and Democracy Foundation, 139
Iran, 39, 44, 67, 83, 169, 185, 188, 212, 217, 223, 239, 244, 264, 281
Iraq, xi, xlv, xlvi, 35, 44, 50, 60, 64, 67, 75, 76, 81, 87, 94, 96, 98, 115, 121, 150, 180, 188, 214, 223, 231, 239, 251, 252, 264, 273, 292
Iraq Veterans Against the War, 252
Ireland, 133, 235
Islam, 140
Italy, 80, 114, 132, 169, 189, 196, 220

Jackson State, 121, 258
Jacques Baud, 69, 71, 73, 75
Jakarta, 50, 172, 175, 207
Jamestown Foundation, 139
Jamie Dimon, 222
Janet Yellen, 170, 180

Japan, v, xliii, xlvii, 111, 126, 128, 132, 150, 159, 169, 170, 173, 210, 213
Jean-Bertrand Aristide, 242
Jeffrey Mackler, 42
Jeffrey Sachs, l, 106, 156, 186, 194, 201, 203, 216
Jens Plötner, 80
JFK, 206, 213, 228
Jill Stein, 95, 96
João Goulart, 206
Joe Lombardo, 68
John Foster Dulles, 128, 210
John Kiriakou, 204
John Mearsheimer, 37, 41, 63
John Parker, xlii
Jonathan Hutto, 250
Joy Damiani, 251
Juan Guaidó, 219
Julian Assange, xlv, 75, 205, 255, 273
Julie Tang, 110, 129, 135, 148

Kashgar, 141
Katherine Graham, 211
Kazakhstan, 137, 140
Kennedy, 206, 213
Kenneth Hammond, 139
Kent State, 121, 258
Kenya, 47, 142
Kevin Tillman, 254
Kherson, 47
Kissinger, 218, 220, 230
Korea, xlvii, 113, 121, 128, 132, 164, 169, 172, 175, 239, 280
Kramatorsk, 71, 73

Kristalina Georgieva, 222
Kuomintang, 111, 128, 210
Kusturica, 61
Kwame Nkrumah, 208

Labor Against the War, 262
La France Insoumise, 113
LA Progressive, xii, 227, 291
Latin America, xlii, 38, 49, 175, 176, . 208, 211, 218, 236, 244, 264, 286
Laurent-Désiré Kabila, 208
Lavrov, 40, 46, 122, 171, 188
Left Party, 195, 197
Le Monde, 83
LGBTQ, 262
Liberal Democratic Party, 213
Liberia, 142, 239
Libya, 36, 44, 60, 63, 67, 81, 87, 94, 142, 219, 223, 239
Lisa Kenna, 287
Liz Theoharis, 105, 108
Liz Truss, 113
Lloyd Austin, 52, 101
Luc Mélanchon, 113
Lugansk, 45, 54

Macky Sall, 46
Macron, 80, 113, 132, 174, 181, 185, 196
Madrid, 80, 81, 89
Malaysia, 140
Mali, 142, 239
Manolo de Los Santos, 94, 102
Margaret Flowers, 68

Margaret Kimberley, xlviii, 36, 76, 199
Margaret Thatcher, 218
Mario Draghi, 196
Mariupol, 70
Marshall Plan, 213
Martha Harnecker, 237
Martin Luther King, xlii, 94, 98, 104, 196, 259
Max Parry, 75
Maxwell Taylor, 206
Medicare for All, 264
Michael Hudson, xi, 39, 44, 63, 195, 216, 280
Michael Pompeo, 75, 90, 270
Middle East, xlii, 49, 67, 85, 94
Milton Friedman, 218, 230
Minneapolis Anti-War Committee, 115
Minsk II, xli, l, 56, 96, 100, 182
Morales, 50, 161, 231
Moreno, 50, 231
Mozambique, 208, 263
Muammar Gaddafi, 87, 219
Multipolarista, 67, 83, 101, 169
Munich, xli, 179, 180, 201

Nancy Pelosi, 112
National Endowment for Democracy, 69, 135, 150, 210
National Security Act of 1947, 209
NATO, iv, xxiv, xli, xlix, 36, 74, 78, 93, 97, 111, 113, 115, 121, 131, 175, 179, 181, 185, 194, 196, 198, 213, 217, 220, 223, 242, 243, 280, 281

NED, 135, 138, 210
Negotiations, 47
Nelson Mandela, 264
Neoliberalism, xiv, 217, 227, 230
New Cold War, iv, 221, 285
New York Times, xlviii, 40, 45, 54, 56, 67, 83, 120, 138, 171, 176, 197, 264
New Zealand, 171
NICA, 241
Nicholas Davies, xlvii, 40, 100
Nicolas Maduro, 208
Nightingale, 213
Nixon, xliv, 121, 127, 129, 141, 148, 212, 218, 230, 260, 262
Noam Chomsky, 75, 95, 138
Non-Aligned Movement, 175, 286
Nord Stream, 56, 73, 97, 100, 177, 186, 194, 198
Norman Goda, 68
North Korea, 113, 115, 128
Nuremberg, 49, 85, 99, 240

Occupy Wall Street, 109, 234, 236
Odessa, 46, 55, 69, 70
Okinawa, xlvi, 112, 159, 160, 173
Olaf Scholz, 73, 80, 173, 185, 194
Oliver Stone, 203, 209
Operation Defender Europe, xxiv, 53
Operation Gladio, 213
Opium War, 127, 206
Organisation of Islamic Cooperation, 140
Organization for Security and Cooperation in Europe, 49

Organization of Ukrainian Nationalists, 68

Pakistan, 38, 64, 83, 137, 140
Palestine, 115, 184, 239
Paraguay, 50, 207, 231, 239
Party for Socialism and Liberation, 116
PATCO, 230
Paths of Dissent, 249
Peace Summit, 80, 89
Pedro Castillo, 286
Pentagon Papers, xlii, 129
Pepe Escobar, 187
Peter Kuznick, 203, 209
Philippines, 64, 132, 163, 164
Phyllis Bennis, 105
Pinochet, 218, 230
Pivot to Asia, 114
Pivot To Peace, iv, xiii, 110, 114, 130
PLO, 263
Poland, xlvi, xlix, 38, 59, 61, 80, 220
Poor People's Moral March, 103
Popular Resistance, 42, 94
Portugal, 79, 142, 291
Power Shift Africa, 177
Pramila Jayapal, xlv
President Johnson, 206
PR Network, 60
Propaganda, xiii
Putin price hikes, xlviii, 67

Qin Gang, 183

Radhika Desai, iii, xi, 284

RAND Corporation, 199
Real Path to Peace, xiii, 93
Reconstruction, 103, 104, 107, 109
RENACER, 241
Responsible Statecraft, xlvii, 196
Richard Breitman, 68
Richard Helms, 212, 260
Riverside Church, xliv, 282
Robert Kagan, 200
Robert McNamara, 121, 206
Robert Sirvent, 202
Rockefeller Foundation, 208
Romania, xlvi, xlix, 80
Ronald Reagan, xlv, 173, 217, 228, 262
ROTC, 259
Russia, iii, xi, xxiv, xli, 36, 38, 112, 115, 122, 132, 140, 165, 168, 194, 217, 220, 225, 238, 271, 280, 281, 284, 287

Saara Kuugongelwa-Amadhila, 181
Saddam Hussein, 87, 121
Safari Club, 212, 213
Salvador Allende, 207, 218, 230
Samora Machel, 208
Sanctions, xiv, 38, 65, 94, 138, 185, 238
Sanctions Kill, 94, 239
Sandinista, 263, 291
Sara Flounders, xi, xliii, 242
Saudi Arabia, 169, 212, 244
Scott Ritter, xi, 45, 48, 68, 75
SDS, 258, 259
SEATO, 171

Security Council, xli, 41, 56, 60, 73, 182, 186, 209, 242
Serbia, 60, 239
Sergei Ryabkov, 52, 56, 197
Sevim Dagdelen, 195
Shah, 212, 219
Shanghai Cooperation Organization, 223, 244
Slobodan Milošević, 87
SNCC, 258, 259, 260
Somalia, 50, 64, 115, 150, 239
South Africa, 63, 83, 85, 142, 144, 169, 208, 212, 241, 263
Southeast Asia Treaty Organization, 171
South Korea, v, xlvi, 113, 150, 159, 170, 171
Spain, 78, 82, 235
SPIEF, 83, 85
Stanleyville, 207
Stepan Bandera, 68
Stephen Cohen, 54
St. Petersburg International Economic Forum, 83
Struggle/La Lucha, 116
Sufism, 140
Sweden, 79, 89, 133
SWIFT, 38, 225, 243
Syria, 36, 43, 50, 63, 67, 94, 98, 115, 121, 150, 188, 213, 223

Taiwan, 110, 119, 125, 141, 148, 160, 168, 171, 175, 178, 183, 210, 242
Taiwan Labor Party, 111
Taiwan Policy Act, 110

Taiwan Straits, 120, 141, 175

Tax Reform Act, 228

Telford Taylor, 49, 85, 99

THAAD, 113

Thailand, 132, 140, 210

The Destiny of Civilization, 216

The Economist, 142

The Nation, 54, 68

The Untold History of the United States, 203, 209

Third World War, 243

Through Pluripolarity Toward Socialism, 285

Tibet, 127, 141, 210

Timber Sycamore, 214

TIP, 140

Truman, 128, 209, 228

Trump, 90, 98, 121, 141, 148, 210, 219, 228

Tsai Ing-wen, 112

Turkey, 46, 53, 79, 137, 170, 239

Turkistan Islamic Party, 140

UAW, 261

UE, 261

UK, 60, 73, 80, 83, 96, 113, 126, 218, 220

Ukraine, iv, xi, xiii, xxiv, xli, xliii, 36, 73, 93, 95, 170, 179, 193, 213, 217, 220, 222, 271, 280, 284

UN, xi, xli, xlvii, l, 38, 41, 43, 46, 49, 56, 60, 68, 73, 81, 85, 121, 140, 146, 149, 151, 156, 164, 175, 181, 184, 186, 203, 206, 240, 242

UNAC, xi, xliii, 42, 68

United Kingdom, 80, 150, 169

United National Antiwar Coalition, xi, xliii, 42, 94, 116

Ursula von der Leyen, 122

Uruguay, 207, 231

Urumqi, 141

USAID, 144, 170, 210

USAUK, 126

U.S. Defense Strategy, 168

U.S. Indo-Pacific Command, 126

U.S. Peace Council, xxiv, 42, 53, 94, 199

USSR, xliv, 60, 86, 94, 99, 128, 209, 230, 280

U.S. State Department, 119

U.S. war crimes, xlii, 254

U.S. war in Vietnam, xlii

Uyghur American Association, 139

Venezuela, 39, 44, 50, 94, 115, 184, 188, 219, 236, 239, 241, 264

Veterans For Peace, xi, 42, 112, 116, 162, 214, 254, 291

Victoria Nuland, xlvi, 54, 69, 76, 100, 199, 200

Vietnam, iv, xlii, xlv, xlvi, xlix, 66, 75, 83, 96, 98, 120, 171, 206, 210, 228, 250, 258, 262, 280, 291

Vincent Bevins, 50, 175, 207

Vincent Emanuele, 252

VJ Prashad, 95

Vladimir Putin, 46, 57, 84, 87, 121, 198, 226

Wall Street Journal, 56, 185
Wang Wenbin, 63, 120
Wang Wulan, 111
Wang Yi, xli, 41, 143, 181, 182
War in Ukraine: Making Sense of a Senseless Conflict, 100
War on Terror, iii, 249
Washington, xlii, 48, 52, 57, 59, 79, 82, 90, 95, 103, 110, 116, 120, 124, 126, 129, 134, 139, 146, 155, 185, 188, 196, 198, 200, 211, 216, 218, 220, 237, 243, 250, 259, 263, 280, 282
Washington Post, 59, 103, 126, 146, 155, 185, 211
Weapons of Mass Destruction, 75
Wei Yu, 111
Wendy Sherman, 52
Western Europe, 50, 67, 74, 80, 141, 222
White Helmets, 214
White House, xlv, 40, 119, 124, 212, 260
William Barber, 104
William Burns, 60
William Casey, 139

Workers Assembly Against Racism, 116
Workers World Party, 116
Working Class Union, 257
World Bank, 140, 144, 220, 223, 245
World Food Programme, 46, 147
World Uyghur Congress, 139
World War III, xlii, 38, 119, 199, 238

Xi Jinping, 149, 167, 172, 180, 182, 225
Xinhua, 61, 174
Xinjiang, 127, 137, 156, 170, 210

Yemen, 49, 64, 239
Yugoslavia, xliv, 60, 81, 87, 94, 121, 175, 280

Zaporizhzhia, 47
Zelensky, xli, xlviii, 38, 40, 48, 52, 79, 81, 83, 101, 185
Zhou Enlai, 175, 208
Zhun Xu, 138
Zimbabwe, 94, 188, 239, 241
Zoran Milanovic, 194

ENDNOTES

Notes to Preface and Introduction (pp. xxi-li)

1 "US campaign behind the turmoil in Kiev," Ian Traynor, *The Guardian,* 25 Nov. 2004, https://www.theguardian.com/world/2004/nov/26/ukraine.usa.

2 "Victoria Nuland," *Wikipedia,* cited from DeBenedictis, Kent (2022), *Russian 'Hybrid Warfare' and the Annexation of Crimea.* Bloomsbury Publishing. pp. 40–41.

3 U.S. Peace Council, 3 Jan 2022, "Escalating Crisis in Ukraine..." https://uspeacecouncil.org/the-escalating-crisis-in-ukraine-poses-an-imminent-threat-to-world-peace/

4 https://twitter.com/jeremyscahill/status/1737519301454704730

5 *Electronic Intifada,* 5 Dec 2023, "We blew up Israeli houses on 7 October, says Israeli colonel," https://electronicintifada.net/blogs/asa-winstanley/we-blew-is-raeli-houses-7-october-says-israeli-colonel

6 *Wikipedia,* "Bombing of North Korea," https://en.wikipedia.org/wiki/Bombing_of_North_Korea#cite_note-Vick2017-25

7 *Time Web Archive,* "Trump Threatens North Korea," https://web.archive.org/web/20170921032147/https:/time.com/4947990/trump-threatens-north-korea-totally-destroy/

8 https://en.wikipedia.org/wiki/The_Geographical_Pivot_of_History

9 *Al Jazeera,* 19 Dec 2023, "Coups, climate and cost of living: Key issues that shaped 2023 in Africa," https://www.aljazeera.com/news/2023/12/19/coups-climate-and-cost-of-living-key-issues-that-shaped-2023-in-africa

10 *New York Times,* 20 Dec 2023, "Amid Gaza War and Red Sea Attacks, Yemen's Houthis Refuse to Back Down," https://www.nytimes.com/2023/12/20/world/middleeast/israel-hamas-war-yemen-houthis.html?searchResultPosition=1

[11] *Palestine Chronicle,* 20 Dec 2023, https://www.palestinechronicle.com/in-response-to-war-on-gaza-malaysia-bans-israel-flagged-ships-from-its-ports/

[12] *NY Times,* 21 Dec 2023, "U.S. Says It's Ready to Back U.N. Resolution to Allow More Aid Into Gaza," https://www.nytimes.com/2023/12/21/world/middleeast/israel-gaza-un-resolution.html?searchResultPosition=1

[13] *NY Times,* 19 Dec 2023, "Poll Finds Wide Disapproval of Biden on Gaza," https://www.nytimes.com/2023/12/19/us/politics/biden-israel-gaza-poll.html

[14] Kaligny, Khaled, "A Palestinian Revival," *Foreign Affairs, 18 Dec 2023,* https://www.foreignaffairs.com/united-states/palestinian-revival?utm_medium=newsletters&utm_source=fatoday&utm_campaign=A%20Palestinian%20Revival&utm_content=20231218&utm_term=FA%20Today%20-%20112017#author-info

[15] White House Briefing Room, 6 Dec 2023, https://www.whitehouse.gov/briefing-room/speeches-remarks/2023/12/06/remarks-by-president-biden-urging-congress-to-pass-his-national-security-supplemental-request-including-funding-to-support-ukraine/

[16] *Poynter Fact Checking,* "What the White House has said…" https://www.poynter.org/fact-checking/2023/what-the-white-house-has-said-about-sending-troops-to-fight-russia/

[17] *LA Progressive,* 12 Dec 2023, "What Does 'Strategic Defeat Look Like?" https://www.laprogressive.com/war-and-peace/genocidal-israeli-assault

[18] *NY Times,* 27 Dec 2023, "Skepticism Grows About Israel's Ability to Dismantle Hamas," https://www.nytimes.com/2023/12/27/world/middleeast/israel-hamas-war-military.html?searchResultPosition=1

[19] Hedges, Chris, "The Death of Israel," *ScheerPost,* 17 Dec 2023, https://scheerpost.com/2023/12/17/chris-hedges-the-death-of-israel/

[20] U.S. Peace Council, "Report Back by the USPC Delegation to China, https://www.youtube.com/watch?v=sHArPBDbk34

[21] *NBC News,* 27 Jan 2023, "Air Force general predicts war with China in 2025," https://www.nbcnews.com/politics/national-security/us-air-force-general-predicts-war-china-2025-memo-rcna67967

[22] Reed, John, "Surrounded: How the U.S. Is Encircling China with Military Bases," *Foreign Policy,* 20 Aug 2013, https://foreignpolicy.com/2013/08/20/surrounded-how-the-u-s-is-encircling-china-with-military-bases/

23 *NY Times,* 18 Aug 2023, "Looming Over a New Security Pact: China, North Korea and Donald Trump," https://www.nytimes.com/2023/08/18/us/politics/biden-japan-south-korea-summit.html

24 China Ministry of Foreign Affairs, 26 Sept 2023, "A Global Community of Shared Future," https://www.mfa.gov.cn/eng/zxxx_662805/202309/t20230926_11150122.html

25 Tobin, Daniel, "How Xi Jinping's 'New Era' Should have Ended U.S. Debate on Beijing's Ambitions," 8 May 2020, https://www.csis.org/analysis/how-xi-jinpings-new-era-should-have-ended-us-debate-beijings-ambitions

26 *Wikipedia,* "Full-spectrum dominance," https://en.wikipedia.org/wiki/Full-spectrum_dominance

27 Rand Corporation, "War with China, Thinking Through the Unthinkable," https://www.rand.org/pubs/research_reports/RR1140.html

28 *Responsible Statecraft,* 2 Sept 2022, "Diplomacy Watch: Did Boris Johnson help stop a peace deal in Ukraine?" responsiblestatecraft.org/2022/09/02/diplomacy-watch-why-did-the-west-stop-a-peace-deal-in-ukraine/

29 "Wang Yi Attends 59th Munich Security Conference and Delivers a Keynote Speech," *Embassy of the PRC in the... Philippines,* 18 Feb 2023, http://ph.china-embassy.gov.cn/eng/chinew/202302/t20230220_11027395.htm#:~:text=Wang%20Yi%20said%20that%20making,the%20advance%20of%20the%20times.

30 2022 Buffalo Shooting: https://en.wikipedia.org/wiki/2022_Buffalo_shooting

31 Col. Robert Heinl, "Collapse of Armed Forces, 1971": https://alphahistory.com/vietnamwar/robert-heinl-collapse-armed-forces-1971/

32 NY Times, Jan. 3, 2023: *In Romania, U.S. Troops Train Close to Russia's War:* https://www.nytimes.com/2023/01/03/world/europe/us-troops-romania-russia-ukraine-war.html

33 Wisconsin Historical Society GI Press Collection, 1964-1977: https://content.wisconsinhistory.org/digital/collection/p15932coll8/id/95396/

34 Sara Flounders, "Biden Administration Tramples on Japan's Post-WWII Pacifist Constitution by Pushing Country's Rearmament," *Covert Action Magazine,* Jan. 9, 2023, https://covertactionmagazine.com/2023/01/09/biden-administration-tramples-on-japans-post-world-war-ii-pacifist-constitution-by-pushing-countrys-rearmament/

[35] "Sanctuary Movement Supports Surge in GI Resistance," Appendix 2 in *My Whirlwind Lives,* by Dee Knight, Guernica Editions, 2022.

[36] Benjamin and Davies, *LA Progressive,* Oct. 10, 2022: www.laprogressive.com/war-and-peace/chorus-for-peace-in-ukraine-growing

[37] UNPAS, UN Sec-Gen Calls for Peace in Ukraine: https://www.unpas-eu.org/unpas/un-secretary-general-ant%C3%B3nio-guterres-calls-for-peace-on-the-situation-in-ukraine

[38] *UPI*, Oct. 10, 2022: https://www.upi.com/Top_News/World-News/2022/10/02/pope-francis-calls-zelensky-to-be-open-serious-proposals-peace-ukraine-russia/4121664746795/

[39] *Common Dreams,* Sept. 29, 2022: www.commondreams.org/views/2022/09/29/end-war-ukraine-say-66-nations-un-general-assembly

[40] Jack Matlock, "Why the US must press for a ceasefire in Ukraine," *Responsible Statecraft,* 17 Oct 2022, https://responsiblestatecraft.org/2022/10/17/on-ukraine-the-us-is-on-the-hook-to-find-a-way-out/

[41] Margaret Kimberley, *Black Agenda Report,* 20 Apr 2022: https://www.blackagendareport.com/ukraine-crisis-cant-save-biden

[42] Pres. Biden, "What America Will and Will Not Do in Ukraine," *NY Times*, 5 Oct 2022, https://www.nytimes.com/2022/05/31/opinion/biden-ukraine-strategy.html

[43] Douglas MacGregor, *The American Conservative, 20 Dec 2022,* "Washington Is Prolonging Ukraine's Suffering."

[44] *The Economist,* 15 Dec 2022, "An Interview with Gen. Valery Zaluzhny," https://www.economist.com/zaluzhny-transcript

[45] MacGregor, *Op. Cit.*

[46] V. Pietromarchi, *Al Jazeera,* 4 Nov 2022, "As inflation rises, could European support for Ukraine Wobble," https://www.aljazeera.com/news/2022/11/4/hoas-costs-of-living-spike-is-western-stand-on-ukraine-wobbling

[47] Daniel Davis, *1945,* "America Can't Give Ukraine So Many Weapons A Nuclear War Starts," https://www.19fortyfive.com/2022/12/america-cant-give-ukraine-so-many-weapons-a-nuclear-war-starts/

[48] Daniel Conrad, *Courthouse News Service, 15 March 2022,* "Americans Mixed in Views on Russia-Ukraine conflict," https://www.courthousenews.com/americans-enjoy-largely-bipartisan-views-on-russia-ukrainian-war-per-new-pew-survey/

49 *NY Times*, 18 Dec 2022, "Military Spending Surges, Creating Boom for Arms Makers": https://www.nytimes.com/2022/12/18/us/politics/defense-contractors-ukraine-russia.html

50 Jeffrey Sachs, "The West's False Narrative about Russia and China," 22 Aug 2022, www.jeffsachs.org/newspaper-articles/h29g9k7l7fymxp39yhzwxc5f72ancr

Notes to Chapter 1 (pp. 3-12)

1 *Reuters,* 15 Nov 2023, "US public support for Israel drops, majority backs a ceasefire," https://www.reuters.com/world/us-public-support-israel-drops-majority-backs-ceasefire-reutersipsos-2023-11-15/

2 Nassar, Maha, "From the river to the sea," *The Conversation,* 16 Nov 2023, https://theconversation.com/from-the-river-to-the-sea-a-palestinian-historian-explores-the-meaning-and-intent-of-scrutinized-slogan-217491

3 *Petition for the Restoration of Historic Palestine,* https://docs.google.com/forms/d/e/1FAIpQLSdkYR4n_Izsx4QUxTUwbBurc-_p2tlk5uGDEYC-diO8F3mct6A/viewform

4 *South African History Online,* "UN and Apartheid Timeline 1946-1994," https://www.sahistory.org.za/article/united-nations-and-apartheid-timeline-1946-1994

5 *LA Progressive,* 24 Nov 2023, "What Europeans Taught Israel," by Tom Hall, https://www.laprogressive.com/the-middle-east/what-europeans-taught-israel

6 "Israel's One-State Reality," *Foreign Affairs,* 14 April 2023, https://www.foreignaffairs.com/middle-east/israel-palestine-one-state-solution

7 "There Will Be a One-State Solution, But What Kind of State Will It Be?" *Foreign Affairs,* 15 Oct 2019, https://www.foreignaffairs.com/articles/israel/2019-10-15/there-will-be-one-state-solution

8 *Defense for Children Int'l, et al, v. Joseph R. Biden, et al,* Motion for Preliminary Injunction, https://ccrjustice.org/sites/default/files/attach/2023/11/PI%20Motion_w.pdf

9 Cohn, Marjorie, "Palestinians File Emergency Motion to Block US Aid for Israel's Genocide in Gaza," *Truthout,* 17 Nov 2023, https://truthout.org/articles/palestinians-file-emergency-motion-to-block-us-aid-for-israels-genocide-in-gaza/

[10] UN General Assembly Resolution 260 A (III), 9 Dec 1948, "Convention on the Prevention and Punishment of the Crime of Genocide," https://www.un.org/en/genocideprevention/documents/atrocity-crimes/Doc.1_Convention%20on%20the%20Prevention%20and%20Punishment%20of%20the%20Crime%20of%20Genocide.pdf

[11] *18 U.S. Code § 1091 – Genocide,* Cornell Law School Legal Information Institute, https://www.law.cornell.edu/uscode/text/18/1091

[12] Defense for Children International–Palestine, https://www.dci-palestine.org/

[13] AL-Haq Defending Human Rights, https://www.alhaq.org/advocacy/22189.html

[14] *NY Times,* 15 Nov 2023, "'Erase Gaza': War Unleashes Incendiary Rhetoric in Israel," https://www.nytimes.com/2023/11/15/world/middleeast/israel-gaza-war-rhetoric.html

[15] *NY Times,* 23 Nov 2023, "Israel-Hamas War Cease-Fire Will Begin Friday," https://www.nytimes.com/live/2023/11/23/world/israel-hamas-gaza-hostage-war

[16] Palestine Info Center, 23 Nov 23, https://english.palinfo.com/news/2023/11/23/1-000-boats-to-leave-T-rkiye-for-Gaza-in-new-Freedom-Flotilla

[17] "A pause is just that – a pause. We demand a permanent ceasefire," ANSWER, https://www.answercoalition.org/a_pause_is_just_that_a_pause_we_demand_a_permanent_ceasefire

[18] "Ship believed to be Israel-bound leaves Tacoma port," *Seattle Times,* 6 Nov 2023, https://www.seattletimes.com/seattle-news/protesters-block-tacoma-port-to-halt-ship-believed-to-be-israel-bound/

[19] "Stand taller, shout louder…," *Electronic Intifada,* 23 Nov 23, https://electronicintifada.net/content/stand-taller-shout-louder-and-resist-campaign-silence-us/41586

[20] "Harvard billboard accusing students of antisemitism linked to right-wing funder," *The Guardian,* 16 Oct 23, https://www.theguardian.com/us-news/2023/oct/16/harvard-billboard-hamas-informing-america-foundation

[21] "Harvard for Hamas? Something is very twisted…" *USA Today,* 12 Oct 23, https://eu.usatoday.com/story/opinion/columnist/2023/10/12/hamas-attack-harvard-students-blame-israel/71152750007/

22 "Senate condemns student groups as backlash to pro-Palestinian speech grows," *The Intercept,* 27 Oct 23, https://theintercept.com/2023/10/27/palestine-israel-free-speech-retaliation-senate/

23 "Legislatioin targeting advocacy for Pelestinian rights," *Palestine Legal,* 29 Sep 23, https://legislation.palestinelegal.org/#states-map

24 "US professors suspended, probed over Gaza war comments," *Reuters,* 17 Nov 23, https://www.reuters.com/world/us/us-professors-suspended-probed-over-gaza-war-comments-2023-11-17/

25 Kirstein, Peter, "Steven Salaita, the Media, and the Struggle for Academic Freedom," https://www.aaup.org/article/steven-salaita-media-and-struggle-academic-freedom

26 *Democracy Now,* 27 Oct 23, "Palestine Legal Campus Censorship," https://www.democracynow.org/2023/10/27/ palestine_legal_campus_censorship_ryna_workman

27 *Democracy Now,* 14 June 2007, "Norman Finkelstein Denied Tenure," https://www.democracynow.org/2007/6/14/finkelstein_denied_tenure

Notes to Chapter 2 (pp. 13-23)

1 *NY Times,* 1 Dec 23, "Israel Resumes Offensive in Gaza Strip," https://www.nytimes.com/2023/12/01/world/middleeast/01gaza-israel-fighting-resumes.html?searchResultPosition=1

2 *NY Times,* 30 Nov 23, "Blinken Urges Israel to Take Concrete Steps to Aid Civilians," https://www.nytimes.com/2023/11/30/world/middleeast/israel-hamas-peace-process.html?searchResultPosition=1

3 *NY Times,* 2 Dec 23, "Israel Orders Evacuations Amid 'Intense' Attacks," https://www.nytimes.com/2023/12/02/world/middleeast/israel-gaza-evacuations-war.html?searchResultPosition=1

4 *NY Times,* 30 Nov 23, "Israel Knew Hamas's Attack Plan More Than a Year Ago," https://www.nytimes.com/2023/11/30/world/middleeast/israel-hamas-attack-intelligence.html?searchResultPosition=1

5 *NY Times,* 10 Oct 23, "How Israel's Feared Security Services Failed," https://www.nytimes.com/2023/10/10/world/middleeast/israel-gaza-security-failure.html

6 *Kan,* 28 Nov 23, "The Wall of Jericho: Hamas's plan to occupy settlements," https://www.kan.org.il/content/kan/kan-actual/p-591147/628830/

7 "A 'mass assassination factory': Inside Israel's calculated bombing," Yuval Abraham, *+972 Magazine,* 30 Nov 2023, https://www.972mag.com/mass-assassination-factory-israel-calculated-bombing-gaza/

8 "Get to know: power goals," *Israel Defense,* 26 Mar 19, https://www.israeldefense.co.il/node/37949

9 "Operation Al-Aqsa Flood Day 56: Truce ends," *Mondoweiss,* 1 Dec 23, https://mondoweiss.net/2023/12/operation-al-aqsa-flood-day-56-truce-ends-israel-kills-over-100-in-gaza/

10 *NY Times,* 29 Nov 23, "In the West Bank, Release of Prisoners Deepens Support for Hamas," https://www.nytimes.com/2023/11/29/world/middleeast/west-bank-hamas-prisoners.html?searchResultPosition=3

11 *ReliefWeb,* 30 Nov 23, "Call for Submissions on international crimes since 7 Oct 2023, https://reliefweb.int/report/occupied-palestinian-territory/call-submissions-international-crimes-7-october-2023-enarhe

12 Benjamin, Medea and Davies, Nicholas, "Israeli Wa ron Gaza Raising Regional Tensions for US," *Popular Resistance,* 1 Dec 23, https://popularresistance.org/israeli-war-on-gaza-raising-regional-tensions-for-us/

13 *Newsweek,* 15 Dec 23, "Iran-Backed Houthis Cut Israel Off from Critical Lifeline," https://www.newsweek.com/houthis-cut-israel-off-red-sea-gaza-war-1852969#:~:text=%22Our%20operation%20is%20specific%20against,Secretary%20Nasreddin%20Amer%20told%20Newsweek.

14 *The Guardian,* 30 Nov 23, "Spanish prime minister says he doubts Israel is respecting international law," https://www.theguardian.com/world/2023/nov/30/spain-pm-pedro-sanchez-israel-hamas-terror-attacks-gaza

15 *Human Rights Watch,* 16 Nov 23, "Belgium Overcomes EU Struggles to Send Strong Message on Gaza," https://www.hrw.org/news/2023/11/16/belgium-overcomes-eu-struggles-send-strong-message-gaza

16 *Human Rights Watch,* 21 Feb 22, "Europe: Ban Trade with Illegal Settlements," https://www.hrw.org/news/2022/02/21/europe-ban-trade-illegal-settlements

17 *Palestine Info Center,* 23 Nov 23, https://english.palinfo.com/news/2023/11/23/1-000-boats-to-leave-Turkiye-for-Gaza-in-new-Freedom-Flotilla

18 *N Mena,* 30 Nov 23, "China's UN call for end to Palestinian-Israeli conflict," https://www.thenationalnews.com/mena/palestine-israel/2023/11/30/chinas-un-call-for-end-to-palestinian-israeli-conflict-reflects-recent-diplomatic-success/

19 "Our People Cannot Afford for Us to Fail": Palestine Youth Movement," 30 Nov 23, https://therealnews.com/palestinian-youth-movement-gaza-truce-ceasefire-western-left-solidarity

20 Nassar, Maha, https://menas.arizona.edu/person/maha-nassar

21 "From the River to the Sea – a Palestinian historian explores the meaning," *The Conversation,* 16 Nov 23, https://theconversation.com/from-the-river-to-the-sea-a-palestinian-historian-explores-the-meaning-and-intent-of-scrutinized-slogan-217491

22 *ADL,* 26 Oct 23, "Allegation: 'From the River to the Sea Palestine Will be Free'," https://www.adl.org/resources/backgrounder/allegation-river-sea-palestine-will-be-free?gclid=Cj0KCQiAr8eqBhD3ARIsAIe-buNxvQjDx5nWGNcDrO9OE4lECB5 TruGtplZXCVhLsWVFqHWkTf_CqHgaAoBfEALw_wcB

23 "US House censures lone Palestinian-American lawmaker over Israeli comments," *Reuters,* 8 Nov 23, https://www.reuters.com/world/us/us-house-censures-lone-palestinian-american-lawmaker-over-israel-comments-2023-11-08/

Notes to Chapter 3 (pp. 24-32)

1 "Gaza: Ethnic Cleansing of Epic Proportions," *LA Progressive,* 29 Dec 23, https://www.laprogressive.com/the-middle-east/gaza-ethnic-cleansing

2 "Israel risks 'strategic defeat' if civilians aren't protected, Pentagon chief says," *The Hill,* 2 Dec 23, https://thehill.com/policy/defense/4339335-lloyd-austin-israel-risks-defeat-if-civilians-not-protected/#:~:text=Defense-,Israel%20risks%20'strategic%20defeat'%20if%20civilians%20aren',t%20protected%2C%20Pentagon%20chief%20says&text=Secretary%20of%20Defense%20Lloyd%20Austin,group%20Hamas%20in%20the%20region.

3 "Israel Could Lose," *CSIS,* 7 Nov 23, https://www.csis.org/analysis/israel-could-lose

4 "A Vietnam ten times more beautiful," *United World International,* 2 Sep 22, https://uwidata.com/26467-a-vietnam-ten-times-more-beautiful/

5 "Knee-Deep in the Big Muddy," *Swarthmore,* 17 Dec 2009, https://www. swarthmore.edu/feature-stories-archive-2008-2009/knee-deep-big-muddy

6 "Mutiny Brewing Inside State Dept Over Israel-Palestine Policy," 19 Oct 23, https://www.huffpost.com/entry/state-department-gaza_n_6531a23ae4b-0da897ab75ce4?b7p

7 *Politico,* "Hill Staff Ceasefire Open Letter," https://www.documentcloud.org/documents/24041700-hill-staff-ceasefire-open-letter

8 "US State Dept Official Resigns," *Common Dreams,* 19 Oct 23, https://www. commondreams.org/news/state-department-official-resigns

9 *The White House,* 18 Oct 23, https://www.whitehouse.gov/briefing-room/statements-releases/2023/10/18/readout-of-president-joseph-r-biden-jr-meeting-with-prime-minister-benjamin-netanyahu-of-israel-and-the-war-cabinet/

10 "800+ Legal Scholars Say Israel May Be Perpetrating 'Crime of Genocide' in Gaza," *Common Dreams,* 18 Oct 23, https://www.commondreams.org/news/legal-scholars-israel-genocide

11 *NY Times,* 8 Dec 23, "U.S. Vetoes Israel-Hamas Cease-Fire Resolution at UN SC," https://www.nytimes.com/2023/12/08/world/middleeast/israel-hamas-gaza-aid.html

12 *The Guardian,* 30 Nov 23, "Spanish prime minister says he doubts Israel is respecting international law," https://www.theguardian.com/world/2023/nov/30/spain-pm-pedro-sanchez-israel-hamas-terror-attacks-gaza

13 *Human Rights Watch,* 16 Nov 23, "Belgium Overcomes EU Struggles to Send Strong Message on Gaza," https://www.hrw.org/news/2023/11/16/belgium-overcomes-eu-struggles-send-strong-message-gaza

14 *NY Times,* 9 Dec 23, "Pressure Rising on U.S. After Vetoing U.N. Call for a Cease-Fire in Gaza," https://www.nytimes.com/2023/12/09/world/middleeast/us-cease-fire-gaza-criticism.html?searchResultPosition=1

15 *Quinnipiac Univ Poll,* 2 Nov 23, "84% of Voters Concerned The U.S. Will Be Drawn Into Military Conflict In The Middle East," https://poll.qu.edu/poll-release?releaseid=3882

16 "US public support for Israel drops; majority backs a ceasefire," *Reuters,* 15 Nov 23, https://www.reuters.com/world/us-public-support-israel-drops-majority-backs-ceasefire-reutersipsos-2023-11-15/

[17] *N Mena*, 30 Nov 23, "China's UN call for end to Palestinian-Israeli conflict," https://www.thenationalnews.com/mena/palestine-israel/2023/11/30/chinas-un-call-for-end-to-palestinian-israeli-conflict-reflects-recent-diplomatic-success/

[18] "What Vladimir Putin's visit to Saudi and UAE signals," *The Indian Express*, 9 Dec 23, https://indianexpress.com/article/explained/explained-global/what-putins-visit-to-saudi-uae-signals-9060419/

[19] "What Arab states can do to punish Israel," *The Cradle*, 30 Nov 23, https://new.thecradle.co/articles/what-arab-states-can-do-to-punish-israel

[20] *NY Times*, 30 Nov 23, "Israel Knew Hamas's Attack Plan More Than a Year Ago," https://www.nytimes.com/2023/11/30/world/middleeast/israel-hamas-attack-intelligence.html?searchResultPosition=1

[21] "Hundreds of thousands of Israelis flee their homes," *Vatican News, 27 Oct 23*, https://www.vaticannews.va/en/world/news/2023-10/israel-hamas-war-internally-displaced-persons-emergency-humanita.html

[22] "Biden lied about seeing photos of beheaded Israeli children," *Electronic Intitada*, 12 Oct 23, https://electronicintifada.net/blogs/ali-abunimah/biden-lied-about-seeing-photos-beheaded-israeli-children

[23] "Palestine's resistance has already won in Gaza," *Electronic Intitada*, 22 Nov 23, https://electronicintifada.net/content/palestines-resistance-has-already-won-gaza/41456

[24] *CNN*, 15 Oct 23, "US sending 2nd carrier strike group, fighter jets to region," https://edition.cnn.com/2023/10/14/middleeast/us-aircraft-carrier-eisenhower-israel-gaza-intl-hnk-ml/index.html

[25] *Time*, 6 Nov 23, "U.S. Announces Arrival of a Nuclear Submarine in the Middle East," https://time.com/6332014/middle-east-nuclear-submarine/

[26] *Palestine Info Service*, 23 Nov 23, https://english.palinfo.com/news/2023/11/23/1-000-boats-to-leave-T-rkiye-for-Gaza-in-new-Freedom-Flotilla

[27] "Pro-Palestinian Protesters Flood Wall Street," *TheMessenger News*, 8 Dec 23, https://themessenger.com/news/pro-palestinian-protesters-flood-wall-street-comcast-hq-art-basel-claiming-they-support-genocide

28 "Wall Street Analyst Apologizes to Jewish Community for Candalizing Hostage Posers," *TheMessenger News,* 18 Nov 23, https://themessenger.com/news/fired-wall-street-analyst-apologizes-jewish-community-vandalizing-hamas-hostage-posters

29 "Hundreds of pro-Palestinian demonstrators gather outside Biden fundraiser," *Los Angeles Times,* 8 Dec 23, https://www.latimes.com/california/story/2023-12-08/biden-los-angeles-fundraising-visit-protests

Notes to Chapter 4 (pp. 35-44)

1 Wikipedia, "Gulf War" https://en.wikipedia.org/wiki/Gulf_War#Iraqi

2 Watson Institute of International and Public Affairs, Brown Univ., *Costs of War:* https://watson.brown.edu/costsofwar/figures/2021/BudgetaryCosts

3 *Costs of War:* elens.brown.edu/costsofwar/figures/2021/WarDeathToll

4 Margaret Kimberley, "Does Ukraine Expose White Supremacist Foreign Policy?" *LA Progressive,* 4 March 2022, https://www.laprogressive.com/white-supremacist-foreign-policy/

5 Isaac Chotiner, "Why John Mearsheimer Blames the U.S. for the Crisis in Ukraine," *New Yorker,* 1 March 2022: https://www.newyorker.com/news/q-and-a/why-john-mearsheimer-blames-the-us-for-the-crisis-in-ukraine

6 *BBC News,* 28 Feb 2022, "Ukraine Invasion: Misleading Claims Continue to Go Viral": https://www.bbc.com/news/60554910

7 *UN News,* 17 Feb 2022, "Ukraine Crisis: UN Political Affairs Chief calls for 'maximum restraint'": https://news.un.org/en/story/2022/02/1112202

8 Michael Hudson, "America's real adversaries are its European and other allies," *The Saker,* 8 Feb 2022, https://thesaker.is/elensky-real-adversaries-are-its-european-and-other-allies-the-u-s-aim-is-to-keep-them-from-trading-with-china-and-russia/

9 Catherine Belton, *Reuters,* 7 March 2022 "Russia will stop 'in a moment' if Ukraine meets terms."

10 NY Times, 10 March 2022, "What Happened on Day 15 of Russia's Invasion of Ukraine," https://www.nytimes.com/live/2022/03/10/world/elensk-russia-war#talks-fail-to-stop-the-fighting-with-russias-foreign-minister-saying-a-ceasefire-was-never-up-for-discussion

[11] Media Benjamin and Nicholas Davies, *LA Progressive,* 9 March 2022, "How U.S. Empowered Neo-Nazis in Ukraine."

[12] *Moon of Alabama,* 5 March 2022, "Zelensky and the Fascists: 'He Will Hang From Some Tree…'," www.moonofalabama.org/2022/03/elensky-and-the-fascists-he-will-hang-on-some-tree-on-khreshchatyk.html?cid=6a00d-8341c640e53ef0282e147b3c5200b

[13] President of Ukraine Official Website, 26 April 2021, "President of Ukraine calls for revamp of peace process to end Donbas war": https://www.president.gov.ua/en/news/volodimir-zelenskij-zaklikaye-do-modernizaciyi-ta-osuchas-nen-68153

[14] Isaac Chotiner, *New Yorker,* 1 March 2022, "Why John Mearsheimer Blames the U.S. for the Crisis in Ukraine": https://www.newyorker.com/news/q-and-a/why-john-mearsheimer-blames-the-us-for-the-crisis-in-ukraine

[15] *Global Times,* 26 April 2023, "Xi, Zelensky talk on ties, Ukraine crisis on phone," https://www.globaltimes.cn/page/202304/1289838.shtml

[16] Jeff Mackler, *LA Progressive,* 10 March 2022, "Crisis in Ukraine: Major Challenge to the US Antiwar Movement": https://www.laprogressive.com/crisis-in-ukraine/

Notes to Chapter 5 (pp. 45-51)

[1] Scott Ritter, *Consortium News,* 30 May 2022, "Phase Three in Ukraine:" https://consortiumnews.com/2022/05/30/scott-ritter-phase-three-in-ukraine/

[2] Joe Biden, *NY Times,* 31 May 2022, "What America Will and Will Not Do in Ukraine," https://www.nytimes.com/2022/05/31/opinion/biden-ukraine-strate-gy.html

[3] *France 24,* 3 June 2022, "African Union head 'reassured' after talks with Putin on food shortages": https://www.france24.com/en/loomb/20220603-afri-can-union-head-sall-reassured-after-talks-with-putin-on-food-shortages-amid-ukraine-conflict

[4] NY Times, 1 June 2022, "As Food Shortages Loom, a Race to Free Ukraine's Stranded Grain."

[5] World Food Programme, 6 May 2022, "War in Ukraine: WFP calls for ports to reopen": https://www.wfp.org/stories/war-ukraine-wfp-calls-ports-reopen-world-faces-deepening-hunger-crisis

[6] President of Russia website, 3 June 2022, "Interview with Rossiya TV": http://en.kremlin.ru/events/president/news/68571

[7] Dee Knight, "Joe Biden's Saber Rattling…" *Covert Action Mag.,* 8 June 2022 https://covertactionmagazine.com/2022/06/08/joe-bidens-saber-rattling-threatens-world-war-iii-with-china-and-russia/#post-39427-footnote-0

[8] NY Times, 5 June 2022, "Russia Seeks Buyers for Plundered Ukraine Grain, U.S. Warns."

[9] Aaron Smith, *Ag Data News,* 9 March 2022, "We're Not Facing a Global Food Crisis": https://asmith.ucdavis.edu/news/loomb-ukraine

[10] Scott Ritter, *Consortium News,* 30 May 2022, "Phase Three in Ukraine": https://consortiumnews.com/2022/05/30/scott-ritter-phase-three-in-ukraine/

[11] Ellen Taylor, *CounterPunch,* 3 June 2022, "War Crimes, From Nuremberg to Ukraine": https://www.counterpunch.org/2022/06/03/war-crimes-from-nuremberg-to-ukraine/

[12] Dee Knight, *LA Progressive,* 3 June 2022, "Official 'Americas Summit' Sags While People's Summit Surges": https://www.laprogressive.com/latin-america-2/loomber-summit

[13] Dee Knight, "'Summit for Democracy': The Peak of Hypocrisy": www.laprogressive.com/election-reform-campaigns/summit-for-democracy

[14] *AP News,* 20 May 2022, "Biden's approval rating drops to lowest of presidency": https://apnews.com/article/biden-approval-rating-drops-ap-norc-poll-d41bce85e1b062b588a32908b2affa65

[15] *Bloomberg Opinion,* 17 May 2022, "Voters Aren't Worried About Covid. Politicians Should Be": https://www.bloomberg.com/opinion/articles/2022-05-17/covid-and-public-opinion-voters-don-t-fear-the-virus-but-politicians-should

Notes to Chapter 6 (pp. 52-57)

[1] Ray McGovern, antiwar.com, 9 June 2021, "Biden-Putin Summit: Boon or Bust?: https://original.antiwar.com/mcgovern/2021/06/08/biden-putin-summit-boon-or-bust/

[2] Russel Bentley, *Covert Action Magazine,* 11 Jan 2022, "Expect Escalation of Conflict in Donbass and Ukraine Soon…": https://covertactionmagazine.com/2022/01/11/expect-escalation-of-conflict-in-donbass-and-ukraine-soon-says-foreign-correspondent-embedded-in-ukrainian-anti-fascist-brigade/

3 *Defense World,* 3 May 2023, www.defenseworld.net/2023/03/03/news-co-nas-daqnws-shares-sold-by-metlife-investment-management-llc.html#.YdRR5ll-RVhE

4 U.S. Peace Council, 3 Jan 2022, "Escalating Crisis in Ukraine…" https://uspeacecouncil.org/the-escalating-crisis-in-ukraine-poses-an-imminent-threat-to-world-peace/

5 U.S. Senate Committee on Foreign Relations, 7 Dec 2021, Victoria Nuland, "Update on U.S.-Russia Policy": https://www.foreign.senate.gov/imo/media/doc/120721_Nuland_Testimony1.pdf?link_id=0&can_id=33619bca17b-c590e1d6cd0a34928d111&source=email-us-peace-council-statement-no-cold-war-with-china-no-aukus-pact&email_referrer=email_1398472&email_sub-ject=us-peace-council-statement-the-escalating-crisis-in-ukraine-poses-an-im-minent-threat-to-world-peace

6 NY Times, 5 Jan 2022, "Russia Allied Forces to Intervene as Unrest Sweeps Kazakhstan."

7 Steven Cohen, *The Nation,* 2 May 2018, "America's Collusion with Neo-Nazis": https://www.thenation.com/article/archive/americas-collusion-with-neo-Nazis/

8 Lev Golinkin, *The Hill,* 9 Nov 2017, "The Reality of Neo-Nazis in Ukraine…": https://thehill.com/opinion/international/359609-the-reality-of-neo-Nazis-in-the-ukraine-is-far-from-kremlin-propaganda

9 NY Times, 1 April 2017, Opinion, "What Ukraine's Jews Fear": http://nytimes.com/2017/04/1/opinion/what-ukraines-jews-fear.html

10 *New Atlanticist,* 13 June 2014, "'Donbas, the Heart of Russia'": https://www.atlanticcouncil.org/blogs/new-atlanticist/direct-translation-donbas-the-heart-of-russia/

11 Anatole Lieven, *The Nation,* 15 Nov 2021, "Ukraine: The Most Dangerous Problem in the World": https://www.thenation.com/article/world/ukraine-don-bas-russia-conflict/

12 *Wall Street Journal,* 17 Dec 2021, "Russia Lays Out Security Guarantees It Wants from U.S., Europe" https://www.wsj.com/articles/russia-lays-out-secu-rity-guarantees-it-wants-from-u-s-europe-11639753002?mod=article_inline

13 *NY Times,* 16 Dec 2021, "Biden's Stand on Ukraine…" https://www.nytimes.com/2021/12/16/us/politics/biden-russia-ukraine.html?searchResultPosition=1

[14] *Financial Times,* 9 Dec 2021. "Why Nord Stream 2 is at heart of US warnings to Putin over Ukraine" https://www.ft.com/content/650963c2-3e45-4ad0-bc87-0f0b59851a5a

[15] *NY Times,* 18 Feb 2021, *"Biden's Plan to Link Arms With Europe Against Russia and China":* https://www.nytimes.com/2021/02/18/us/politics/biden-europe-russia-china.html

Notes to Chapter 7 (pp. 58-65)

[1] *Washington Post,* 26 March 2022, "How Biden sparked a global uproar with nine ad-libbed words…" www.washingtonpost.com/politics/2022/03/26/biden-putin-regime-change/

[2] *Barrons/AFP News,* 24 March 2022 "Biden's Brussels Triple Summit Big on Unity, Short on Tougher Measures": https://www.barrons.com/news/biden-s-brussels-triple-summit-big-on-unity-short-on-tougher-measures-01648173308?tesla=y

[3] *Washington Post,* 26 March 2022, "How Biden sparked a global uproar…" www.washingtonpost.com/politics/2022/03/26/biden-putin-regime-change/

[4] *Insider,* 10 March 2022, "CIA Director Bill Burns says Putin 'is losing' the information war over Ukraine": https://www.businessinsider.com/cia-director-says-putin-is-losing-information-war-over-ukraine-2022-3

[5] Dan Cohen, *Misión Verdad,* "The vast international network in charge of Ukrainian war propaganda": https://misionverdad.com/traducciones/la-vasta-red-internacional-cargo-de-la-propaganda-de-guerra-ucraniana

[6] The PR Network, https://www.thepr.network/

[7] United Nations *Ukraine:* https://ukraine.un.org/sites/default/files/2022-02/Conflict-related%20civilian%20casualties%20as%20of%2031%20December%202021%20%28rev%2027%20January%202022%29%20corr%20EN_0.pdf%5C

[8] *Misión Verdad,* "23 years after the NATO bombing of Yugoslavia: Lessons about the present": https://misionverdad.com/memoria/23-anos-del-bombardeo-otan-contra-yugoslavia-lecciones-sobre-el-presente

[9] *Global Times,* 11 Oct 2022, "Ukraine Tensions Timeline": https://www.globaltimes.cn/special-coverage/Ukraine-Tensions-Timeline.html

[10] *CounterPunch,* 25 March 2022, "The Blowback from Sanctions on Russia": www.counterpunch.org/2022/03/25/the-blowback-from-sanctions-on-russia/

[11] John Mearsheimer and Ray McGovern, *Committee for the Republic,* 2 March 2022, "Putin's Invasion of Ukraine" youtube.com/watch?v=OeeqooNWO48&t

[12] *BreakThrough News,* 25 March 2022, "Ukraine: The View From Africa": https://www.youtube.com/watch?v=iIiOY_7kPsw

[13] Watson Institute/Brown University, "Estimate of U.S. Post-9/11 War Spending" https://watson.brown.edu/costsofwar/figures/2021/BudgetaryCosts

[14] Center for International Policy, June 2019, "Final Report, Sustainable Defense Task Force" https://static.wixstatic.com/ugd/fb6c59_59a295c780634ce88d-077c391066db9a.pdf

[15] Watson Institute/Brown University, "Costs of War Papers: Summary of Findings" https://watson.brown.edu/costsofwar/papers/summary

Notes to Chapter 8 (pp. 66-77)

[1] *Covert Action Magazine,* 20 March 2022, https://covertactionmagazine.com/2022/04/20/war-in-ukraine-could-be-the-mother-of-all-energy-wars-but-the-media-still-misses-the-context/

[2] *Fox 32/Chicago,* https://www.youtube.com/watch?v=yBWFqmTFoHM

[3] *NY Times,* 11 April 2022, "China's Echoes of Russia's Alternate Reality..." https://www.nytimes.com/2022/04/11/technology/china-russia-propaganda.html?searchResultPosition=1

[4] United National Antiwar Coalition: https://www.unacpeace.org/

[5] *Scott Ritter: A Conversation About Ukraine Part 1* (with Margaret Flowers and Joe Lombardo of the United National Antiwar Coalition-UNAC): https://www.youtube.com/watch?v=-fNrnWxXhP0

[6] *ShadowProof,* 9 Aug 2014, "CIA intervention in Ukraine has been taking place for decades," https://shadowproof.com/2014/08/09/cia-intervention-in-ukraine-has-been-taking-place-for-decades/

[7] Richard Breitman and Norman J.W. Goda, *Hitler's Shadow: Nazi War Criminals, U.S. Intelligence, and the Cold War,* The National Archives, https://www.archives.gov/files/iwg/reports/hitlers-shadow.pdf

[8] Paul H. Rosenberg and Foreign Policy in Focus, *The Nation,* 28 March 2014, "Seven Decades of Nazi Collaboration: America's Dirty Little Ukraine Secret," https://www.thenation.com/article/archive/seven-decades-nazi-collaboration-americas-dirty-little-ukraine-secret/

9 "Far-Right Group Made Its Home in Ukraine's Major Western Military Training Hub," *Institute for European, Russian, and Eurasian Studies, GW University,* Sept 2021, https://www.illiberalism.org/wp-content/uploads/2021/09/IERES-Papers-no-11-September-2021-FINAL.pdf

10 Will Carless, *USA Today,* 5 March 2022, "A regiment of Ukraine's military was founded by white supremacists. Now It's battling Russia on the front lines." https://www.usatoday.com/story/news/world/2022/03/05/russia-invasion-ukraine-attention-extremist-regiment-nazi/9368016002/?gnt-cfr=1

11 *War crimes of the armed forces and security forces of Ukraine: torture and inhumane treatment, Second report,* OSCE Foundation for the Study of Democracy, 15 April 2016: www.osce.org/files/f/documents/e/7/233896.pdf

12 "Noam Chomsky: Propaganda Wars Are Raging…," *Truthout,* 28 April 2022, https://truthout.org/articles/noam-chomsky-propaganda-wars-are-raging-as-russias-war-on-ukraine-expands/?eType=EmailBlastContent&eId=0dc-d487c-2617-4818-9515-dcef7f95bc99

13 Max Parry, "Synthetic Left Joins Corporate Right in Getting Ukraine War Wrong," *Covert Action Magazine,* 22 April 2022, https://covertactionmagazine.com/2022/04/22/the-synthetic-left-joins-the-corporate-right-in-getting-the-ukraine-war-wrong/

14 Margaret Kimberley, "The Ukraine Crisis Can't Save Biden," *Black Agenda Report,* 20 April 2022, https://www.blackagendareport.com/ukraine-crisis-cant-save-biden

15 Quinnipiac Poll, 12 Jan 2022, "Political instability, not U.S. adversaries, seen as bigger threat" https://poll.qu.edu/images/polling/us/us01122022_ubjw88.pdf

Notes to Chapter 9 (pp. 78-90)

1 *NY Times,* 24 June 2022, "U.S.-Led Alliance Faces Frustration, and Pain of Its Own, Over Russia Sanctions" https://www.nytimes.com/2022/06/24/us/politics/russia-ukraine-biden-sanctions.html?searchResultPosition=1

2 *Business Insider,* 11 June 2022, "Cases of desertion are growing among Ukrainian forces…" https://www.businessinsider.com/ukraine-troops-deserting-russias-artillery-onslaught-takes-toll-report-says-2022-6

[3] Alexander Mercouris, "Ukraine Announces Tactical Withdrawals…" https://www.youtube.com/watch?v=-tKUE1Qlm0M

[4] *USA Today,* 19 May 2022, "Senate approves $40 billion in Ukraine assistance as last aid package runs out" https://www.usatoday.com/web-stories/us-aid-ukraine-53-billion-congress/

[5] *Washington Post,* 29 June 2022, "Turkey drops opposition to Finland, Sweden joining NATO."

[6] *Washington Post,* 30 June 2022, "U.S. to increase military presence in Europe"

[7] Peace Summit Madrid 2022, Declaration, peacesummitmadrid.org/#declaration

[8] Peace In Ukraine: https://www.peaceinukraine.org/

[9] *CNBC,* 21 May 2022, "Biden signs $40 billion aid package to Ukraine" https://www.cnbc.com/2022/05/21/biden-signs-40-billion-aid-package-for-ukraine-during-trip-to-asia.html

[10] Canada-wide Peace and Justice Network https://peaceandjusticenetwork.ca/stopnato/

[11] Ben Norton, *Multipolarista,* 22 June 2022, "Only 4 of 55 African leaders attend Zelensky call, showing neutrality on Ukraine and Russia: geopoliticaleconomy.com/2022/06/22/africa-zelensky-call-neutrality-ukraine/

[12] *LeMonde,* 22 June 2022, "Zelensky seeks support from the African Union" https://www.lemonde.fr/en/le-monde-africa/article/2022/06/22/volodymyr-zelensky-seeks-african-union-support_5987621_124.html

[13] Ben Norton, *Multipolarista,* 24 March 2022, "Ex US oficial admits Ukraine conflicto is NATO 'proxy war' with Russia" geopoliticaleconomy.com/2022/03/24/us-official-ukraine-nato-proxy-war-russia/

[14] Norton, *Multipolarista,* 22 June 2022 geopoliticaleconomy.com/2022/06/22/africa-zelensky-call-neutrality-ukraine/

[15] *NY Times,* 24 June 2022, "U.S.-Led Alliance Faces Frustration, and Pain of Its Own, Over Russia Sanctions." 1

[16] St. Petersburg International Economic Forum: https://forumspb.com/en/

[17] Roger Annis, *A Socialist In Canada*, April 23, 2022, "Civilian and military casualties in Donbass since 2014": https://socialistincanada.ca/civilian-and-military-casualties-in-donbass-since-2014/

[18] Ellen Taylor, "War Crimes, From Nuremberg to Ukraine," *CounterPunch,* 3 June 2022, https://www.counterpunch.org/2022/06/03/war-crimes-from-nuremberg-to-ukraine/

[19] Wikipedia, "Reponsibility to Protect," wikipedia.org/wiki/Responsibility_to_protect

[20] Wikipedia, "Donbas" https://en.wikipedia.org/wiki/Donbas

[21] Ben Norton, "Ex VP Dick Cheney confirmed US goal is to break up Russia, not just the USSR," 22 Jan 2022: geopoliticaleconomy.com/2022/02/01/dick-cheney-us-goal-break-up-russia/

[22] Zbigniew Brzezinski, *Foreign Affairs,* Sept/Oct 1997, "A Geostrategy for Asia," https://archive.ph/bSSkm#selection-1815.417-1815.483

[23] Ben Norton, "US gov't body plots to break up Russia in name of 'decolonization'," 23 June 2022, https://geopoliticaleconomy.com/2022/06/23/us-government-decolonize-russia/

[24] Wikipedia, "Slobodan Milošević" https://en.wikipedia.org/wiki/Slobodan_Milo%C5%A1evi%C4%87

[25] Frente Antiimperialista Internacionalista, "Political Foundations of the Front": https://frenteantiimperialista.org/fai/documentacion/documentos/fundamentos-politicos-del-frente/

[26] Ben Norton, 30 June 2022, "NATO seeks to prevent Eurasian challenger to US world dominance, admits ex CIA chief Mike Pompeo" geopoliticaleconomy.com/2022/06/30/nato-eurasia-us-hegemony-mike-pompeo/

[27] Hudson Institute, "War, Ukraine, and a Global Alliance for Freedom," 24 June 2022: https://www.hudson.org/events/2122-virtual-event-war-ukraine-and-a-global-alliance-for-freedom62022

[28] Ben Norton, 23 June 2022, "US gov't body plots to break up Russia in name of 'decolonization'" https://geopoliticaleconomy.com/2022/06/23/us-government-decolonize-russia/

Notes to Chapter 10 (pp. 93-102)

[1] *The Real Path to Peace in Ukraine,* 19 Nov 2022 https://www.youtube.com/watch?v=asndac1ETFk

[2] Norman Solomon, "Worried About Nuclear Power? Do Something…" www.laprogressive.com/war-and-peace/dont-just-worry-about-nuclear-war

[3] Ellen Taylor, "War Crimes, From Nuremberg to Ukraine," *CounterPunch,* 3 June 2022, https://www.counterpunch.org/2022/06/03/war-crimes-from-nuremberg-to-ukraine/

[4] Irena Chalupa, *"Direct Translation*: 'Donbas, the Heart of Russia'," *New Atlanticist,* 13 June 2014, https://www.atlanticcouncil.org/blogs/new-atlanticist/direct-translation-donbas-the-heart-of-russia/

[5] Ellen Taylor, "War Crimes..." *CounterPunch* 3 June 2022

[6] Robert M. Gates, *Duty: Memoirs of a Secretary of War,* Jan 2014. e

[7] Ben Norton, 1 Feb 2022, "Ex VP Dick Cheney confirmed US goal is to break up Russia, not just USSR" http://geopoliticaleconomy.com/2022/02/01/dick-cheney-us-goal-break-up-russia/

[8] Zbigniew Brzezinski, "A Geostrategy for Eurasia," *Foreign Affairs,* Sept/Oct 1997, https://archive.ph/bSSkm#selection-1815.417-1815.483

[9] *NY Times,* 22 May 2022, "The War in Ukraine Is Getting Complicated, and America Isn't Ready"

Notes to Chapter 11 (pp. 103-109)

[1] *Washington Post,* 18 June 2022, "Poor People's Campaign marches, rallies in District" https://www.washingtonpost.com/dc-md-va/2022/06/18/poor-peoples-campaign-dc-march/

[2] Poor People's March on Washington Saturday Demands "Moral Reset" on Poverty, Voting Rights, Climate | Democracy Now!

Notes to Chapter 12 (pp. 110-116)

[1] Wikipedia, "History of Taiwan" https://en.wikipedia.org/wiki/History_of_Taiwan

[2] Wikipedia, "Chinese Nationalist Party retreat to Taiwan" https://en.wikipedia.org/wiki/Chinese_Nationalist_Party_retreat_to_Taiwan

[3] Wikipedia, "Chiang Kai-shek" https://en.wikipedia.org/wiki/Chiang_Kai-shek

[4] *Politico,* "Senators seek billions more in military aid for Taiwan," 12 Oct 2022, https://www.politico.com/news/2022/10/12/senators-more-military-aid-taiwan-00061549

[5] *NY Times,* 19 Oct 2022, " 'Yankees Go Home!': Seoul Gets Squeezed Between the U.S. and China."

⁶ Wikipedia, La France Insoumise, en.wikipedia.org/wiki/La_France_Insoumise

⁷ Pivot To Peace, Mission Statement, https://peacepivot.org/mission/

⁸ "'Say No to US Wars!': Back to the streets, October 15-22," United National Antiwar Coalition (UNAC) https://popularresistance.org/say-no-to-u-s-wars-back-to-the-streets-october-15-23/

⁹ Minneapolis march says 'No to U.S. wars' | Fight Back! (fightbacknews.org)

¹⁰ Minnie Bruce Pratt, *Workers World,* 18 Oct 2022 www.workers.org/2022/10/67272/

Notes to Chapter 13 (pp. 119-122)

¹ White House Briefing, 23 May 2022: https://www.whitehouse.gov/briefing-room/speeches-remarks/2022/05/23/remarks-by-president-biden-and-prime-minister-fumio-kishida-of-japan-in-joint-press-conference/

² Patrick Lawrence, *Consortium News, 31 May 2022,* ""Biden's Taiwan Talk": https://consortiumnews.com/2022/05/31//loombe-lawrence-bidens-taiwan-talk/

³ U.S. State Department Fact Sheet, 28 May 2022, "U.S. Relations with Taiwan": https://www.state.gov/u-s-relations-with-taiwan/

⁴ *War Games: The Battle for Taiwan:* https://www.youtube.com/watch?v=qY-fvm-JLhPQ

⁵ Patrick Lawrence, *Consortium News, 31 May 2022,* ""Biden's Taiwan Talk"

⁶ Paul D. Shinkman, *U.S. News and World Report,* 23 May 2022, "China Expresses Outrage at Biden's Comments That U.S. Would Defend Taiwan": https://www.usnews.com/news/world-report/articles/2022-05-23/china-expresses-outrage-at-bidens-comments-that-u-s-would-defend-taiwan

⁷ National Defense Strategy Commission, January 2018: "Providing for the Common Defense": https://www.usip.org/sites/default/files/2019-07/providing-for-the-common-defense.pdf

⁸ Graham Allison, *The National Interest,* 29 Oct 2021, "Could the U.S. Lose a War with China Over Taiwan?": https://nationalinterest.org/feature/could-us-lose-war-china-over-taiwan-195686

⁹ *The War Monger's Legacy,* www.youtube.com/watch?v=Jkb1f5eqUpM

¹⁰ *The Battle at Lake Changjin,* Bloomberg.org/wiki/The_Battle_at_Lake_Changjin

Notes to Chapter 14 (pp. 123-130)

[1] *NY Times,* 7 Oct 2021, "China's Power Crunch Exposes Tensions…" https://www.nytimes.com/2021/10/07/climate/china-cop26-blackouts-coal.html?-searchResultPosition=1

[2] *NY Times, 15 Oct 2021,* "Key To Biden's Energy Agenda Likely to Be Cut…" https://www.nytimes.com/2021/10/15/climate/biden-clean-energy-manchin.html

[3] People vs Fossil Fuels.org, *Press Release* Oct 15, 2021

[4] *NPR,* 13 July 2021, "Biden Promised to End New Drilling on Federal Land…" https://www.npr.org/2021/07/13/1015581092/biden-promised-to-end-new-drilling-on-federal-land-but-approvals-are-up

[5] *Oil Change Int'l,* Oct 2021, "Greenhouse Gas Emission Estimates of Proposed U.S. Fossil Fuel Infrastructure Projects": priceofoil.org/content/uploads/2021/10/Biden_GHG_emissions_briefing.pdf

[6] Watson Institute, Brown Univ., "Pentagon Fuel Use, Climate Change, and the Costs of War": https://watson.brown.edu/costsofwar/papers/ClimateChangeandCostofWar

[7] *Science Daily,* 20 June 2019, "U.S. military consumes more hydrocarbons than most countries…" https://www.sciencedaily.com/releases/2019/06/190620100005.htm

[8] *NY Times,* 9 Oct 2021, "Starting a Fire?" https://www.nytimes.com/2021/10/09/world/asia/united-states-china-taiwan.html?searchResultPosition=1

[9] *NY Times,* 17 Sept 2020, "U.S. Pushes Large Arms Sale to Taiwan": https://www.nytimes.com/2020/09/17/us/politics/us-arms-sale-taiwan-china.html?-searchResultPosition=1

[10] *Washington Post,* 11 Oct 2021, "Congress must untie Biden's hands on Taiwan": https://www.washingtonpost.com/opinions/2021/10/11/elaine-luria-congress-biden-taiwan/

[11] *Stars & Stripes,* 12 Oct 2021, "Retired Marine colonel says U.S. should weigh nuclear war with China over Taiwan": https://www.stripes.com/branches/marine_corps/2021-10-12/taiwan-china-invasion-nuclear-war-united-states-3214248.html

[12] *Southern China Morning Post,* 8 Oct 2021, "China demands Answers on US nuclear submarine accident": https://www.scmp.com/news/china/diplomacy/article/3151724/china-demands-answers-us-nuclear-submarine-accident-south

13 *Insider,* 17 Sept 2021, "China is furious over a new US-UK-Australia nuclear submarine deal…" https://www.insider.com/china-furious-us-uk-nuclear-submarine-deal-australia-2021-9

14 *Wikipedia,* "CIA Tibetan program": https://en.wikipedia.org/wiki/CIA_Tibetan_program

15 *LA Progressive,* 31 Jul 2021, "Stop Escalating U.S./NATO Cold War Against China": https://www.laprogressive.com/cold-war-against-china/

16 *Global Times,* 8 Oct 2021, "US' revelation of troops in Taiwan will only hasten cross-straits war": www.globaltimes.cn/page/202110/1235814.shtml

17 *NY Times,* 22 May 2021, "Risk of Nuclear War Over Taiwan in 1958…Greater Than Publicly Known": www.nytimes.com/2021/05/22/us/politics/nuclear-war-risk-1958-us-china.html

18 *Pivot To Peace,* Mission Statement: https://peacepivot.org/mission/

19 *CodePink,* "China Is Not Our Enemy": https://www.codepink.org/china

Notes to Chapter 15 (pp. 131-148)

1 *NY Times,* 15 June 2021, "China… Accuses NATO of Hypocrisy" https://www.nytimes.com/2021/06/15/world/asia/china-nato-military.html?searchResultPosition=1

2 *Politico,* 14 June 2021, "Decoding the NATO Summit" https://news.yahoo.com/decoding-nato-summit-163910282.html

3 "The crisis of American power: How Europeans see Biden's America," European Council on Foreign Relations, 19 Jan 2021, https://ecfr.eu/publication/the-crisis-of-american-power-how-europeans-see-bidens-america/

4 *The Guardian,* 5 May 2021, "US seen as bigger threat to democracy than Russia or China, global poll finds" https://www.theguardian.com/world/2021/may/05/us-threat-democracy-russia-china-global-poll

5 *Alliance of Democracies,* "Democracy Perception Index 2020" https://www.allianceofdemocracies.org/initiatives/the-copenhagen-democracy-summit/dpi-2020/

6 Harvard/Ash Center for Democratic Governance and Innovation, "Understanding CCP Resilience: Surveying Chinese Public Opinion Through Time," July 2020, https://ash.harvard.edu/publications/understanding-ccp-resilience-surveying-chinese-public-opinion-through-time

[7] Bernie Sanders, "Washington's Dangerous New Consensus on China," *Foreign Affairs*, 17 June 2021, www.foreignaffairs.com/articles/china/2021-06-17/washingtons-dangerous-new-consensus-china

[8] "Myths & Facts about genocide: What's happening in Xinjiang, China," Pivot To Peace, 12 June 2021, //www.facebook.com/watch/live/?v=1078871589265868&ref=watch_permalink

[9] "Why is the National Endowment for Democracy fueling Hong Kong protests?" *News CGTN,* 27 Aug 2019, https://news.cgtn.com/news/2019-08-27/Why-is-the-NED-fueling-the-Hong-Kong-protests--JtMb2yKKWc/index.html

[10] *Human Freedom Index 2020,* Fraser Institute, 17 Dec 2020, https://www.fraserinstitute.org/studies/human-freedom-index-2020

[11] Nury Vittachi, *The Other Side of the Story: A Secret War in Hong Kong,* 2020, ASIN

[12] James Griffiths and Jessie Yeung, *CNN,* "A Generation Criminalized," //www.cnn.com/interactive/2019/12/asia/hong-kong-6-months-intl-hnk/

[13] "Myths & Facts about genocide: What's happening in Xinjiang, China," Pivot To Peace, 12 June 2021, //www.facebook.com/watch/live/?v=1078871589265868&ref=watch_permalink

[14] *CNN World,* 10 July 2021, "Some Hong Kongers are glorifying a man who knifed a cop…" https://www.cnn.com/2021/07/09/asia/hong-kong-stabbing-aftermath-intl-hnk-dst/index.html

[15] *NY Times,* 19 Jan 2021, "U.S. Says China's Repression of Uyghurs Is 'Genocide'," https://www.nytimes.com/2021/01/19/us/politics/trump-china-xinjiang.html

[16] *USA Today,* 6 April 2021, "U.S. says China is committing genocide against the Uyghurs," https://www.usatoday.com/in-depth/news/politics/2021/04/02/is-china-committing-genocide-what-you-need-know-uyghurs/7015211002/

[17] Daniel Drumbrill, "Xinjiang, Hong Kong, Media Lies and the War On China," 30 Aug 2021, https://www.youtube.com/watch?v=BENky0V_qDM

[18] *NY Times,* 23 April 2021, "Ezra Klein Interviews Noam Chomsky," https://www.nytimes.com/2021/04/23/podcasts/ezra-klein-podcast-noam-chomsky-transcript.html

[19] "Myths & Facts about genocide: What's happening in Xinjiang, China," Pivot To Peace, 12 June 2021, www.facebook.com/watch/live/?v=1078871589265868&ref=watch_permalink

[20] Reese Erlich, "What's Really Going on with China's Uighurs?" *The Progressive Magazine,* 19 Feb 2021, https://progressive.org/latest/whats-going-on-china-uighurs-erlich-210219/

[21] Ajit Singh, " 'Forced labor' stories on China brought to you by US gov, NATO, arms industry to drive Cold War PR blitz," 26 March 2020, thegrayzone.com/2020/03/26/forced-labor-china-us-nato-arms-industry-cold-war/

[22] *Ibid.*

[23] "Myths & Facts about genocide: What's happening in Xinjiang, China," Pivot To Peace, 12 June 2021, www.facebook.com/watch/live/?v=1078871589265868&ref=watch_permalink

[24] "Demographic Situation in Xinjiang-Uigur Autonomous Area in the Last Quarter of the Twentieth Century," *Global Media Journal,* 5 May 2016 https://www.globalmediajournal.com/open-access/demographic-situation-in-xinjianguigur-autonomous-area-in-the-last-quarter-of-the-twentieth-century.php?aid=77746

[25] "Education in Xinjiang," *Borgen Magazine,* 4 Dec 2017, https://www.borgenmagazine.com/education-in-xinjiang/

[26] "A growing economy is key to China's control of Xinjiang," *The Article,* 1 March 2020, https://www.thearticle.com/a-growing-economy-is-key-to-chinas-control-of-xinjiang

[27] Ethnic minorities in China - Wikipedia

[28] Wikipedia, "Islam in China," https://en.wikipedia.org/wiki/Islam_in_China

[29] Beijing's Decades-Long Policies in Xinjiang, CIA Interference, Funding of Separatist and Terrorist Groups – Orinoco Tribune – News and opinion pieces about Venezuela and beyond

[30] Wikipedia, "Abdul Haq al-Turkistani" en.wikipedia.org/wiki/Abdul_Haq_ (ETIP)

[31] Luiz Alberto Moniz Bandeira, *The Second Cold War Geopolitics and the Strategic Dimensions of the USA,* 2017, https://lib.ugent.be/catalog/ebk01:3710000001388793

[32] *Xinjiang: A Report and Resource Compilation,* Qiao Collective, Sept 2021 https://www.qiaocollective.com/en/education/xinjiang

[33] *CodePink,* "Empire, Racism, & Propaganda: Preventing the US's War on China," Episode 103, August 2021, https://www.codepink.org/episode_103

34 *Reuters,* 5 Aug 2021, "U.S.approves potential sale of howitzers to Taiwan" https://www.reuters.com/world/asia-pacific/us-approves-potential-sales-howitzers-taiwan-pentagon-2021-08-04/

35 *CodePink,* "China Is NOT Our Enemy" https://www.codepink.org/china

36 *XinhuaNet,* Sept 2018, "2018 Beijing Summit, Forum on China-Africa Cooperation" www.xinhuanet.com/english/cnleaders/2018BeijingSummit/ej.htm?pagename=pl

37 China's vaccine map: Aid to more countries with 1st EU GMP certificate, CGTN, 5 April 2021

38 U.S. Census: www.census.gov/foreign-trade/balance/c7910.html

39 "Is American 'Aid' Assistance or Theft? The Case of Africa," in *American Exceptionalism and American Innocence,* by Roberto Sirvent and Danny Haiphong, Skyhorse, New York, 2019.

40 *PRC State Council,* 10 Jan. 2021, "China's Int'l Development Cooperation in the New Era," English.www.gov.cn/archive/whitepaper/202101/10/content_WS5ffa6bbbc6d0f72576943922.html

41 Deborah Bräutigam, "U.S. politicians get China in Africa all wrong," *Washington Post,* 12 April 2018, www.washingtonpost.com/news/theworldpost/wp/2018/04/12/china-africa/

42 Amadou Sy, "What Do We Know About the Chinese Land Grab in Africa?" Brookings Institution, November 5, 2015.

43 *China's International Development Cooperation in the New Era,* State Council White Paper, 10 January 2021, http://english.www.gov.cn/

44 Yiping Huang, "Understanding China's Belt & Road Initiative: Motivation, Framework and Assessment," *China Economic Review,* Vol. 40, Sept. 2016, pp. 314-321

Notes to Chapter 16 (pp. 149-158)

1 *White House,* "Remarks by Pres. Biden before the 77th UN GA," www.whitehouse.gov/briefing-room/speeches-remarks/2022/09/21/remarks-by-president-biden-before-the-77th-session-of-the-united-nations-general-assembly/

2 *Transcript,* "Chinese Pres. Xi Jinping UN GA 2021 Speech," https://www.rev.com/blog/transcripts/chinese-president-xi-jinping-un-general-assembly-2021-speech-transcript

³ "Serve the People: The Eradication of Extreme Poverty in China," Tricontinental Research Institute, 23 July 2021, https://thetricontinental.org/studies-1-socialist-construction/

⁴ *Xinhua,* "Xi Jinping's Report at 19ᵗʰ CPC National Congress," 3 Nov 2017, http://www.xinhuanet.com/english/special/2017-11/03/c_136725942.htm

⁵ Harvard/Ash Center for Democratic Governance and Innovation, "Understanding CCP Resilience: Surveying Chinese Public Opinion Through Time," July 2020, https://ash.harvard.edu/publications/understanding-ccp-resilience-surveying-chinese-public-opinion-through-time

⁶ Yu Keping, *Democracy in China: Challenge or Opportunity?"* Harvard As Center, *https://ash.harvard.edu/files/ash/files/democracyinchina_0.pdf*

⁷ "Serve the People: The Eradication of Extreme Poverty in China," Tricontinental Research Institute, 23 July 2021, https://thetricontinental.org/studies-1-socialist-construction/

⁸ *Washington Post,* 5 May 2021, "Did the pandemic shake Chinese citizens' trust in their government," Cary Woo, www.washingtonpost.com/politics/2021/05/05/did-pandemic-shake-chinese-citizens-trust-their-government/

⁹ Fraser Institute, *Human Freedom Index 2020, www.fraserinstitute.org/resource-file?nid=13803&fid=15258*

¹⁰ "UN urged to help wipe out colonial legacies," *CGTN,* 23 Sept 2021, https://newseu.cgtn.com/news/2021-09-23/UN-urged-to-help-wipe-out-colonial-legacies-13LWxpDdX0I/index.html

¹¹ *XinhuaNet,* 25 June 2021, "China, like-minded countries voice concern over military interventions against sovereign states," http://www.xinhuanet.com/english/2021-06/25/c_1310027120.htm

¹² Yu Keping, *Democracy in China: Challenge or Opportunity?"* Harvard As Center, *https://ash.harvard.edu/files/ash/files/democracyinchina_0.pdf*

Notes to Chapter 17 (pp. 159-166)

¹ *NY Times,* 19 Oct 2022, " 'Yankees, Go Home!': Seoul Gets Squeezed Between the U.S. and China," https://www.nytimes.com/2022/10/19/world/asia/korea-china-us-thaad-missiles.html?searchResultPosition=1

[2] Hideki Yoshikawa, *Open Letter to Senate Armed Services Committee co-signed by 57 Groups & Organizations in Okinawa and Japan, and 45 Groups & Organizations outside Okinawa and Japan,* 31 Oct 2022, https://drive.google.com/file/d/1kRYFzRqoB-zGxoKi1aPCSLzK5ipDpA2h/view

[3] "Congress to Shut Down US Military Bases in Okinawa," *DSA International Committee Statement,* 20 Oct 2022, https://international.dsausa.org/zenko-henoko-anti-base-project/#okinawa

[4] *"Jabari Brisport solidarity message against construction of new US military base in Okinawa,"* DSA Int'l Committee, Oct 2022, https://www.youtube.com/watch?v=XNuPQvVPl2g

[5] C. Douglas Lummis, "Futenma: 'The Most Dangerous Base in the World'," 30 March 2018, *The* Diplomat, https://thediplomat.com/2018/03/futenma-the-most-dangerous-base-in-the-world/

[6] *US Military in the Pacific,* DSA Int'l Committee Webinar, https://international.dsausa.org/us-military-pacific/

[7] Mark Tseng-Putterman, "China and the American Lake," *Monthly Review,* 1 July 2021, https://monthlyreview.org/2021/07/01/china-and-the-american-lake/

[8] Jon Letman, "Guam: Where the US Military Is Revered and Reviled," 19 Aug 2016, *The Diplomat,* https://thediplomat.com/2016/08/guam-where-the-us-military-is-revered-and-reviled/

[9] "Shut Down Red Hill," *O'ahu Water Protectors,* https://oahuwaterprotectors.org/

[10] Gavan McCormack, "There Will Be No Stopping the Okinawan Resistance," an Interview with Yamashiro Hiroji, *The Asia-Pacific Journal, 1 Aug 2017* https://apjjf.org/2017/15/McCormack.html

[11] *NY Times,* 27 Oct 2022, "Pnetagon's Strategy Says China and Russia Pose Very Different Challenges," https://www.nytimes.com/2022/10/27/us/politics/biden-military-russia-china.html?searchResultPosition=1

[12] *White House,* 26 April 2023, "Washington Declaration," https://www.whitehouse.gov/briefing-room/statements-releases/2023/04/26/washington-declaration-2/

¹³ *Rodong Sinbun (via KCNA Watch),* 2 May 2023, "Truth of Dangerous Trip for Nuclear War Disclosed," https://kcnawatch.org/newstream/1682926334-453855128/truth-of-dangerous-trip-for-nuclear-war-disclosed-kcna-commentary/

¹⁴ "US Flies Nuclear-Capable Bombers Amid Tensions with North Korea," *Military.com,* 5 April 2023, https://www.military.com/daily-news/2023/04/05/us-flies-nuclear-capable-bombers-amid-tensions-north-korea.html

¹⁵ "Yoon Suk Yeol's State Visit: U.S. Backing of Far-Right Leader Bad for South Korea," Simon Chun, *Common Dreams,* 27 April 2013, https://www.common-dreams.org/opinion/yoon-suk-yeol-state-visit

¹⁶ "Philippines, US start largest ever drills in South China Sea," *Aljazeera,* 11 April 2023, https://www.aljazeera.com/news/2023/4/11/philip-pines-and-us-start-largest-ever-annual-military-drills

¹⁷ *Reuters,* 3 April 2023, "Philippines reveals locations of 4 new strategic sites for U.S. military pact," https://www.reuters.com/world/asia-pacific/philippines-re-veals-locations-4-new-strategic-sites-us-military-pact-2023-04-03/

¹⁸ "Japan, Philippines agree to boost defence ties amid China tension," *Aljazeera,* 10 Feb 2023, https://www.aljazeera.com/news/2023/2/10/japan-philippines-agree-to-boost-defence-ties-amid-china-tension

Notes to Chapter 18 (pp. 167-178)

¹ *NY Times,* "For Biden and Xi, a Long Relationship…" 11 Nov 2022 https://www.nytimes.com/2022/11/11/us/politics/biden-china-g20-bali.html?-searchResultPosition=1

² *NY Times,* "Pentagon's Strategy Says China and Russia Pose Very Different Challenges," 27 Oct 2022 www.nytimes.com/2022/10/27/us/politics/biden-military-russia-china.html?searchResultPosition=1

³ *Xinhua,* "Report to the 20ᵗʰ National Congress…," 26 Oct 2022, http://en-glish.scio.gov.cn/20thcpccongress/2022-10/26/content_78486016.html

⁴ *Xinhua,* 15 Nov 2022, "Xi, Biden candid, in-depth exchange…" english.news.cn/20221115/72c2d122221e4c9e94cc483654981aea/c.html

⁵ *Global Times,* "Long-awaited scene between China and the US gives the world relief," 15 Nov 2022 www.globaltimes.cn/page/202211/1279524.shtml

[6] *Global Times,* "Anyone who deviates from G20 theme will be booed," 13 Nov 2022, https://www.globaltimes.cn/page/202211/1279423.shtml

[7] *IMF,* "World Economic Outlook Press Briefing," 11 Oct 2022, https://www.imf.org/en/News/Articles/2022/10/12/tr101122-weo-transcript

[8] Ben Norton, "IMF warns of 'wave of debt crises'…" *GeoPolitical/Economy Report,* 13 Nov 2022, https://geopoliticaleconomy.com/2022/11/13/imf-debt-crises-global-south-interest-dollar/

[9] "The BRICS countries: where next and what impact on global economy?" *Economics Observatory,* 20 Oct 2022, https://www.economicsobservatory.com/the-brics-countries-where-next-and-what-impact-on-the-global-economy

[10] *NY Times,* "U.S. Seeks Closer Ties With India as Tension With China and Russia Builds," 11 Nov 2022, www.nytimes.com/2022/11/11/business/us-india-relations.html?searchResultPosition=1

[11] ASEAN member states: https://asean.org/member-states/

[12] *Politico,* "Russia's Lavrov: Western leaders want to militarize Southeast Asia," 13 Sept 2022, www.politico.eu/article/russia-foreign-minister-sergei-lavrov-western-leaders-militarize-southeast-asia-asean-g20-bali-indonesia/

[13] Hu Xijin, "US better give up attempt to contain China by utilizing Southeast Asian countries," *Global Times,* 3 Nov 2022 www.globaltimes.cn/page/202211/1278649.shtml

[14] *NY Times,* "In His 3rd Summit With SE Asian Leaders, Biden Bets on Face Time," 12 Nov 2022, https://www.nytimes.com/2022/11/12/us/politics/biden-asean-summit.html?searchResultPosition=1

[15] *Global Times,* "US woos ASEAN with fancy words; actions don't stand up," 12 Nov 2022, https://www.globaltimes.cn/page/202211/1279350.shtml

[16] "Indonesia Gears Up to Start its First High-Speed Rail Line," *The Diplomat,* 14 Oct 2022 https://thediplomat.com/2022/10/indonesia-gears-up-to-start-its-first-high-speed-rail-line/

[17] "U.S. and South Korea warplanes begin largest ever air drills," *Reuters,* 31 Oct 2022, https://www.reuters.com/world/us-south-korean-warplanes-begin-largest-ever-air-drills-2022-10-31/

[18] "US aircraft carrier starts joint military drills in South Korea," *Aljazeera,* 26 Sept 2022, https://www.aljazeera.com/news/2022/9/26/us-aircraft-carrier-starts-joint-military-drills-in-south-korea

19 "Opposition Grows to US Bases Poised Against China," *LA Progressive,* 5 Nov 2022, https://www.laprogressive.com/asia/us-bases-poised-against-china

20 Mark Tseng-Putterman, "China and the American Lake," *Monthly Review,* 1 July 2021, https://monthlyreview.org/2021/07/01/china-and-the-american-lake/

21 "Germany's Olaf Scholz meets China's Xi Jinping as trade in focus," *Aljazeera,* 4 Nov 2022, https://www.aljazeera.com/news/2022/11/4/germany-chancellor-olaf-scholz-visits-china-with-eye-on-trade

22 "Xi meets French President Macron," *Xinhua,* 15 Nov 2022, english.news.cn/20221115/6521ac3498f24426b79256d4fc529bbb/c.html

23 *Wikipedia,* "Non-Aligned Movement" https://en.wikipedia.org/wiki/Non-Aligned_Movement#:~:text=The%20Non%2DAligned%20Movement%20(NAM,of%20the%20Non%2DAligned%20Movement.

24 "The assassination attempt of Zhou Enlai," *The China Project,* 14 April 2021, thechinaproject.com/2021/04/14/the-assassination-attempt-of-zhou-enlai/

25 "The Taiwan Strait Crisis of 1954-55 and specter of nuclear war," *The China Project,* 2 Sept 2020, https://thechinaproject.com/2020/09/02/the-taiwan-straits-crisis-of-1954-55/

26 "The Battle at Lake Changjin," *Wikpedia,* https://en.wikipedia.org/wiki/The_Battle_at_Lake_Changjin

27 "Indonesian mass killings of 1965-66," *Wikipedia,* en.wikipedia.org/wiki/Indonesian_mass_killings_of_1965%E2%80%9366

28 *NY Times,* "Biden Casts America as Climate Leader..." 11 Nov 2022, https://www.nytimes.com/2022/11/11/climate/biden-cop27-climate-speech.html?-searchResultPosition=1

29 "2022 Nord Stream pipeline sabotage," *Wikipedia,* https://en.wikipedia.org/wiki/2022_Nord_Stream_gas_leaks

30 Seymour Hersh, "How America Took Out The Nord Stream Pipeline," 8 Feb 2023, seymourhersh.substack.com/p/how-america-took-out-the-nord-stream

31 "What is the financial cost of loss and damage from climate change?" *Land & Climate Review,* 12 June 2022, https://elc-insight.org/what-is-the-financial-cost-of-loss-and-damage-from-climate-change/

32 *NY Times,* "Biden Casts America as Climate Leader..." 11 Nov 2022, https://www.nytimes.com/2022/11/11/climate/biden-cop27-climate-speech.html?-searchResultPosition=1

[33] *NY Times,* "U.S. Seeks Closer Ties With India as Tension With China and Russia Builds," 11 Nov 2022, www.nytimes.com/2022/11/11/business/us-india-relations.html?searchResultPosition=1

[34] *NY Times,* "In His 3rd Summit With SE Asian Leaders, Biden Bets on Face Time," 12 Nov 2022, https://www.nytimes.com/2022/11/12/us/politics/biden-asean-summit.html?searchResultPosition=1

[35] *Global Times,* "Anyone who deviates from G20 theme will be booed," 13 Nov 2022, https://www.globaltimes.cn/page/202211/1279423.shtml

Notes to Chapter 19 (pp. 179-189)

[1] Ben Norton, "West tells Global South 'you can't be neutral' in Ukraine war..." *Global Political Economy,* 20 Feb 2023 https://geopoliticaleconomy.com/2023/02/20/west-global-south-neutral-ukraine/

[2] "Nearly 90 Percent of the World Isn't Following Us on Ukraine," *Newsweek,* 15 Sept 2022 https://www.newsweek.com/nearly-90-percent-world-isnt-following-us-ukraine-opinion-1743061

[3] "Yellen affirms push for stronger Russia sanctions at G-20," *AP News,* 23 Feb 2023, https://apnews.com/article/g-20-summit-bangalore-janet-yellen-china-india-54d46cf97ab66a6325ccc259e62e36b2

[4] "Host India doesn't want G20 to discuss further Russia sanctions," *Reuters,* 22 Feb 2023, https://www.reuters.com/world/host-india-does-not-want-g20-discuss-more-sanctions-russia-sources-2023-02-22/

[5] "In Munich: West sounds alarm over Global South stances," *The Cradle,* 23 Feb 2023, https://thecradle.co/article-view/21844/in-munich-west-sounds-alarm-over-global-south-stances

[6] *Ibid.*

[7] *Munich Security Conference 2023,* "Main Stage 1: Defending the UN Charter," 18 Feb 2023, https://securityconference.org/mediathek/asset/main-stage-i-defending-the-un-charter-and-the-rules-based-international-order-20230218-0917/

[8] Namibian PM Saara Kuugongelwa-Amadhilahttps, *Tweet:* "The bottom line is that this money that is used to buy weapons could be better utilised..." // twitter.com/NoColdWar/status/1628379083104202754

9 "Wang Yi Attends 59th Munich Security Conference and Delivers a Keynote Speech," *Embassy of the PRC in the... Philippines,* 18 Feb 2023, http://ph.china-embassy.gov.cn/eng/chinew/202302/t20230220_11027395.htm#:~:text=Wang%20Yi%20said%20that%20making,the%20advance%20of%20the%20times.

10 "China's Position on the Political Settlement of the Ukraine Crisis," *Ministry of Foreign Affairs of the PRC,* 24 Feb 2023, https://www.mfa.gov.cn/eng/zxxx_662805/202302/t20230224_11030713.html

11 "Sen. Lindsey Graham likens China supporting Russia to 'buying a ticket on the Titanic'," *Vanity Fair,* 19 Feb 2023, https://www.vanityfair.com/news/2023/02/sen-lindsey-graham-likens-china-supporting-russia-to-buying-a-ticket-on-the-titanic

12 "Why Did Biden Snub China's Ukraine Peace Plan?" *LA Progressive,* 2 March 2023 https://www.laprogressive.com/war-and-peace/ukraine-peace-plan

13 "Pres. Biden blasts China's Peace Plan: 'Putin is applauding it, so how can it be any good?" *Vanity Fair,* 26 Feb 2023 www.vanityfair.com/news/2023/02/president-biden-blasts-chinas-peace-plan

14 "Zelensky open to China's peace plan..." *The Guardian,* 24 Feb 2023, https://www.theguardian.com/world/2023/feb/24/zelenskiy-open-to-chinas-peace-plan-but-rejects-compromise-with-sick-putin

15 "China and Russia won't be swayed by others, Beijing's top diplomat tells Putin," *South China Morning Post,* 22 Feb 2023, https://www.scmp.com/news/china/diplomacy/article/3211061/china-russia-relations-rock-solid-ahead-ukraine-war-anniversary

16 *Xinhua,* "The Global Security Initiative Concept Paper," 21 Feb 2023, english.news.cn/20230221/75375646823e4060832c760e00a1ec19/c.html

17 "Implementing the Global Security Initiative..." *Ministry of Foreign Affairs of the PRC,"* 22 Feb 2023, www.fmprc.gov.cn/mfa_eng/zxxx_662805/202302/t20230222_11029589.html

18 "US Hegemony and Its Perils," *Ministry of Foreign Affairs of the PRC,* 20 Feb 2023 www.fmprc.gov.cn/mfa_eng/wjbxw/202302/t20230220_11027664.html

19 "Biden warns of 'hard and bitter days' ahead..." *APNews,* 21 Feb 2023, apnews.com/article/ap-news-alert-warsaw-771f1860ad94345cf0b327c4d8a8f55a

20 "An awkward tension lies beneath the West's support for Ukraine," *Washington Post-Today's Worldview,* 22 Feb 2023, https://s2.washingtonpost.com/camp-rw/?trackId=602ed7709bbc0f73f69e20b8&s=63fc3c0c1b79c-61f87abaaeb&linknum=5&linktot=73

21 "NATO's Biggest European Members Float Defense Pact With Ukraine," *Wall Street Journal,* 24 Feb 2023, https://www.wsj.com/articles/natos-biggest-european-members-float-defense-pact-with-ukraine-38966950

22 Alastair Crooke, "Icarus defies hubris: Are Biden's 'Wings' melting?" *Al Mayadeen English,* 26 Feb 2023, https://english.almayadeen.net/articles/analysis/icarus-defies-hubris:-are-bidens-wings-melting

23 "Prof. Jeffrey Sachs and Ray McGovern address UN Security Council on Nord Stream investigations," *Consortium News,* 22 Feb 2023, https://www.youtube.com/watch?v=R_EX-VwKjng

24 *Ibid.*

25 *Ibid.*

26 *President of Russia,* "Presidential Address to Federal Assembly," 21 Feb 2023, http://en.kremlin.ru/events/president/news/70565

27 Pete Escobar, "Putin's 'civilizational' speech frames conflict between east and west," *The Cradle,* 22 Feb 2023, https://thecradle.co/article-view/21772/putins-civilizational-speech-frames-conflict-between-east-and-west

28 *Peace in Ukraine,* "Protest on the 20th anniversary of the U.S. invasion of Iraq," peoplesforum.org/events/peace-in-ukraine-say-no-to-endless-u-s-wars/

Notes to Chapter 20 (pp. 193-201)

1 "Reaching a Just and Lasting Peace in Ukraine: A Conversation with Jeffrey Sachs," IPB International, 25 Jan 2023, https://www.youtube.com/watch?v=z-FaMVZzueEU

2 "German tanks in Russia? The US wants to send Germany into the line of fire," *Liberation Newsletter,* 18 Jan 2023, https://liberationorg.co.uk/uncategorized/german-tanks-in-russia-the-us-wants-to-send-germany-into-the-line-of-fire/

3 Michael Hudson, "Germany's position in America's New World Order," *https://michael-hudson.com/2022/11/germanys-position-in-americas-new-world-order/*

4 "Europeans want peace, not sanctions," and "An overwhelming majority in Europe is pro-peace," https://szazadveg.hu/en/2022/12/20/europeans-want-peace-not-sanctions-n3420

5 "Growing US Divide on How Long to Support Ukraine," *Chicago Council on Global Affairs,* 5 Dec 2022, https://globalaffairs.org/research/public-opin-ion-survey/growing-us-divide-how-long-support-ukraine

6 "Mission Creep? How the US role in Ukraine has slowly escalated," *Responsible Statecraft,* 23 Jan 2023, https://responsiblestatecraft.org/2023/01/23/how-the-us-role-in-ukraine-has-slowly-but-steadily-escalated/?highlight=Mission%20Creep

7 *CNN Politics,* "Here's what Biden has said about sending US troops to Ukraine," 24 Feb 2022, https://www.cnn.com/2022/02/24/politics/us-troops-ukraine-rus-sia-nato/index.html

8 *NY Times,* "U.S. Warms to Helping Ukraine Target Crimea," 18 Jan 2023, https://www.nytimes.com/2023/01/18/us/politics/ukraine-crimea-military.html

9 *Newsweek,* "Ukraine Testing Weapons With Range Longer Than Biden Willing to Provide," 13 Jan 2023, https://www.newsweek.com/ukraine-testing-longer-range-drones-biden-willing-provide-1773753

10 "German tanks in Russia? The US wants to send Germany into the line of fire," *Liberation Newsletter,* 18 Jan 2023, https://liberationorg.co.uk/uncategorized/german-tanks-in-russia-the-us-wants-to-send-germany-into-the-line-of-fire/

11 Seymour Hersh, "How America Took Out The Nord Stream Pipeline," 8 Feb 2023, seymourhersh.substack.com/p/how-america-took-out-the-nord-stream

12 *Tass,* "German elites lose memory of Nazism victims, but ordinary Germans remember – Putin," 2 Feb 2023, https://tass.com/politics/1570735

13 *Rand Corp.,* "Avoiding a Long War…" https://www.rand.org/pubs/perspectives/PEA2510-1.html

14 *NATO,* "Weapons are – in fact – the way to peace," 5 Jan 2023, https://www.nato.int/cps/en/natohq/news_210447.htm?selectedLocale=en

15 Margaret Kimberley, "The US Continues Escalating in Ukraine," *Black Agenda Report,* 1 Feb 2023, https://www.blackagendareport.com/us-continues-escalat-ing-ukraine

16 Roger D. Harris, "Nostalgia for the Cuban Missile Crisis," *Popular Resistance,* 2 Feb 2023, https://popularresistance.org/nostalgia-for-the-cuban-missile-crisis/

[17] Rick Sterling, "Rand Report Prescribed US Provocations Against Russia...," *Antiwar.com,* 28 March 2022, https://original.antiwar.com/rick_sterling/2022/03/27/rand-report-prescribed-us-provocations-against-russia-and-predicted-russia-might-retaliate-in-ukraine/

[18] "US defense to its workforce: Nuclear war can be won," *bulletin of the Atomic Scientists,* 2 Feb 2022, https://thebulletin.org/2022/02/us-defense-to-its-workforce-nuclear-war-can-be-won/

[19] *National Security Archive,* "Nuclear War Planning and the Challenge of Civilian Oversight," 22 Jan 2020, nsarchive.gwu.edu/briefing-book/nuclear-vault/2020-01-22/nuclear-war-planning-challenge-civilian-oversight

[20] Robert Kagan, "The Price of Hegemony: Can America Learn to Use Its Power?" *Foreign Affairs,* May/June 2022, www.foreignaffairs.com/articles/ukraine/2022-04-06/russia-ukraine-war-price-hegemony

[21] "With Its Doomsday Clock at 100 Seconds to Midnight, ...Calls for Escalating US Aggression Against Russia," *Mintpress News,* https://www.mintpressnews.com/doomsday-clock-100-seconds-midnight-bulletin-atomic-scientists-calls-escalating-us-aggression-russia/279669/

Notes to Chapter 21 (pp. 202-215)

[1] *Wikipedia,* "João Goulart," https://en.wikipedia.org/wiki/Jo%C3%A3o_Goulart

[2] *Wikipedia,* "Military dictatorship in Brazil," https://en.wikipedia.org/wiki/Brazilian_military_government

[3] *Wikipedia,* "Zaire," https://en.wikipedia.org/wiki/Zaire

[4] "Hugo Chavez Cancer Conspiracy Theories Resurface After Death," *Forbes,* 6 March 2013, https://www.forbes.com/sites/kenrapoza/2013/03/06/hugo-chavez-cancer-conspiracy-theories-resurface-after-death/?sh=d473eeb4f1a3

[5] *Washington Post,* "Maduro promises to investigate Chavez 'assassination'," 5 Mar 2013, www.washingtonpost.com/news/worldviews/wp/2013/03/05/maduro-promises-to-investigate-chavez-assassination/?print=1

[6] *Wikipedia,* "Kashmir Princess," https://en.wikipedia.org/wiki/Kashmir_Princess

[7] "Untold History: The Coup Against Wallace and What Might Have Been," *Truthout,* 11 Jan 2013, https://truthout.org/video/untold-history-the-coup-against-wallace-and-what-might-have-been/

[8] *Wikipedia,* "Golden Triangle," https://en.wikipedia.org/wiki/Golden_Triangle_(Southeast_Asia)

[9] "Does China's Rise Really Threaten the U.S...," *Covert Action Magazine,* 14 Aug 2021, https://covertactionmagazine.com/2021/08/14/does-chinas-rise-really-threaten-the-u-s-or-just-its-sociopathic-power-elite-who-want-to-keep-ruling-the-world-even-if-it-drags-us-into-ww-iii/

[10] *National Security Archive,* "Gerald Ford White House Altered Rockefeller Commission Report in 1975; Removed Section on CIA Assassination Plots," 29 Feb 2016, https://nsarchive.gwu.edu/briefing-book/intelligence/2016-02-29/gerald-ford-white-house-altered-rockefeller-commission-report

Notes to Chapter 22 (pp. 216-226)

[1] Ellen Brown, "Predicted Global Economic Crash," *LA Progressive,* 22 May 2022, https://www.laprogressive.com/economic-equality/predicted-global-economic-crash

[2] Michael Hudson, *Articles,* https://michael-hudson.com/category/articles/

[3] *Henry Kissinger Quotes,* in Quotefancy.com/henry-kissinger-quotes

Notes to Chapter 23 (pp. 227-237)

[1] "History of Federal Income Tax Rates: 1913-2023," *Bradford Tax Institute,* https://bradfordtaxinstitute.com/Free_Resources/Federal-Income-Tax-Rates.aspx

[2] Vijay Prashad, "A Map of Latin America's Present," *Tricontinental Dossier no. 49,* 7 Feb 2022, thetricontinental.org/dossier-hector-bejar-latin-america/

[3] "Keynesian Economics vs. Monetarism: What's the Difference?" *Investopedia,* 12 April 2022, https://www.investopedia.com/ask/answers/012615/what-difference-between-keynesian-economics-and-monetarist-economics.asp

Notes to Chapter 24 (pp. 238-245)

[1] "U.S. Economic War Waged at Home and Abroad," *SanctionsKill.org,* https://docs.google.com/presentation/d/1rY9pj9g3nMSrRfSap5bdcs3CpPkjj5VI3E-7m1ALbQjM/edit#slide=id.gb9c5a1e4dd_0_19

[2] "Haiti in the Caribbean: A Political Economy Perspective on the Urgent Crisis of Imperialism," *Black Agenda Report,* 23 Nov 2022, https://blackagendareport.com/haiti-caribbean-political-economy-perspective-urgent-crisis-imperialism

[3] "Haiti: Neocolonial Dictatorshipi, Paramilitary and Police Terror," *Counterpunch,* 4 Dec 2022, https://popularresistance.org/neocolonial-dictatorship-paramilitary-and-police-terror-in-haiti-today/

[4] *Ibid.*

Notes to Chapter 25 (pp. 249-255)

[1] *Joy Damiani, Words and Music,* http://joydamiani.com/

[2] *P.A.R.C. Politics-Art-Roots-Culture,* www.facebook.com/1713FranklinSt

Notes to Chapter 26 (pp. 256-265)

[1] "Red Oklahoma," *Jacobin,* 13 April 2018, www.jacobinmag.com/2018/04/teachers-strikes-oklahoma-socialism-sanders-unions

[2] "Working Class Union," *Encyclopedia of Oklahoma History and Culture,* https://www.okhistory.org/publications/enc/entry.php?entry=WO021

[3] *Direct Action: Protest and the Reinvention of American Radicalism,* Verso, https://www.versobooks.com/books/2331-direct-action

Notes to Part VII (pp. 267-288)

[1] *Washington Pose, 14 May 2021,* "Israeli tactic of 'mowing the grass' returns to Gaza," https://www.washingtonpost.com/world/2021/05/14/israel-gaza-history/

[2] *CBS News,* 30 Dec 2023, "Israel-Hamas war will go on for "many more months,' Netanyahu," https://www.cbsnews.com/news/israel-hamas-war-will-go-on-for-many-more-months-netanyahu-says/#:~:text=Prime%20Minister%20Benjamin%20Netanyahu%20said,displacement%20in%20the%20besieged%20enclave.

[3] *Electronic Intifada,* 12 Oct 2023, "Biden lied about seeing photos of beheaded Israeli children," https://electronicintifada.net/blogs/ali-abunimah/biden-lied-about-seeing-photos-beheaded-israeli-children

[4] *Electronic Intifada,* 22 Nov 2023, "Palestine's resistance has already won in Gaza," https://electronicintifada.net/content/palestines-resistance-has-already-won-gaza/41456

[5] Sachs, Jeffrey, "The West's False Narrative About Russia and China," 22 Aug 2022, https://www.jeffsachs.org/newspaper-articles/h29g9k7l7fymxp39yhzwx-c5f72ancr

[6] *New York Times*, 5 Jan 2024, "Blinken Returns to Middle East as Tensions Grow With Israel," https://www.nytimes.com/2024/01/05/us/politics/blinken-israel-gaza-war.html?searchResultPosition=1

[7] "Pro-Palestine activists protest in front of Blinken's house in Virginia," *AA*, 4 Jan 2024, https://www.aa.com.tr/en/americas/pro-palestine-activists-protest-in-front-of-blinkens-house-in-virginia/3100563

[8] *The Times of Israel*, 15 Jan 24, "Netanyahu touts his role blocking 2-state solution," https://www.timesofisrael.com/pointing-to-hamass-little-state-netanyahu-touts-role-blocking-2-state-solution/

[9] *New York Times*, 5 Jan 24, "As Pressure Mounts, Israeli Minister Proposes Plan for Postwar Gaza," https://www.nytimes.com/2024/01/05/world/middleeast/israel-plan-gaza.html?searchResultPosition=1

[10] *New York Times*, 27 Dec 2023, "Skepticism Grows Over Israel's Ability to Dismantle Hamas," https://www.nytimes.com/2023/12/27/world/middleeast/israel-hamas-war-military.html?searchResultPosition=1

[11] "Senior Hamas member says group open to cease-fire but against US, Israeli interference," *AA*, 29 Dec 23, https://www.aa.com.tr/en/middle-east/senior-hamas-member-says-group-open-to-cease-fire-but-against-us-israeli-interference/3095151

[12] *The Times of Israel*, 3 Jan 24, "Nasrallah vows response to Arouri, warns of fight 'without limits' if Israel goes to war," https://www.timesofisrael.com/nasrallah-threatens-israel-over-arouri-hit-warns-of-war-without-rules-or-limits/

[13] *New York Times*, 20 Dec 23, "Amid Gaza War and Red Sea Attacks, Yemen's Houthis Refuse to Back Down," https://www.nytimes.com/2023/12/20/world/middleeast/israel-hamas-war-yemen-houthis.html?searchResultPosition=1

[14] *The Duran: Episode 1794*, "Middle East escalation; Hardline neocons vs moderate neocons," https://twitter.com/TheDuranReal/status/1742813122866430405?ref_src=twsrc%5E%20google%7Ctwcamp%5Eserp%7Ctwgr%5Etweet

[15] *New York Times*, 7 Jan 24, "From Lebanon to the Red Sea, a Broader Conflict With Iran Looms," https://www.nytimes.com/2024/01/07/us/politics/iran-us-israel-conflict.html

[16] *Foreign Affairs,* 17 Nov 23, "Redefining Success in Ukraine," https://www.foreignaffairs.com/ukraine/redefining-success-ukraine

[17] *Global Times,* 10 Apr 23, "US uneasiness over Macron's 'strategic autonomy' statement shows Washington's declining ability to maintain hegemony," https://www.globaltimes.cn/page/202304/1288825.shtml

[18] *New York Times,* 14 Apr 23, "Brazil's Lula Meets Xi in China as They Seek Path to Peace in Ukraine," http://www.nytimes.com/2023/04/14/world/asia/brazil-china-russia-ukraine.html?searchResultPosition=1

[19] *France 24,* 14 Apr 23, "Brazil's Lula criticizes US dollar and IMF during China visit," https://www.france24.com/en/americas/20230414-brazil-s-lula-criticises-us-dollar-and-imf-during-china-visit

[20] *The Real News Network,* 30 Nov 23, "'Our People Cannot Afford for Us to Fail'," https://therealnews.com/palestinian-youth-movement-gaza-truce-cease-fire-western-left-solidarity

[21] Michael Hudson, *Articles,* https://michael-hudson.com/category/articles/

[22] Ben Norton, "Michael Hudson on New cold war, super imperialism, China, Russia, de-dollarization," *GeoPolitical Economy,* 5 Dec 2021, geopoliticaleconomy.com/2021/05/12/michael-hudson-new-cold-war-china-russia/

[23] Ben Norton, "China 'counters US dollar hegemony' with gold reserves, Argentina yuan currency swap deal," *GeoPolitical Economy,* 8 Jan 2023, https://geopoliticaleconomy.com/2023/01/08/china-dollar-gold-reserves-argentina-yuan/

[24] "Ajamu Baraka: The Left Must Draw Clear Political and Ideological Lines," *Clearing the Fog,* 2 Jan 2023, https://popularresistance.org/ajamu-baraka-the-left-must-draw-clear-political-and-ideological-lines/

[25] Desai, Radhika, *Capitalism, Coronavirus and War: A Geopolitical Economy,* https://www.routledge.com/Capitalism-Coronavirus-and-War-A-Geopolitical-Economy/Desai/p/book/9781032059501

[26] *International Manifesto Group,* https://internationalmanifesto.org/about/

[27] *Wikipedia,* "Coups d'état in Bolivia," https://en.wikipedia.org/wiki/Coups_d%27%C3%A9tat_in_Bolivia#:~:text=Bolivia%20has%20experienced%20more%20than,transition%20to%20democracy%20in%201980.

28 Ben Norton, "Peru's natural resources: CIA-linked US ambassador meets with mining and energy ministers to talk 'investments'," *GeoPolitical Economy*, 19 Jan 2023, https://geopoliticaleconomy.com/2023/01/19/peru-resources-mining-gas-investment/

29 "Socialista Pedro Castillo apunta a renegociar convenios tributarios de mineras en Peru," *La República*, 22 marzo 2023, https://www.larepublica.co/globoeconomia/socialista-pedro-castillo-apunta-a-renegociar-convenios-tributarios-de-mineras-en-peru-3179618

30 *Pedro Castillo Terrones, Tweet,* 16 Feb 2023, https://twitter.com/PedroCastilloTe/status/1361683551448662018

31 *Presidencia de la República de Perú,* "Presidente Castillo: rescatamos los recursos naturales del país para todos los peruanos..." 27 Feb 2022, https://www.gob.pe/institucion/presidencia/noticias/586636-presidente-castillo-rescatamos-los-recursos-naturales-del-pais-para-todos-los-peruanos-en-el-marco-de-la-segunda-reforma-agraria

32 "Queremos que nuestros recursos naturales beneficien al pueblo..." *Gestión,* 28 Oct 2021, https://gestion.pe/peru/politica/pedro-castillo-queremos-que-nuestros-recursos-naturales-beneficien-directamente-al-pueblo-nndc-noticia/

33 Ben Norton, "Peru rises up after coup against elected President Pedro Castillo," *GeoPolitical Economy*, 10 Dec 2022, geopoliticaleconomy.com/2022/12/10/peru-coup-president-pedro-castillo/

34 Ben Norton, "Peru's natural resources: CIA-linked US ambassador meets with mining and energy ministers to talk 'investments'," *GeoPolitical Economy*, 19 Jan 2023, https://geopoliticaleconomy.com/2023/01/19/peru-resources-mining-gas-investment/